BACKSTAGE HANDBOOK
An Illustrated Almanac of Technical Information

BACKSTAGE
HANDBOOK

an Illustrated Almanac of Technical Information

Third Edition

By

Paul Carter

Illustrations by

George Chiang

Broadway Press
Louisville, Kentucky
1994

Carter, Paul.
    Backstage handbook : an illustrated almanac of technical
information / by Paul Carter ; illustrations by George Chiang. --
3rd ed.
    p. cm.
Includes bibliographical references and index.
ISBN 0-911747-39-7

    1. Theaters--Stage-setting and scenery--Handbooks, manuals, etc.
2. Theatre architecture--Handbooks, manuals, etc. 3. Stage
machinery--Handbooks, manuals, etc.   I. Title.

PN2091.S8C32 1994   792'.025
                                     QBI94-2022

Second Edition

© 1988 Paul Carter

Third Edition

© 1994 Sally Friedman
All rights reserved.

ISBN: 0-911747-39-7
Fifth printing of third edition: March, 1999,
including corrections on page 200 and price change.
Printed in the United States of America

CONTENTS

PREFACE

Preface to Third Edition:

Paul Douglas Carter
September 29, 1956 - August 9, 1990

The third edition of the Backstage Handbook was put together from notes Paul had left in various places, letters with suggestions he had saved, and remembered conversations. I like to think that even though this is ostensibly a book of facts and figures, it is actually much more than that, and affords the careful reader a glimpse of the extraordinary person Paul Carter was. There is intelligence tempered by wit, order leavened by whimsicality, complexity elucidated by simplicity. There is a boyish fascination with how things work transformed by the desire to teach others, to pass information along, to leave something behind.

There were the beginnings of other books in the computer, and another book published, but it is by the Backstage Handbook that he must now be remembered by those who never had the good fortune to meet him. For those of us who knew him, and loved him, it is but a small souvenir of his unique sensibility.

There are many people I would like to thank for making this edition possible. First, and foremost, Monique Mitchell and Andy Day, for all their work on the new grip equipment and film lighting sections; Betsy Tanner, Joe Valentino, and Steve Nelson, for patiently answering all our questions; Allan Trumpler, Leo Schlosser, Jeffrey C. Gay, Bill Raoul, Jim Smith, Bob Mumm, Rachel Keebler, and Lisa LoCurto at Rose Brand for supplying us with various bits and pieces of information which made it into the book. Once again, I would like to thank David Rodger and Deborah Hazlett, the publishers, and George Chiang the ever-brilliant illustrator–with extra thanks to Sheri and Ariel for their gracious sharing of George's limited time. I would like to thank the Thompsons, on a professional note, for the unlimited, 24-hour use of their Xerox machine, and on a personal note, for their many kindnesses.

My most heartfelt, and personal gratitude goes to my family and friends, Paul's family, my forever pal Leslie, and most especially, my sister, Laurie, for keeping me going with all those care packages and phone calls.

Sally Friedman Carter, a.k.a. Li'l Sal

Preface to First and Second Editions:

The seeds for this book were planted about eight years ago while I was working as a stagehand. I needed to know which pin of a standard stage plug was the hot pin and which was the neutral. No one I asked was sure, so I went to look it up. I searched through several stagecraft books and was surprised to discover that this basic piece of information was no where to be found.

On several other occasions I had to look much too hard to find information which I thought would or should be readily available. For instance: What was the strength of $^3/_4$ inch manila rope? How do you tie a sheetbend? How much does a sheet of $^3/_4$ inch plywood weigh? I eventually found what I needed, but it was usually in some highly specialized and expensive book of which only three or four pages were really useful to me. I started saving these scraps of information in a notebook. That was the beginning of this book.

After several years of gathering facts and figures I realized that if I could organize all this information and get it published it would probably be appreciated by a lot of people. Deciding what to include and what to omit was the hard part. I knew I didn't want to write a "how to" book, I wanted a "what is" book – facts and figures only.

The book is divided into seven chapters: tools, hardware, materials, shop math, electrics, and architecture.. It was impossible to find just the right chapter for all this information. For instance, what chapter do you put chain in – Tools, Hardware, or Materials? Should pulleys go with tools or rope? I've gone around and around with this. With the help of the index and trying to decipher my logic, I hope you will be able to find everything you need.

I welcome your comments and suggestions. Please send me your thoughts care of Broadway Press.

There are many people who helped to make this book possible. The readers: Ned Bowman, Cameron Fruit, Paul Garrity, Doug Lebrecht, Seth Orbach, Russ Swift, Betsy Tanner, Dick Ventre, and the exceptional proof reader, John Tissot; Artec Consultants Inc, for the use of their resources; David Rodger, my publisher and George Chiang, the skillful and patient illustrator, for making this book more polished and complete than I ever envisioned it; my father for teaching me how things work; and of course L'il Sal.

Paul Carter

TOOLS

MEASURING AND MARKING TOOLS

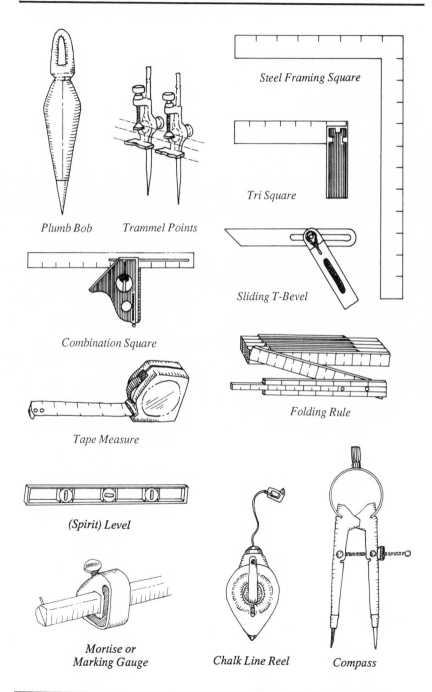

Plumb Bob

Trammel Points

Steel Framing Square

Tri Square

Sliding T-Bevel

Combination Square

Tape Measure

Folding Rule

(Spirit) Level

Mortise or
Marking Gauge

Chalk Line Reel

Compass

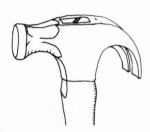

Claw Hammer

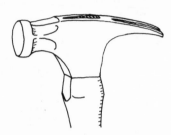

Ripping or Framing Hammer

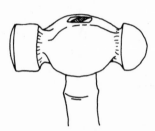

Ball Peen Hammer

Mallet

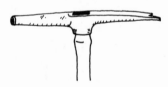

Tack Hammer

Nail Set

Sledge Hammer

Pin Fastener & Charge

Power Hammer

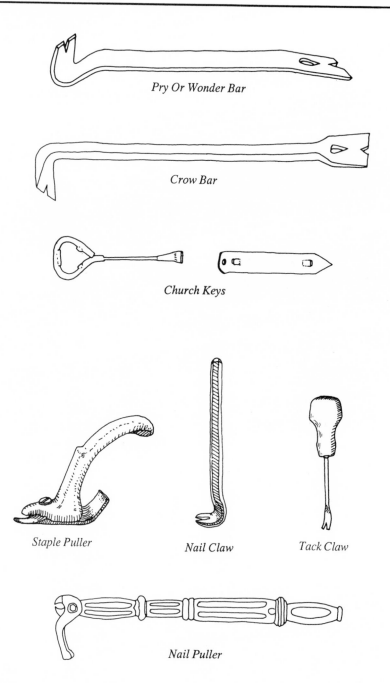

Pry Or Wonder Bar

Crow Bar

Church Keys

Staple Puller

Nail Claw

Tack Claw

Nail Puller

*"Crescent", "C" or
Adjustable Wrench*

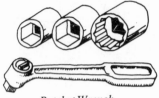

*Ratchet Wrench
with Sockets*

Nut Driver

*Folding Hex or
Allen Keys*

*Hex or Allen Wrench,
Hex Driver*

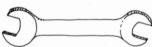

Open End Wrench

Closed End or Box Wrench

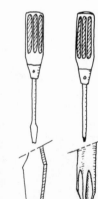

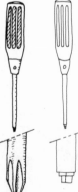

Flat   *Phillips*

*Robertson
or
Square
Drive*

*Ratcheting Box or
Speed Wrench*

*Ratchet or "Yankee"
Screw Driver*

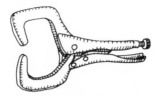
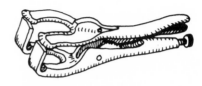

Assorted "Vise-Grip" Locking Pliers

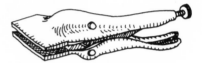

Needle Nose Plier

*Slip Joint or
Sheep Nose Plier*

*Side Cutting or
Linesman's Plier*

Channel Locks

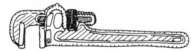
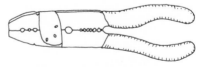

Pipe Wrench

Wire Tool or Wire Stripper

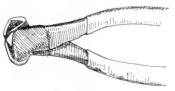
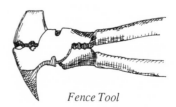

End Nipper

Fence Tool

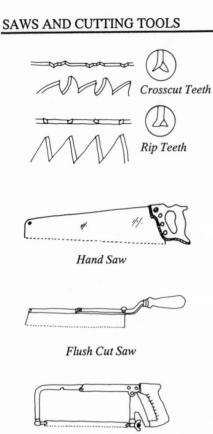

Crosscut Teeth

Rip Teeth

Hand Saw

Flush Cut Saw

Coping Saw

Miter Box with Back Saw

Hack Saw

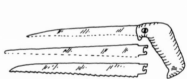
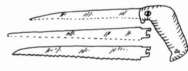

Key Hole Saw

Mat or Utility Knife

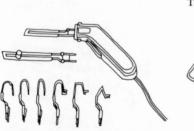

Hot Wire Cutter with various Blades

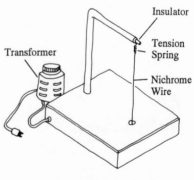

Insulator

Transformer

Tension Spring

Nichrome Wire

Benchtop Hot Wire Cutter

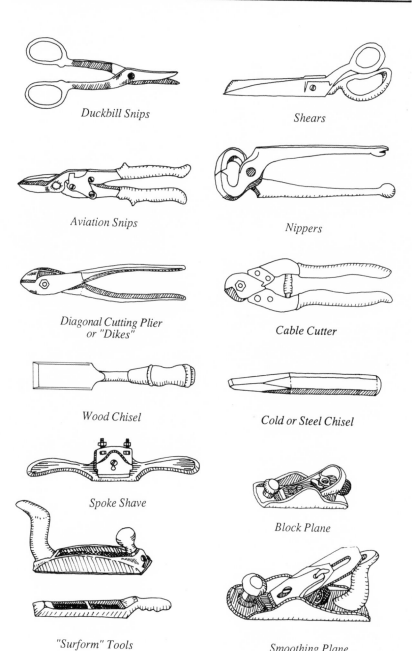

Duckbill Snips

Shears

Aviation Snips

Nippers

Diagonal Cutting Plier or "Dikes"

Cable Cutter

Wood Chisel

Cold or Steel Chisel

Spoke Shave

Block Plane

"Surform" Tools

Smoothing Plane

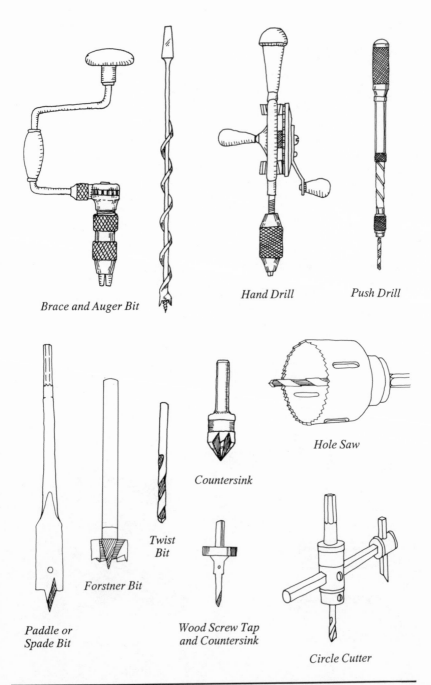

Brace and Auger Bit

Hand Drill

Push Drill

Hole Saw

Countersink

Paddle or
Spade Bit

Forstner Bit

Twist
Bit

Wood Screw Tap
and Countersink

Circle Cutter

TWIST DRILL SIZES

Size* Desig.	Decimal Equivalent	Size* Desig.	Decimal Equivalent	Size* Desig.	Decimal Equivalent	Size* Desig.	Decimal Equivalent
80	0.0135	49	0.073	20	0.161	I	0.272
79	0.0145	48	0.076	19	0.166	J	0.277
1/64	0.0156	5/64	0.0781	18	0.1695	K	0.281
78	0.016	47	0.0785	11/64	0.1719	9/32	0.2813
77	0.018	46	0.081	17	0.173	L	0.290
76	0.020	45	0.082	16	0.177	M	0.295
75	0.021	44	0.086	15	0.180	19/64	0.2969
74	0.0225	43	0.089	14	0.182	N	0.302
73	0.024	42	0.0935	13	0.185	5/16	0.3125
72	0.025	3/32	0.0938	3/16	0.1875	O	0.316
71	0.026	41	0.096	12	0.189	P	0.323
70	0.028	40	0.098	11	0.191	21/64	0.3281
69	0.0292	39	0.0995	10	0.1935	Q	0.332
68	0.031	38	0.1015	9	0.196	R	0.339
1/32	0.0313	37	0.104	8	0.199	11/32	0.3438
67	0.032	36	0.1065	7	0.201	S	0.348
66	0.033	7/64	0.1094	13/64	0.2031	T	0.358
65	0.035	35	0.110	6	0.204	23/64	0.3594
64	0.036	34	0.111	5	0.2055	U	0.368
63	0.037	33	0.113	4	0.209	3/8	0.375
62	0.038	32	0.116	3	0.213	V	0.377
61	0.039	31	0.120	7/32	0.2188	W	0.386
60	0.040	1/8	0.125	2	0.221	25/64	0.3906
59	0.041	30	0.1285	1	0.228	X	0.397
58	0.042	29	0.136	A	0.234	Y	0.404
57	0.043	28	0.1405	15/64	0.2344	13/32	0.4063
56	0.0465	9/64	0.1406	B	0.238	Z	0.413
3/64	0.0469	27	0.144	C	0.242	27/64	0.4219
55	0.052	26	0.147	D	0.246	7/16	0.4375
54	0.055	25	0.1495	1/4	0.250	29/64	0.4531
53	0.0595	24	0.152	E	0.250	15/32	0.4689
1/16	0.0625	23	0.154	F	0.257	31/64	0.4844
52	0.0635	5/32	0.1562	G	0.261	1/2	0.500
51	0.067	22	0.157	17/64	0.2656		
50	0.070	21	0.159	H	0.266		

* Twist drills are designated in one of three ways: by number, by letter, or by the drill's fractional diameter.

SAFE DRILLING SPEEDS FOR MILD STEEL

Drill Size	------------------R.P.M.------------------	
	(hand feed with little or no lubrication)	
	Carbon Bit	**High-speed Bit**
1/16"	920 (1,830)	3,060 (6,110)
3/32"	610 (1,220)	2,060 (4,075)
1/8"	460 (920)	1,530 (3,060)
3/16"	310 (610)	1,020 (2,040)
1/4"	230 (460)	760 (1,530)
5/16"	180 (370)	610 (1,220)
3/8"	150 (310)	510 (1,020)
1/2"	115 (230)	380 (764)

Note: The figures in parentheses are drilling speeds which are safe under industrial conditions: machine-fed equipment where the material is flooded with lubricant.

SAFE DRILLING SPEEDS FOR OTHER METALS

Safe drilling speeds of the metals listed below can be determined by multiplying the safe drilling speed of mild steel from the preceding table by the multiplying factor listed next to the metal below. For example: the safe drilling speed for stainless steel using a 3/8" high-speed bit is 150 x 0.30 = 50 R.P.M.

Die castings (zinc base)	3.5	Cast iron, hard	0.80
Aluminum	2.5	Tool steel	0.60
Brass and bronze	2.0	Stainless steel, hard	0.30
Cast iron, soft	1.15	Chilled cast iron	0.20
Malleable iron	0.85	Manganese steel	0.15

TAP AND DIE

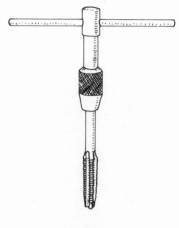

Tap
(in Tap Wrench)

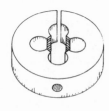

Die

TAP DRILL SIZES - USA Standard Unified Thread Series

Nominal Diameter	Coarse UNC		Fine UNF		Extra Fine UNEF	
	Threads per inch	Tap Drill	Threads per inch	Tap Drill	Threads per inch	Tap Drill
0 (.060)	---	---	80	$3/64$	---	---
1 (.073)	64	No. 53	72	No. 53	---	---
2 (.086)	56	No. 50	64	No. 50	---	---
3 (.099)	48	No. 47	56	No. 45	---	---
4 (.112)	40	No. 43	48	No. 42	---	---
5 (.125)	40	No. 38	44	No. 37	---	---
6 (.138)	32	No. 36	40	No. 33	---	---
10 (.190)	24	No. 25	32	No. 21	---	---
12 (.216)	24	No. 16	28	No. 14	32	No. 13
$1/4$	20	No. 7	28	No. 3	32	$7/32$
$5/16$	18	F	24	I	32	$9/32$
$3/8$	16	$5/16$	24	Q	32	$11/32$
$7/16$	14	U	20	$25/64$	28	$13/32$
$1/2$	13	$27/64$	20	$29/64$	28	$15/32$
$9/16$	12	$31/64$	18	$33/64$	24	$33/64$
$5/8$	11	$17/32$	18	$37/64$	24	$37/64$
$11/16$	---	---	---	---	24	$41/64$
$3/4$	10	$21/32$	16	$11/16$	20	$45/64$
$13/16$	---	---	---	---	20	$49/64$
$7/8$	9	$49/64$	14	$13/16$	20	$53/64$
$15/16$	---	---	---	---	20	$57/64$
1	8	$7/8$	12	$59/64$	20	$61/64$
$11/16$	---	---	---	---	18	1
$11/8$	7	$63/64$	12	$13/64$	18	$15/64$
$13/16$	---	---	---	---	18	$19/64$
$11/4$	7	$17/64$	12	$111/64$	18	$13/16$
$15/16$	---	---	---	---	18	$117/64$
$13/8$	6	$17/32$	12	$119/64$	18	$15/16$
$17/16$	---	---	---	---	18	$13/8$
$11/2$	6	$111/32$	12	$127/64$	18	$17/16$
$19/16$	---	---	---	---	18	$11/2$
$15/8$	---	---	---	---	18	$19/16$
$111/16$	---	---	---	---	18	$15/8$
$13/4$	5	$19/16$	---	---	16	$111/16$
2	$41/2$	$125/32$	---	---	16	$115/16$
$21/4$	$41/2$	$21/32$	---	---	---	---
$21/2$	4	$21/4$	---	---	---	---
$23/4$	4	$21/2$	---	---	---	---
3	4	$23/4$	---	---	---	---
$31/4$	4	3	---	---	---	---
$31/2$	4	$31/4$	---	---	---	---
$33/4$	4	$31/2$	---	---	---	---
4	4	$33/4$	---	---	---	---

FILES

American Pattern files are generally used for fast material removal where a precision finish is not required.

Coarseness grades are identified as:
Bastard Cut: for heavy removal with coarse finish.
Second Cut: for light removal with fair finish.
Smooth Cut: for fine finishing work.
Cut types include:
Single Cut: used with light pressure for finishing or sharpening.
Double Cut: used with heavier pressure for rougher finishes.

Swiss Pattern files are made to more exacting measurements than American Pattern files to assure precision smoothness. They are primarily finishing tools used on delicate and intricate parts. Uses include removing burrs, shaping and finishing narrow grooves, notches and keyways and enlarging small holes.

Swiss Pattern files come in grades of coarseness (cut No.) ranging from No. 00, the coarsest, to No. 4, the finest.

FILE SHAPES

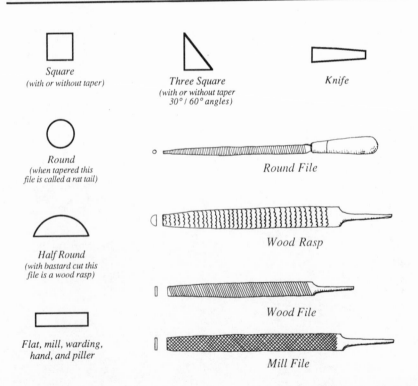

Square
(with or without taper)

Three Square
(with or without taper 30° / 60° angles)

Knife

Round
(when tapered this file is called a rat tail)

Round File

Half Round
(with bastard cut this file is a wood rasp)

Wood Rasp

Wood File

Flat, mill, warding, hand, and piller

Mill File

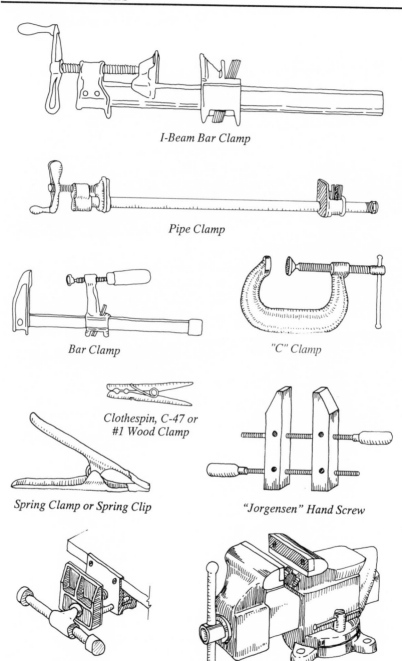

I-Beam Bar Clamp

Pipe Clamp

Bar Clamp

"C" Clamp

Clothespin, C-47 or #1 Wood Clamp

Spring Clamp or Spring Clip

"Jorgensen" Hand Screw

Carpenter's Vise

Steel Vise

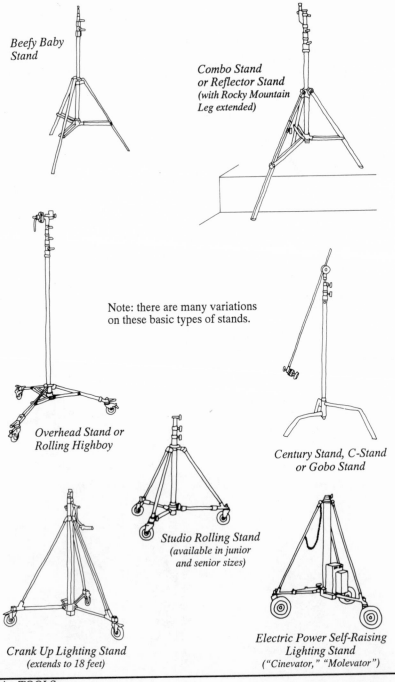

Beefy Baby Stand

Combo Stand or Reflector Stand (with Rocky Mountain Leg extended)

Note: there are many variations on these basic types of stands.

Overhead Stand or Rolling Highboy

Century Stand, C-Stand or Gobo Stand

Studio Rolling Stand (available in junior and senior sizes)

Crank Up Lighting Stand (extends to 18 feet)

Electric Power Self-Raising Lighting Stand ("Cinevator," "Molevator")

GRIP CLAMPS, HEADS AND HANGING HARDWARE

Grid Clamp or
Big Ben Clamp

Mafer Clamp

Times Square C-Clamp
or Baby Matth Pipe Adapter

Grip Head or Bull Head
(2¹/₂" Grip Head)

4¹/₂ or Combi Head
(4¹/₂" Grip Head)

Baby Pipe Clamp

Junior Pipe Clamp

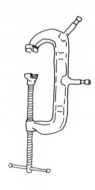

Studded C-Clamp

Matthews Magic Finger

Matthews Pop-up Stud

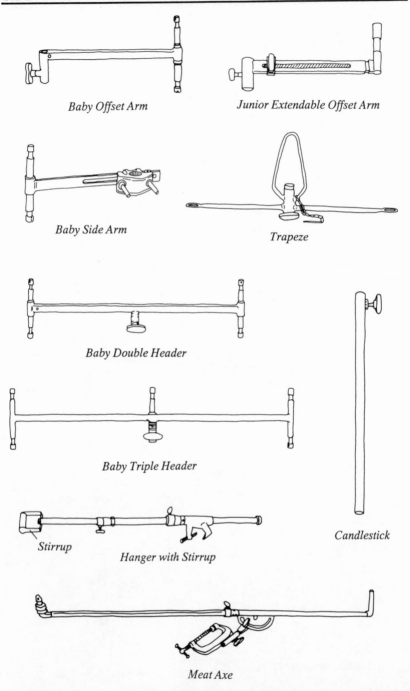

Baby Offset Arm

Junior Extendable Offset Arm

Baby Side Arm

Trapeze

Baby Double Header

Candlestick

Baby Triple Header

Stirrup

Hanger with Stirrup

Meat Axe

Junior Trombone

Set Claw Wall Hanger
Matth Becky Adjustable Hanger

Set Wall Bracket

Junior Hanger
with 750 Studs

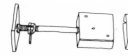

Wall Stretcher or Wall Spreader
(accepts either 2x4 or 2x6 lumber)

Pole Cat or
Matth Pole

Baby Plate or 1K Pigeon

Junior Wall Plate or 2K Pigeon

T-Bone or Turtle

Chain Vise Grip

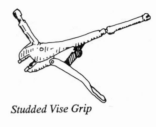

Studded Vise Grip

Drop Ceiling Scissor
or Scissor Clamp

Putty Knife

Gaffer Grip or Gator Grip

Tubing Hanger

Bailin Bracket

Stud Adapter (1$^{1}/_{8}$" to $^{5}/_{8}$")

Junior Grip Helper

Sandbag

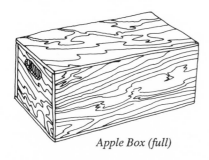

Apple Box (full)

Apple Box (eighth or pancake)

Basso Blocks

Apple Box Dimensions

Matthews

Full	20" x 12" x 8"
Half	20" x 12" x 4"
Quarter	20" x 12" x 2"
Eighth (pancake)	20" x 12" x 1"

Mole Richardson

Full	18" x 12" x 12"
Half	18" x 12" x 6"
Quarter	18" x 12" x 3"
Eighth	18" x 12" x $1^{1}/_{2}$"

Matthews Minis

Full	12" x 10" x 8"
Half	12" x 10" x 4"
Quarter	12" x 10" x 2"
Eighth (pancake)	12" x 10" x 1"

Basso Blocks

Full	10" x $6^{1}/_{2}$" x 4"
Half	10" x $6^{1}/_{2}$" x 2"

Doughnut

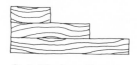

Stair Blocks or Step Up
(stacked 2x4s)

Cribbing
1x3s x 10" or 2x4s x 10"

Cup Block

Wedge or Camera Wedge
10"x4" tapered $^{1}/_{16}$" to 1"

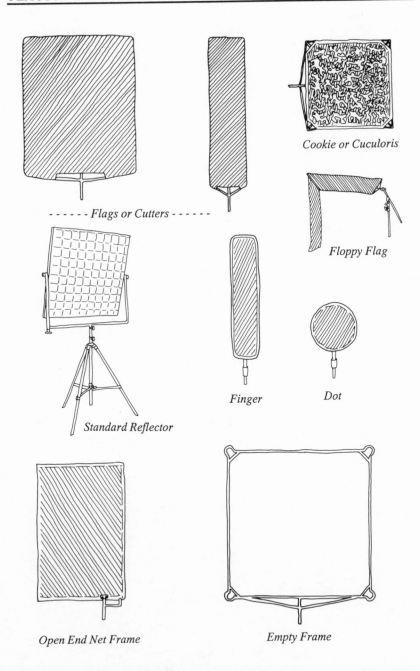

------ *Flags or Cutters* ------

Cookie or Cuculoris

Floppy Flag

Standard Reflector

Finger

Dot

Open End Net Frame

Empty Frame

FLAGS, CUTTERS AND SCRIM SPECIFICATIONS

Type	Covering Material	Basic Sizes	Notes
Flag	Black duvetyne	12"x18", 18"x24", 24"x30", 24"x36", 30"x36", 48"x48"	Most common sizes are 18"x24", 24"x36", 48"x48". Flags are often called Cutters, since they also "cut" light
Cutter	Black duvetyne	10"x12", 12"x20", 10"x42", 12"x48", 18"x48", 24"x72"	Most common sizes are 12"x48" 18"x48"–small meat axe 24"x72"–meat axe
Net	Bobbinet: –black, white, lavender –single, double, triple	12"x18", 18"x24", 24"x30", 24"x36", 30"x36", 48"x48"	Colored border designates type of net, single, double, triple, etc. (See Net /Scrim Characteristics table below.)
Dot or Target	Single net, double net, solid, silk, lavender, white bobbinet, stopsilk	3", 6", 8", 10" diameter	Used mainly for table top shoots in small or confined areas.
Finger	Same as Dots	2"x12", 4"x12", 4"x14"	
Butterfly or Overhead	Silk, griffolyn, grid cloth, muslin (bleached or unbleached), single or double net, black duvetyne, or solid	6'x6', 8'x8', 12'x12', 20'x20'	
Reflector board	Hard side: –mirror, mylar, silvered plexi, hard reflector Soft side: –silver or gold leaf	42"x42"	Never point reflected light into someone's eyes without warning them.
Scrim	Stainless steel screen	Diameters match lens size of various lights.	
Silk	China silk or nylon	12"x18", 18"x24", 24"x30", 24"x36", 30"x36", 48"x48"	Diffusion or reduction of light source.
Open or Empty Frames	Any diffusion or cutting material, or gel	18"x24", 24"x36", 48"x48"	Useful when gels can't be put directly on lights.
McGrid	Black honeycomb	18"x24" or 40"x40"	Makes a soft light directional.

NET / SCRIM CHARACTERISTICS

Type	Edge Color	Approximate Light Reduction
Single	White (Green on West Coast)	$1/2 f$ stop
Double	Red	$1 f$ stop
Triple	Blue	$1 1/2 f$ stop
Silk	Gold	$1 3/4 f$ stop
$1/4$ Stop Silk	Gold	$1/4 f$ stop
Lavender	Lavender	$1/3 f$ stop

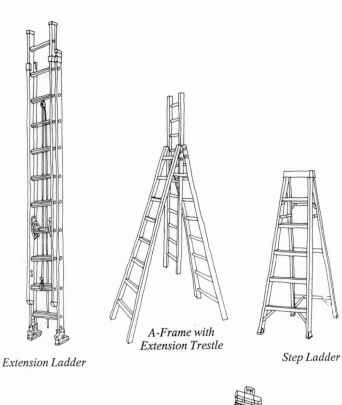

Extension Ladder

A-Frame with Extension Trestle

Step Ladder

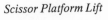

Scissor Platform Lift

"Genie" Lift

Boom Lift, "Condor," "JLG"

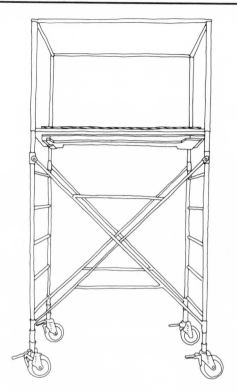

Rule of Thumb:
The maximum height of
free standing scaffolding
should not exceed 4 times
the narrow dimension of
the base.

Matthews Parallel

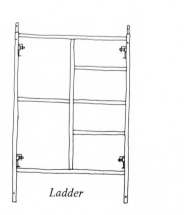

Ladder

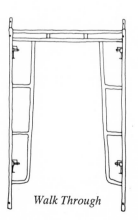

Walk Through

Scaffold Frame Types

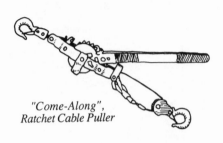

"Come-Along",
Ratchet Cable Puller

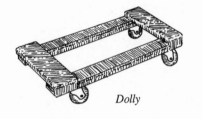

Dolly

Chain Hoist

Capacity (Bushels)	Inside Dimensions		
	L	W	D
6	30"	20"	$20^{1}/_{2}$"
8	34"	22"	23"
10	36"	24"	25"
12	36"	26"	$27^{1}/_{2}$"
14	40"	28"	$27^{1}/_{2}$"
16	40"	28"	30"
20	48"	32"	30"

Canvas Hamper,
Scenery Cart

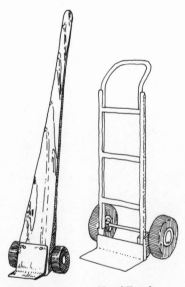

Johnson or
"J" Bar

Hand Truck

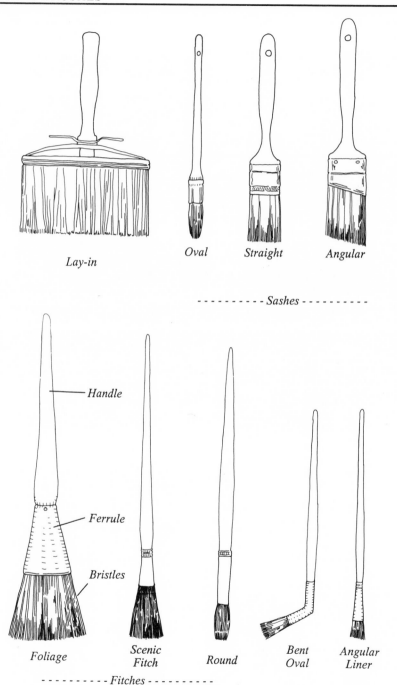

Lay-in

Oval Straight Angular

- - - - - - - - - - Sashes - - - - - - - - - -

Handle

Ferrule

Bristles

Foliage Scenic Fitch Round Bent Oval Angular Liner

- - - - - - - - - - Fitches - - - - - - - - - -

Grainer / Scumbler

Graining Brushes

Over Grainer

Heel

Rubber Grainer

Tufted Fan
Over Grainer

Fan
Blender

Steel Comb

Mottler

Flogger

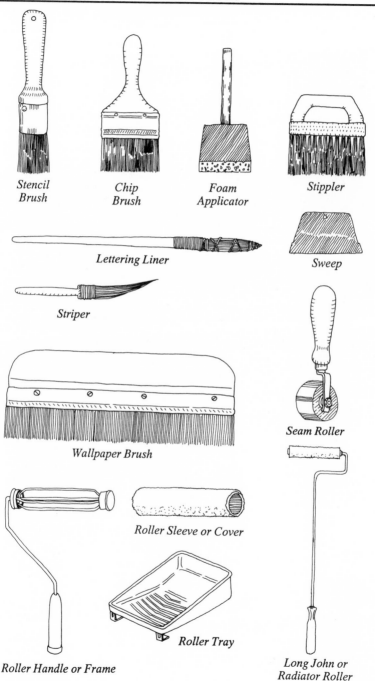

Stencil Brush

Chip Brush

Foam Applicator

Stippler

Lettering Liner

Sweep

Striper

Wallpaper Brush

Seam Roller

Roller Sleeve or Cover

Roller Handle or Frame

Roller Tray

Long John or Radiator Roller

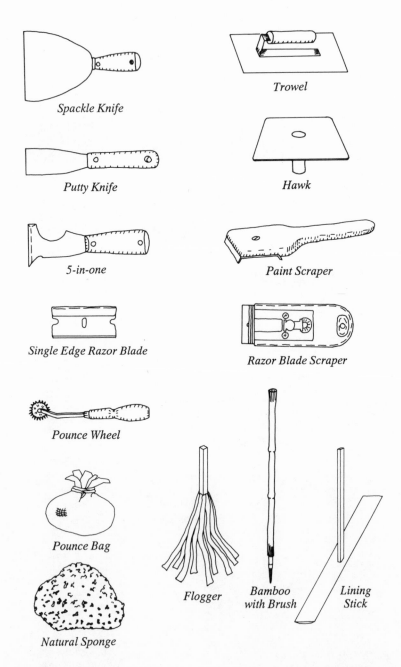

Spackle Knife

Trowel

Putty Knife

Hawk

5-in-one

Paint Scraper

Single Edge Razor Blade

Razor Blade Scraper

Pounce Wheel

Pounce Bag

Flogger

Bamboo
with Brush

Lining
Stick

Natural Sponge

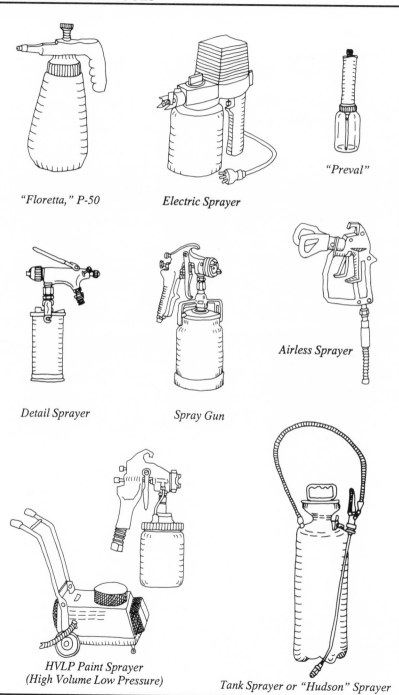

"Floretta," P-50

Electric Sprayer

"Preval"

Detail Sprayer

Spray Gun

Airless Sprayer

HVLP Paint Sprayer
(High Volume Low Pressure)

Tank Sprayer or "Hudson" Sprayer

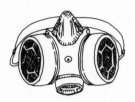

Respirator

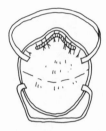

Disposable Dust Mask

Goggles

Face Fold Faceshield

Ear (Muffs) Protectors

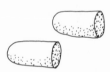

Ear Plugs

Fire Extinguisher

FIRE EXTINGUISHER RATING TERMS

Fire extinguishers are rated by size of fire (number) and by type of fire (letter). The most common type is "10 ABC."

No. 1: Will extinguish a stack of fifty burning sticks, 20 inches long; or will put out a 2.5 sq. ft. area of burning naptha.

No. 10: Will extinguish a fire 10 times larger than a No. 1 fire.

Type A: For wood, paper, etc. Puts out fires by absorbing heat, or by smothering.

Type B: For gas, paint, etc. Puts out fires by smothering.

Type C: For electrical equipment. Smothering chemicals are non-conductive.

RESPIRATOR FILTERS AND CARTRIDGES

Contaminants	*Abbreviations*	
	Cartridges	*Filters*
Acid Gas: evaporating acids, bleaches, or some photographic chemicals	AG	
Ammonia: cleaners, diazo copier chemicals	NH3	
Organic Vapor: evaporating solvents	OV	
Formaldehyde: emitted from plywood, urea formaldehyde glues	FOR	
Paint, Lacquer, Enamel Mist: spray, airbrush, aerosol paints	PLE*	
Pesticides: sprays	PEST	
Asbestos: (should never need to be used)		A
Dusts**: powders or dust from sanding, sawing, etc.		D
Mists**: water-based spray products		M
Fumes**: from heating, casting, melting metals		F

* An organic vapor cartridge with a spray paint pre-filter.
** Designed as respiratory protection against dusts, mists, and metal fumes having a permissible exposure level (measured as time weighted average) not less than 0.05 milligrams per cubic meter or dusts and mists having an air contamination level not less than 2 million particles.

Adapted from: COH1

SELECTION CHART FOR FILTERS AND CARTRIDGES

Substance or Process	*Cartridge*		*Filter*
Aerosol sprays - see Spraying below			
Air brush - containing solvents	PLE		
- water based			M
Ammonia	NH3		
Asbestos (protects only against asbestosis)			A
Dusts: wood, plaster, clay, fiber, and other toxic dusts			D or DM
Dye powders			D or DM
Fiberglass wool or insulation			D or DM
Formaldehyde	FOR		
Hydrochloric (muriatic) or acids	AG		
Lacquers and fixatives - if evaporating	OV		
- if sprayed	PLE		
Metal melting or casting			F or DMF
Metal fumes from welding			
(will not protect wearer from welding *gases*)			DMF
Metal powder			D or DM
Paint strippers (solvent-containing)	OV		
Photo-print-making solvents (evaporating)	OV		
Pigments (powdered)			D or DM
Plastic cements and glues	OV		
Plastic resin casting (except for urethane)	OV		
Plastic sanding, grinding, cutting (except for urethane and PVC)	OV	and	D or DM
PVC (polyvinyl chloride) sanding and grinding	AG/OV	and	D
Silk screen wash ups	OV		
Soldering			DMF
with acid, fluoride, and zinc chloride flux	AG	and	DMF
Solvents (evaporating)	OV		
Spray adhesives	PLE		
Spraying toxic water-based paints, dyes, and other materials			DM
Spraying solvent-containing paints, dyes and other materials	PLE		

Adapted from: COH1

Sheathing Stapler

Wrench

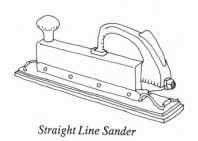

Straight Line Sander

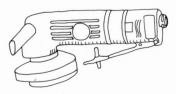

Angle Grinder

Female   Male

Air Line Couplers

Female   Male

Air Line Plugs

AIR TOOLS AVERAGE AIR REQUIREMENTS

Tool	CFM	Tool	CFM
Nailer, framing	9	Impact wrench, 1/2"	4
Nailer, roofing	5	Impact wrench, 3/4"	10
Nailer, finish	6	Angle grinder	9
Nailer, brads	1.5	Orbital sander	6
Stapler, sheathing, decking	7	Straight-line sander	8
Stapler, roofing	4.5	Needle scaler	6
Spray gun, 15 to 50 psi	3		
Spray gun, 40 to 85 psi	10		

Note: CFM requirements vary widely depending on usage and manufacturer. Actual requirement may be less, especially with tools like nailers and staplers where hits per minute determine air requirements.

HAND POWER TOOLS

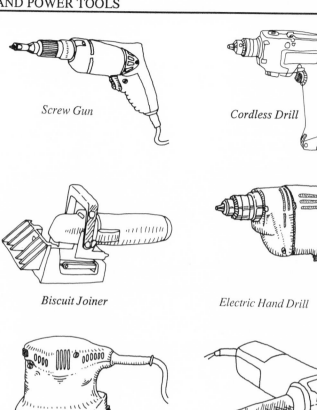

Screw Gun

Cordless Drill

Biscuit Joiner

Electric Hand Drill

Orbital Sander

Grinder

Reciprocating Sander

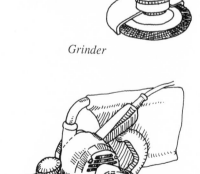

Belt Sander

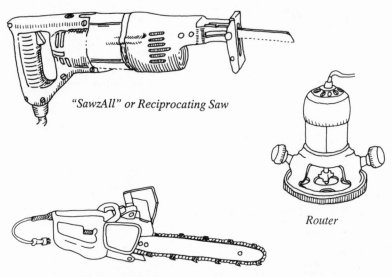

"SawzAll" or Reciprocating Saw

Router

Electric Chain Saw

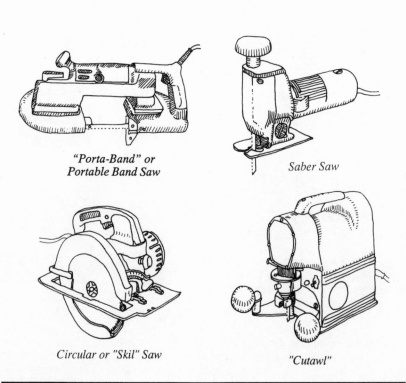

"Porta-Band" or
Portable Band Saw

Saber Saw

Circular or "Skil" Saw

"Cutawl"

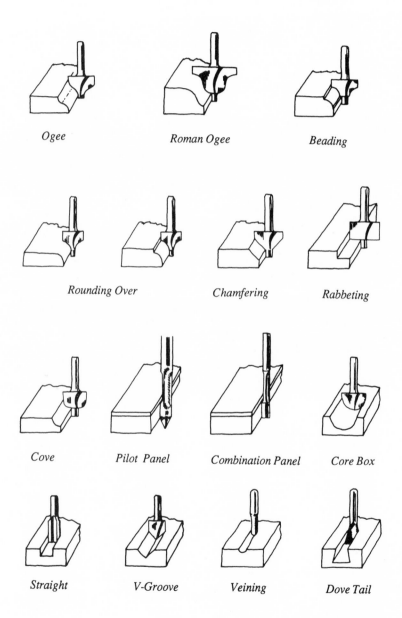

Ogee

Roman Ogee

Beading

Rounding Over

Chamfering

Rabbeting

Cove

Pilot Panel

Combination Panel

Core Box

Straight

V-Groove

Veining

Dove Tail

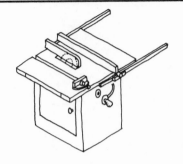

Circular or Table Saw

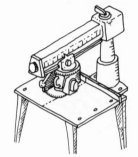

Radial Arm or Pull Over Saw

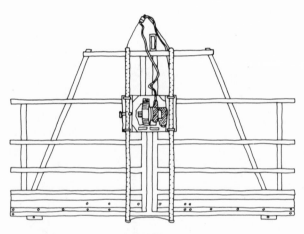

Panel Saw

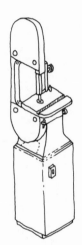

Band Saw

**Power Miter Box Saw
or Chop Saw**

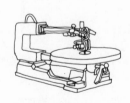

Scroll Saw

*Metal Cutting Band Saw
or "Kalamazoo" Saw*

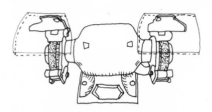

Bench Grinder

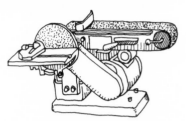

Belt and Disk Sander

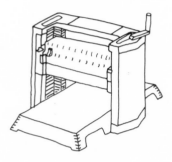

Portable Planer

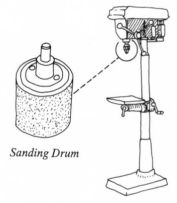

Sanding Drum

Drill Press

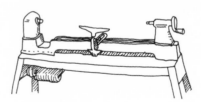

Wood Lathe

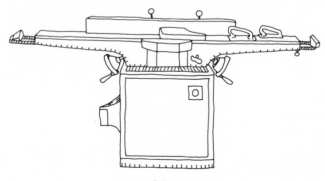

Jointer

Welding Helmet

Welding Goggles

Oxyacetylene Torch and Tips

Chipping Hammer

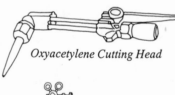

Oxyacetylene Cutting Head

Striker

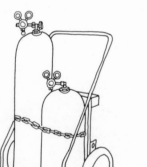

Oxyacetylene Welding Tanks

MIG Welder

ARC WELDING ELECTRODES FOR MILD STEEL

Electrode No.	Description	Current Range (Amps)* 1/16	3/32	1/8	5/32
E6011	Use for welding dirty, rusty material in all positions. Also for cutting and piercing.	---	50-90	70-130	120-180
E6013	General purpose welding; produces a soft arc.	40-70	30-80	80-120	120-190
E7014	General purpose, especially short, irregular welds. Rod contains iron powder, allowing drag technique.	---	80-110	110-150	140-190
E7018	Use for skip and tack welding. Low hydrogen.	---	70-120	100-150	120-200

* Given current ratings are estimates. Please verify correct amperages for specific electrodes with manufacturer.

A.W.S. CLASS NUMBERING SYSTEM

Electrode numbers indicate the tensile strength of the weld metal, the appropriate welding position, AC and/or DC as well as such features as low hydrogen and iron powder coating.

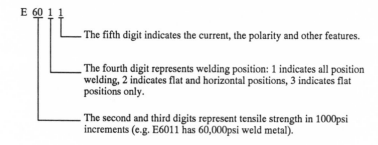

E 60 1 1

The fifth digit indicates the current, the polarity and other features.

The fourth digit represents welding position: 1 indicates all position welding, 2 indicates flat and horizontal positions, 3 indicates flat positions only.

The second and third digits represent tensile strength in 1000psi increments (e.g. E6011 has 60,000psi weld metal).

ELECTRIC ARC WELDING: SIMPLIFIED DIAGRAM

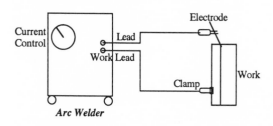

Soldering Iron

Soldering Pencil

Soldering Gun

Hot Glue Gun

Propane Torch

Nozzles

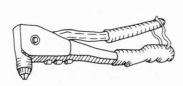

*Hand Rivet Tool
or Rivet Gun*

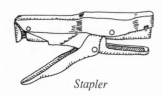

Stapler

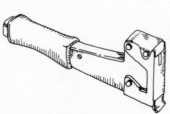

Hammer Stapler

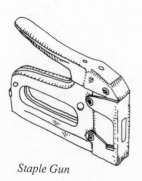

Staple Gun

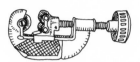

Tubing Cutter

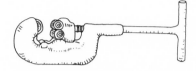

Pipe Cutter

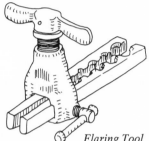

Flaring Tool

Pipe Reamer

Plastic Pipe and Tube Cutter

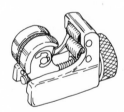

Midget Tubing Cutter

Pipe Threader

Conduit Bender

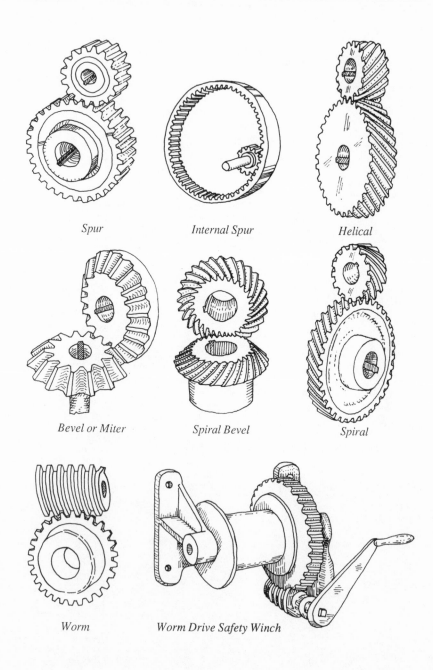

Spur

Internal Spur

Helical

Bevel or Miter

Spiral Bevel

Spiral

Worm

Worm Drive Safety Winch

JACKS

Hydraulic Jack: This jack employs the tremendous power of hydraulics. A given pressure exerted on a small area of incompressible fluid is transmitted undiminished to a larger area in the same closed circuit, thus multiplying the exerted force. This jack is not as fast in operation as the ratchet type, but it provides great power for easy lifting of heavy loads.

Ratchet Jack: A simple, fast acting jack that operates on the lever and fulcrum principle. A downward stroke of the jack handle raises the rack bar one stroke at a time. The pawls spring into position to hold the load and release the lever for the next lifting stroke. Used for loads up to 20 tons.

Screw Jack: A powerful screw and nut principle permits infinite height adjustment. There are two general types: regular for lighter loads where a simple lever bar will apply enough power to turn the screw, and inched devices which multiply the operator's strength for heavy loads.

Scissor Jack: The scissor action allows this type of jack to raise a considerable distance compared to its profile height. A drawback for this type of jack is that it requires a large amount of power at the start of its extension and provides a varying speed through its extension.

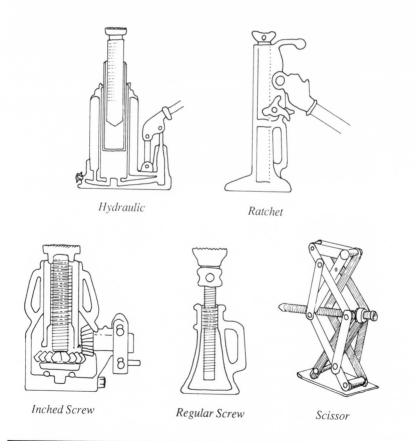

Hydraulic   *Ratchet*

Inched Screw   *Regular Screw*   *Scissor*

VALVES

Globe Valve: Named for its shape, the globe valve can operate fully open or fully closed, or set in an intermediate position to regulate flow. Often used to throttle flow, as in a bypass around a pressure regulator or other automatic device. Used for water, oil, gas. A common type of Globe Valve used in plumbing systems is the **Hose Bib** which is threaded for standard pipe fittings on one side and garden hose fittings on the other.

Needle Valve: Similar in design to a globe valve, a needle valve has a long tapered disc instead of a flat seating surface. This valve permits very close regulation and metering of flow. Used for water, oil, gas.

Gate Valve: Has a gate or wedge disc that can be raised or lowered, like a castle gate. A fully open valve offers little resistance to flow, reducing pressure drop to a minimum. If partially closed, all throttling is done at the bottom of discs and seats, subjecting them to erosion. A gate valve should be used only fully open or fully closed. Used for water, oil, gas.

Ball Valve: Used when a low profile valve is necessary to fit into confined quarters. A 90° turn opens or closes the valve, and the handle position indicates whether the valve is open or closed. Used for water, oil, gas.

Check Valve: Used to prevent backflow in lines. Line pressure forces the disc or ball to open and allow flow in forward direction. When pressure drops, gravity and line back pressure force disc or ball against seat, preventing backflow.

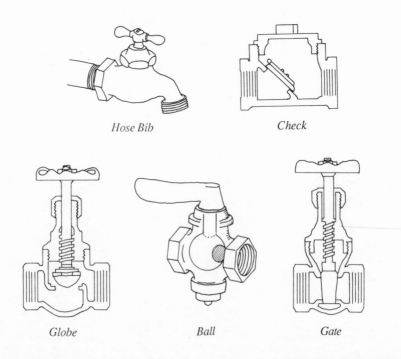

Hose Bib   *Check*

Globe   *Ball*   *Gate*

LIQUID PUMPS

Centrifugal: Used for high gallonage at low pressures. Generally not self-priming. Can handle abrasive-laden chemicals as well as water.

Rotary: Applicable for pressures up to 150 PSI. Self-priming and will handle a wide range of chemicals because of the many body materials and seal choices available. Can handle viscous liquids and liquids that will attack rubber or plastic. Not for use with abrasives.

Flexible Impeller: Self-priming and for use with viscous and abrasive liquids. Basic pressure limit is 60 PSI. Comes with several different materials and, as such, can handle water and many chemicals.

Peristaltic (Tubing): Used for low gallonage, sanitary applications and some fog machines. Nothing comes in contact with the liquid other than the tubing itself. No seals or gaskets to leak or contaminate. Self-priming and will handle light abrasives.

Diaphragm: Ideal for slurries, soft solids and light abrasives. Can be run dry for long periods without a great deal of damage.

Piston: Generally used for pumping low to medium viscous liquids at high pressures. Self-priming at short distances.

Roller or Vane: Self-priming. Used for pressures up to 200 PSI. Handles light slurries as well as viscous and abrasive liquids.

PUMP TERMS

Flow: The liquid capacity of a pump is often expressed in gallons per hour (GPH), gallons per minute (GPM) or cubic centimeters per minute (CC/MIN).

Pressure: The force exerted on the walls of a container of liquid. Measured in pounds per square inch (PSI).

Head: A measure of pressure expressed in feet. Indicates the height of a column of water lifted by the pump disregarding friction loss. For water, 1 PSI equals 2.31 feet of head.

Suction Lift: A condition that exists when the source of liquid is lower than the pump. A partial vacuum is created by pump action, and atmospheric pressure forces liquid up to the pump. The theoretical limit of suction lift is 34 feet: the practical limit is 30 feet or less, depending upon the type of pump used and the height above sea level.

Total Head: The head plus suction lift and friction loss.

Self-Priming: The ability of a pump to lift any liquid from a depth lower than the suction port of the pump.

Specific Gravity: The ratio of the weight of a given volume of liquid to the same volume of water.

Viscosity: The thickness of a liquid usually measured in *Saybolt Seconds Universal* (SSU) or *Centipoises* (CP). As temperature increases, viscosity usually decreases. The more viscous the liquid, the slower the pump speed required.

AIR COMPRESSOR TERMS AND LAWS

Cubic Feet Per Minute (CFM): A measure of a compressor's capacity or a measure of the air flow requirements of air-driven devices. Compressors have two ratings: *Displacement CFM* and *Free Air CFM*. All air driven devices are rated in *Free Air CFM*.

Displacement CFM: Calculated by multiplying the volume of the pump cylinder(s) by the pump's speed in RPM. This applies to reciprocating units and does not take into account the compressor's mechanical efficiency.

Free Air CFM: Actual air delivery of a compressor, as measured in pounds per square inch (PSI).

Pressure (PSI)*: Force exerted by the compressed air, as measured in pounds per square inch (PSI).

Determining Air Requirement: Add up the Free Air CFM requirements for all of the air powered devices that the compressor will be required to operate at the same time. To this total, add 25% or more to allow for any system variables and to provide the capacity for future needs.

Boyle's Law: At constant temperature, the absolute pressure of a gas varies inversely to the volume.

Charles's Law: At constant pressure, the volume of gas is proportional to its absolute temperature.

* Manufacturers sometimes use the term PSIG (pounds per square inch at gauge) which allows for losses in the system.

ENERGY CONVERTING MACHINES

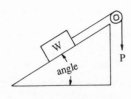

Incline Plane

P = W x Sine of Angle + Friction

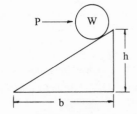

*Incline Plane
(horizontal push)*
P = W x h ÷ b

HARDWARE

ACTUAL COMMON NAIL SIZES

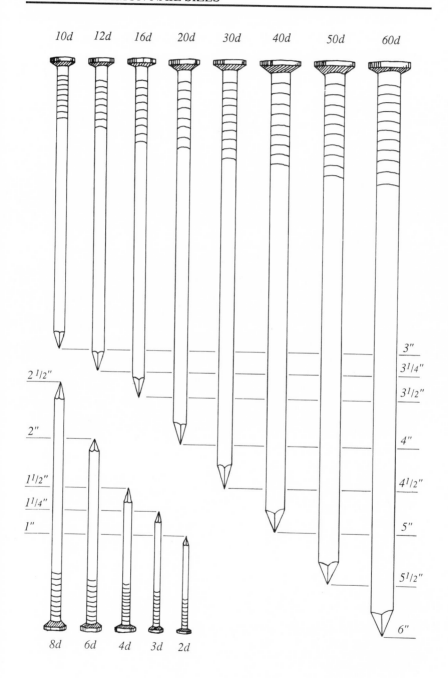

10d 12d 16d 20d 30d 40d 50d 60d

3"
3¹/4"
3¹/2"
4"
4¹/2"
5"
5¹/2"
6"

2¹/2"
2"
1¹/2"
1¹/4"
1"

8d 6d 4d 3d 2d

NAIL TYPES

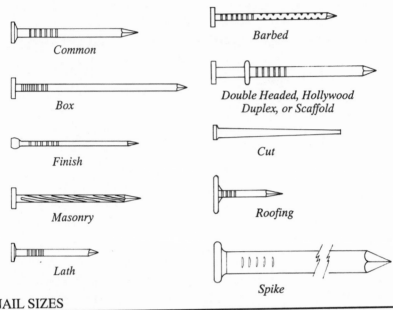

Common

Barbed

Box

Double Headed, Hollywood
Duplex, or Scaffold

Finish

Cut

Masonry

Roofing

Lath

Spike

NAIL SIZES

Size	Length (inches)	Common Nails No. per lb.	Common Nails Gauge	Box Nails No. per lb.	Box Nails Gauge	Finish Nails No. per lb.	Finish Nails Gauge
2d	1	876	15	1010	$15^1/2$	1351	$16^1/2$
3d	$1^1/4$	568	14	635	$14^1/2$	807	$15^1/2$
4d	$1^1/2$	316	$12^1/2$	473	14	584	15
5d*	$1^3/4$	271	$12^1/2$	406	14	500	15
6d	2	181	$11^1/2$	236	$12^1/2$	309	13
7d*	$2^1/4$	161	$11^1/2$	210	$12^1/2$	238	13
8d	$2^1/2$	106	$10^1/4$	145	$11^1/2$	189	$12^1/2$
9d*	$2^3/4$	96	$10^1/4$	132	$11^1/2$	172	$12^1/2$
10d	3	69	9	94	$10^1/2$	121	$11^1/2$
12d*	$3^1/4$	64	9	87	$10^1/2$	113	$11^1/2$
16d	$3^1/2$	49	8	71	10	90	11
20d	4	31	6	52	9	62	10
40d	5	18	4	---	---	---	---
60d	6	11	2	---	---	---	---

* Not very common.

The Penny System: There are several explanations as to how the *penny* system of designating nail sizes was adopted. One explanation asserts that since four or six penny nails, for instance, once cost four pence or six pence per hundred the abbreviation for penny, *d* (being the first letter of the Roman coin denarius), was also adopted to designate nail sizes. Another commonly accepted theory is that one thousand eight penny nails, for instance, weighed eight pounds. Since the ancient symbol for the English pound (in weight) was *d*, it is thought that the same symbol was used for nails.

NAIL SPECIFICATIONS

Nail	Uses	Type of Point	Type of Head	Special Features	Standard Sizes & (Gauges)
Box, Grooved Box	General construction, carpentry	Diamond	Large flat	Available with grooved shank, often coated.	2d (15¹/₂), 3d (14¹/₂), 4d & 5d (14), 6d & 7d (12¹/₂), 8d & 9d (11¹/₂), 10d & 12d(10¹/₂), 16d (10), 20d (9)
Common, Grooved Common	General construction, carpentry	Diamond	Flat	Available with grooved shank.	2d (15), 3d (14), 4d & 5d (12¹/₂), 6d & 7d (11¹/₂), 8d & 9d (10¹/₄), 10d & 12d (9),16d (8), 20d (6), 30d (5), 40d (4), 50d (3) 60d (2)
Casing	Fine finish work	Diamond	Deep counter-sunk		4d (14), 6d (12¹/₂), 8d (11¹/₂), 10d (10¹/₂), 16d (10)
Wall Board (Dry Wall)	Installing gypsum wallboard	Diamond	Flat	Smooth or grooved shank. Also available with coating for extra holding power.	Smooth shank: 4d (14), 5d (13¹/₂), 6d (13) Grooved shank: 1¹/₄", 1³/₈", 1¹/₂" (all 12¹/₂)
Double-Head (Duplex)	Temporary lumber construction	Diamond	Dual	Easily removed.	6d (11¹/₂), 8d (10¹/₄), 10d (9), 16d (8), 20d (6)
Finishing	General construction, carpentry	Diamond	Brad		2d (16¹/₂), 3d (15¹/₂), 4d & 5d (15), 6d & 7d (13), 8d & 9d (12¹/₂), 10d & 12d (11¹/₂), 16d (11), 20d (10)
Blue Lath	Various	Needle	Flat		3/4" (15)
Clout	Scenery (flats)	Clout	Flat	Soft end bends over.	4, 6, 8, 10
Concrete (Masonry)	Fastening to concrete or masonry	Diamond	Flat or square	Some with fluted shanks.	Available in fractional lengths of ¹/₂" to 3" and in various gauge sizes.
Flooring	Floor construction	Diamond	Deep counter-sunk		Standard flooring nail: 8d (10) Hardwood flooring nail: 8d (11¹/₂)
Grooved Flooring	Floor construction	Blunt Diamond	Flat counter-sunk	Special grooved shank helps reduce squeaks.	6d, 7d, 8d, (all 11¹/₂)

NAIL HEADS

Flat Common

Large Flat

*Large Flat
Reinforced*

Wire Spike

Brad

Cut Nail

Finish

Cupped Finish

*Double
Headed*

*Checkered
Roofing*

Oval

Round

NAIL POINTS

Blunt Diamond

Diamond

Long Diamond

Round

Needle

Chisel

*Front
Sheared*

*Side
Bevel*

*(Front)   (Side)
Cut Nail*

ACTUAL WOOD SCREW SIZES

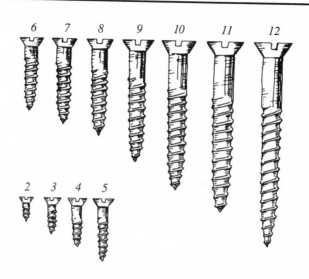

SCREW HEADS

| Lag | Fillister | Oval | Pan | Bugle | Round Head (R.H.) | Flat Head (F.H.) |

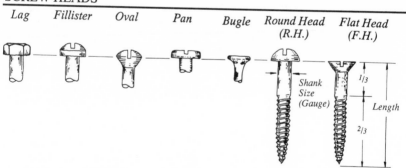

Shank Size (Gauge)

1/3

2/3

Length

One-Way   "Torx"   "Pozidriv"   Clutch Head

Plain Slotted   Phillips   Phillips/Slot   Robertson

WOOD SCREW SPECIFICATIONS

Screw Size	Screw Diameter	Threads per inch	Head Diameter			Lead Hole Drill Sizes	
			Flat	Round	Oval	Hardwoods	Softwoods
0	0.060	32	0.112	0.106	0.112	70(1/32)	---
1	0.073	28	0.138	0.130	0.138	66(1/32)	71(1/32)
2	0.086	26	0.164	0.154	0.164	56(3/64)	65(1/32)
3	0.099	24	0.190	0.178	0.190	54(1/16)	58(3/64)
4	0.112	22	0.216	0.202	0.216	52(1/16)	55(3/64)
5	0.125	20	0.242	0.228	0.242	49(5/64)	53(1/16)
6	0.138	18	0.268	0.250	0.268	47(5/64)	52(1/16)
7	0.151	16	0.294	0.274	0.294	44(3/32)	51(1/16)
8	0.164	15	0.320	0.298	0.320	40(3/32)	48(5/64)
9	0.177	14	0.346	0.322	0.346	37(7/64)	45(5/64)
10	0.190	13	0.371	0.346	0.371	33(7/64)	43(3/32)
12	0.216	11	0.424	0.395	0.424	30(1/8)	38(7/64)
14	0.242	10	0.476	0.443	0.476	25(9/64)	32(7/64)
16	0.268	9	0.485	0.476	0.485	18(5/32)	29(9/64)
18	0.294	8	0.534	0.523	0.534	13(3/16)	26(9/64)
20	0.320	8	0.582	0.570	0.582	4(13/64)	19(11/64)
24	0.372	7	0.679	0.664	0.679	1(7/32)	15(3/16)

Note: Lead holes aren't usually required for No. 0 and No. 1 screws. For sizes smaller than No. 6, lead holes can be eliminated in softwoods, except near the edges and ends of boards.

WOOD SCREWS - Stock Sizes

Length (inches)	0	1	2	3	4	5	6	7	8	9	10	11	12	14	16	18	20	24
1/4	x	x	x	x														
3/8	•	•	x	•	•	•	•	x	•	•								
1/2		•	x	•	x	•	x	•	x	•	•	•	•					
5/8		•	•	x	•	•	•	•	•	x	•	•	•					
3/4			•	x	•	•	•	x	•	•	x	x	•	•				
7/8			•	•	•	•	x	•	•	•	•	x	•	•				
1				•	•	•	x	•	•	•	•	•	x	•	•	•		
1 1/4					•	•	•	x	•	•	•	•	•	x	•	•	•	
1 1/2					•	•	x	•	•	•	•	•	•	•	x	•	•	
1 3/4						•	•	x	•	•	•	•	•	•	•	x	•	
2						•	•	x	•	•	•	•	•	•	•	x	•	•
2 1/4							•	•	x	•	•	•	•	•	•	x	•	•
2 1/2								•	•	•	•	x	•	•	•	x	•	•
2 3/4								•	•	•	•	•	x	•	•	x	•	•
3										•	•	•	•	x	•	x	•	•
3 1/2												•	•	•	x	•	x	x
4												•	•	•	x	•	x	x
4 1/2														•	x	•	x	x
5														•	x	•	x	x
6														•	x	•	x	x

* x's are most commonly available.

PHILLIPS SCREWDRIVER POINT SIZES

Screw Size	Use Point Number		Screw Size	Use Point Number
0	0		10	3
1	0		11	3
2	1		12	3
3	1		14	3
4	1		16	3
5	2		18	4
6	2		20	4
7	2		24	4
8	2			
9	2			

OTHER SCREW TYPES

Dowel Screw

Lag Screw

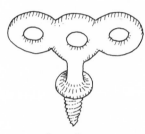

Stage Screw
(see also page 64)

Screw Hook

Screw Eye

Cup Hook Screw

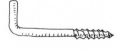

"L" Screw Hook

Hanger Screw

Sheet Metal Screws

SCREW EYE SIZES

Size Designation	Overall Length (inches)	Wire Size	Thread Length (inches)	Eye Inside Dia. (inches)
217^1/$_2$	^{15}/$_{32}$	15	^{3}/$_{32}$	^{1}/$_8$
216^1/$_2$	^{1}/$_2$	16	^{5}/$_{32}$	^{1}/$_8$
214^1/$_2$	^{11}/$_{16}$	14	^{7}/$_{32}$	^{3}/$_{16}$
212^1/$_2$	^{13}/$_{16}$	12	^{5}/$_{16}$	^{3}/$_{16}$
210	1^1/$_8$	10	^{1}/$_2$	^{3}/$_{16}$
206	1^5/$_8$	6	^{3}/$_4$	^{1}/$_4$
114	^{13}/$_{16}$	14	^{5}/$_{16}$	^{1}/$_4$
112	1^1/$_8$	12	^{7}/$_{16}$	^{9}/$_{32}$
110	1^1/$_4$	10	^{1}/$_2$	^{5}/$_{16}$
108	1^7/$_{16}$	8	^{5}/$_8$	^{3}/$_8$
106	1^{13}/$_{16}$	6	^{3}/$_4$	^{7}/$_{16}$
104	2^3/$_{16}$	4	^{15}/$_{16}$	^{15}/$_{32}$
14	1^1/$_{16}$	14	^{11}/$_{32}$	^{11}/$_{32}$
12	1^3/$_{16}$	12	^{7}/$_{16}$	^{3}/$_8$
10	1^3/$_8$	10	^{1}/$_2$	^{13}/$_{32}$
8	1^5/$_8$	8	^{5}/$_8$	^{15}/$_{32}$
6	1^{15}/$_{16}$	6	^{3}/$_4$	^{17}/$_{32}$
4	2^3/$_{16}$	4	^{7}/$_8$	^{5}/$_8$
2	2^5/$_8$	2	^{15}/$_{16}$	^{23}/$_{32}$
0	2^7/$_8$	0	1	^{13}/$_{16}$
000	3^7/$_8$	000	1^5/$_8$	1^1/$_8$

ROTO-LOCK

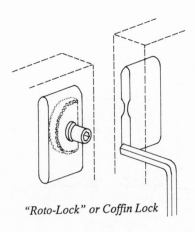

"Roto-Lock" or Coffin Lock

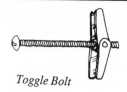

Toggle Bolt

Lag Screw Shield

"Scru 'N' Grip"

Plastic Anchor

Fiber Anchor

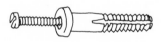

Nylon Drive Anchor

Machine Bolt Shield

*Expansion Bolt or
Molly® Fastener*

Machine Screw Anchor

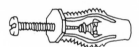

Nylon Expansion Bolt

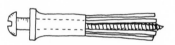

Lead Screw Anchor

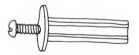

Neoprene Sleeve

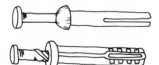

Nail Anchors

Definition of a Bolt: A bolt is a fastener which is externally threaded. It is designed to be inserted through holes in assembled parts, and is normally tightened or released by torquing a nut. A screw, on the other hand, is mated with a preformed internal thread or forms its own thread in the material. A screw is tightened or released by torquing the head.

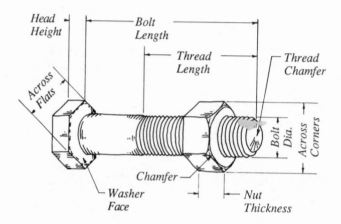

BOLT SPECIFICATIONS

Nominal Size	Diameter (inches)	Nut & Head Diameter	T.P.I.* (UNC)	T.P.I.* (UNF)	
No. 2	.0860	3/16"	56	64	
No. 3	.0990	3/16"	48	56	
No. 4	.1120	1/4"	40	48	
No. 6	.1380	5/16"	32	40	machine
No. 8	.1640	11/32"	32	36	screws **
No. 10	.1900	3/8"	24	32	
No. 12	.2160	7/16"	24	28	
1/4"	.2500	7/16"	20	28	
5/16"	.3125	1/2"	18	24	
3/8"	.3750	9/16"	16	24	
7/16"	.4375	5/8"	14	20	hex bolts,
1/2"	.5000	3/4"	13	20	cap screws,
5/8"	.6250	15/16"	11	18	stove bolts
3/4"	.7500	1 1/8"	10	16	
7/8"	.8750	1 5/16"	9	14	
1"	1.0000	1 1/2"	8	12	

*TPI = Threads Per Inch, UNC = Unified National Coarse, UNF = Unified National Fine.
** Machine screws are typically fully threaded, slotted, round head bolts of less than 1/4" diameter. They are ordered by specifying size number and threads per inch (T.P.I.).

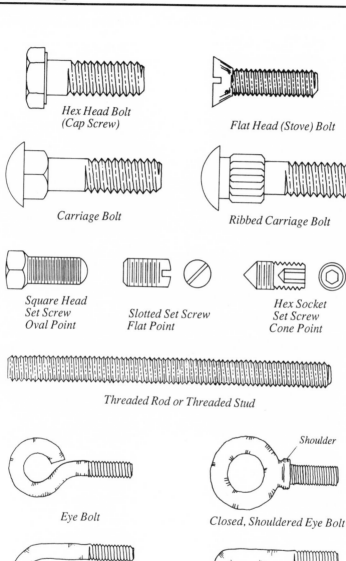

Hex Head Bolt
(Cap Screw)

Flat Head (Stove) Bolt

Carriage Bolt

Ribbed Carriage Bolt

Square Head
Set Screw
Oval Point

Slotted Set Screw
Flat Point

Hex Socket
Set Screw
Cone Point

Threaded Rod or Threaded Stud

Eye Bolt

Shoulder

Closed, Shouldered Eye Bolt

Round U-Bolt

Square U-Bolt

HEX-HEAD BOLTS - Stock Sizes

Length (inches)	\multicolumn{8}{c}{Diameters Available* (in inches)}							
	1/4	5/16	3/8	7/16	1/2	5/8	3/4	7/8
1/2	•							
3/4	x	x	x	---	•			
1	x	x	x	---	x			
1 1/4	x	x	x	---	x	•	•	
1 1/2	x	x	x	---	x	x	x	
1 3/4	•	•	x	---	x	x	x	
2	x	•	x	---	x	x	x	•
2 1/4	---	---	---	---	•	•	•	---
2 1/2	•	•	x	---	x	•	x	•
2 3/4	---	---	---	---	•	---	---	---
3		•	•	---	•	x	•	•
3 1/2			•	---	•	x	•	•
4			•	---	•	•	x	•
4 1/2			---	---	•	•	•	•
5			•	---	•	x	x	•
5 1/2				---	•	•	•	---
6				---	•	•	•	•

* x's are most common sizes. Note: you may find hex-head machine bolts in sizes other than are marked in this table, but they are not considered *standard* sizes.

SQUARE-HEAD BOLTS - Stock Sizes

Length (inches)	\multicolumn{11}{c}{Diameters Available (in inches)}										
	1/4	3/8	7/16	1/2	9/16	5/8	3/4	7/8	1	1 1/8	1 1/4
3/4	x	x									
1	x	x	x	x	x	x					
1 1/4	x	x	x	x	x	x					
1 1/2 - 9 1/2*	x	x	x	x	x	x	x	x	x		
10 - 20**	x	x	x	x	x	x	x	x	x	x	x

* Available in 1/2 inch intervals.
** Available in 1 inch intervals.

CARRIAGE BOLTS - Stock Sizes

Length (inches)	\multicolumn{9}{c}{Diameters Available (in inches)}								
	3/16	1/4	5/16	3/8	7/16	1/2	9/16	5/8	3/4
3/4	x	x	x	x					
1	x	x	x	x	x	x			
1 1/4	x	x	x	x	x	x	x	x	
1 1/2 - 9 1/2*	x	x	x	x	x	x	x	x	
10 - 20**	x	x	x	x	x	x	x	x	x

* Available in 1/2 inch intervals.
** Available in 1 inch intervals.

UNIFIED NATIONAL THREAD SERIES

Threads on bolts, nuts and screws are classified by the Unified National Thread Series. This standard was adopted in 1948, superseding the American Standard. The three most common thread series are described below.

Unified National Coarse - UNC: This series is the most common. It is usually provided if no other series is specified.

Unified National Fine - UNF: A finer thread series than UNC. Accidental loosening of bolts is less likely to occur.

Unified National Extra Fine - UNEF: As the name implies, this series has a very fine pitch of threads. Used in specialized applications only – thin walled tubes, ferrules, etc.

The Unified Standard establishes limits of tolerance called *classes*:

Classes 1A, 2A & 3A are for *external* threads (bolts).
Classes 1B, 2B & 3B are for *internal* threads (nuts).

Classes 1A and 1B are used where liberal fit is required; e.g. dirty or bruised threads. Classes 2A and 2B are standard class of fit, providing optimum fit allowance. Classes 3A and 3B provide the closest fit.

The standard method for designating screw threads specifies 1) the nominal size, 2) the number of threads per inch, 3) the thread series symbol and 4) the thread class symbol. For example, a common $^3/_4$" fastener, with coarse threads would be designated as follows:

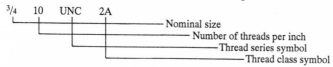

THREAD TYPES

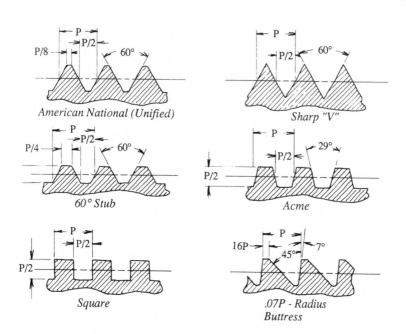

American National (Unified)

Sharp "V"

60° Stub

Acme

Square

.07P - Radius
Buttress

MECHANICAL FASTENER POINTS

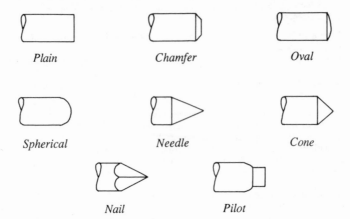

Plain   Chamfer   Oval

Spherical   Needle   Cone

Nail   Pilot

NUTS

Nominal Sizes:*   1/4" 5/16" 3/8" 7/16" 1/2"

Width at Flats: 7/16" 1/2" 9/16" 5/8" 11/16"

* The nominal size of a nut is the same as the bolt size that fits the nut.

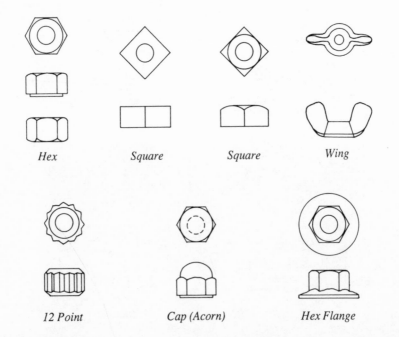

Hex   Square   Square   Wing

12 Point   Cap (Acorn)   Hex Flange

WASHER TYPES

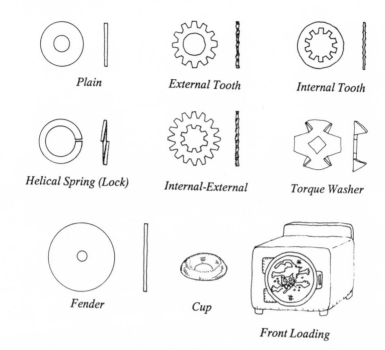

Plain   External Tooth   Internal Tooth

Helical Spring (Lock)   Internal-External   Torque Washer

Fender   Cup

Front Loading

PLAIN WASHER SPECIFICATIONS

Nominal Size of Bolt	Outside Diameter	Size of Hole	Thickness (wire gauge)	Nominal Size of Bolt	Outside Diameter	Size of Hole	Thickness (wire gauge)
3/16"	9/16"	1/4"	No. 18	1 1/8"	2 3/4"	1 1/4"	No. 8
1/4"	3/4"	5/16"	No. 16	1 1/4"	3"	1 3/8"	No. 8
5/16"	7/8"	3/8"	No. 16	1 3/8"	3 1/4"	1 1/2"	No. 7
3/8"	1"	7/16"	No. 14	1 1/2"	3 1/2"	1 5/8"	No. 7
7/16"	1 1/4"	1/2"	No. 14	1 5/8"	3 3/4"	1 3/4"	No. 7
1/2"	1 3/8"	9/16"	No. 12	1 3/4"	4"	1 7/8"	No. 7
9/16"	1 1/2"	5/8"	No. 12	1 7/8"	4 1/4"	2"	No. 7
5/8"	1 3/4"	11/16"	No. 10	2"	4 1/2"	2 1/8"	No. 7
3/4"	2"	13/16"	No. 9	2 1/4"	4 3/4"	2 3/8"	No. 5
7/8"	2 1/4"	15/16"	No. 8	2 1/2"	5"	2 5/8"	No. 4
1"	2 1/2"	1 1/16"	No. 8	2 3/4"	5 1/4"	2 7/8"	No. 3
				3"	5 1/2"	3 1/8"	No. 2

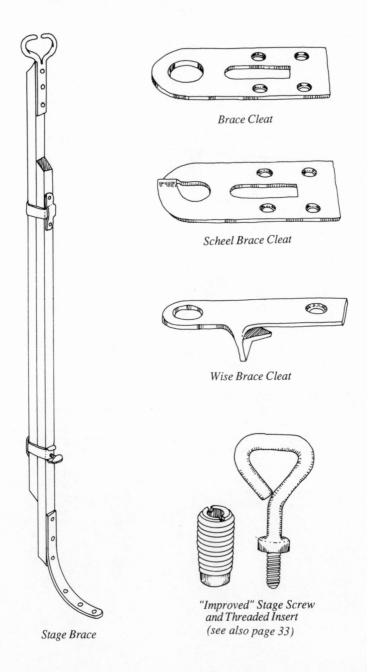

Brace Cleat

Scheel Brace Cleat

Wise Brace Cleat

Stage Brace

"Improved" Stage Screw
and Threaded Insert
(see also page 33)

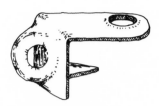

Wise Eye Cleat

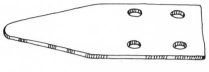

Lash Cleat

Wise Lash Line Cleat

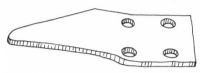

Improved Lash Cleat

Round Lash Line Cleat

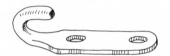

Towel Lash Line Hook

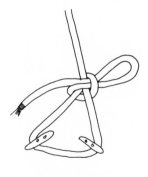

Lash Knot

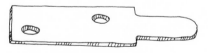

Tie Off Cleat

Steel Stop Cleat

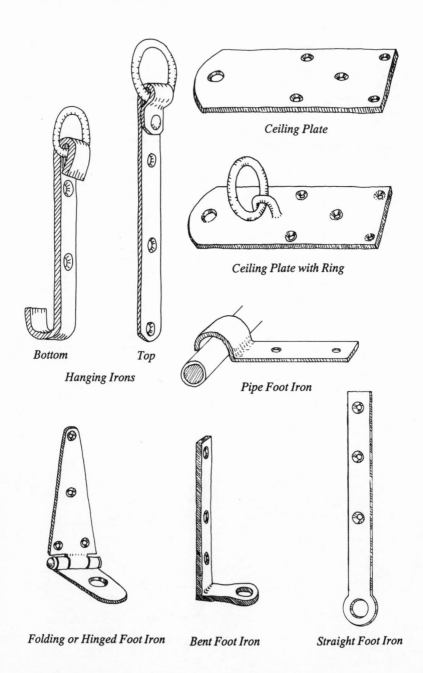

Ceiling Plate

Ceiling Plate with Ring

Bottom   *Top*

Hanging Irons

Pipe Foot Iron

Folding or Hinged Foot Iron   *Bent Foot Iron*   *Straight Foot Iron*

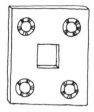

Carriage Bolt Plate

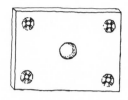

Threaded Bolt Plate

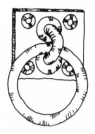

Ring on a Plate

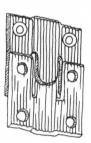

Picture Hanger

Threaded Box Bolt

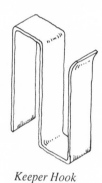

Keeper Hook

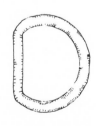

D-Ring and Keeper,
D-Ring and Strap or
Oblong Floor Plate

Picture Hanger

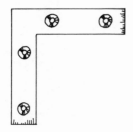

Flat Corner Iron

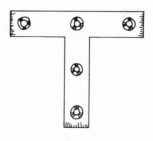

T-Iron

Bent Corner Iron

Mending Iron

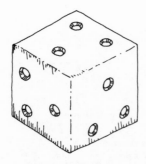

3-Way Box Corner

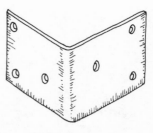

2-Way Box Corner

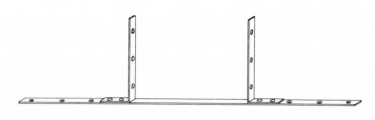

Saddle Iron

Sill Iron

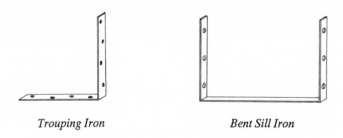

Trouping Iron   *Bent Sill Iron*

Hinged Sill Iron

BLOCK AND TACKLE

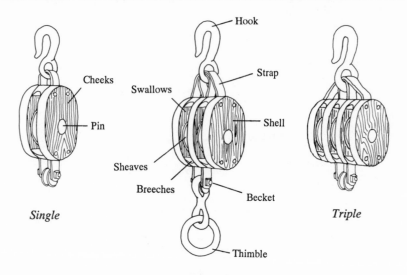

Cheeks

Pin

Hook

Swallows

Strap

Shell

Sheaves

Breeches

Becket

Thimble

Single

Double
Wood Blocks with Single Becket

Triple

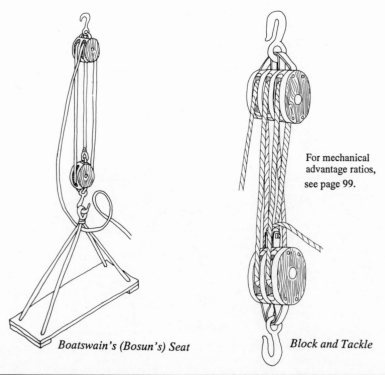

For mechanical
advantage ratios,
see page 99.

Boatswain's (Bosun's) Seat

Block and Tackle

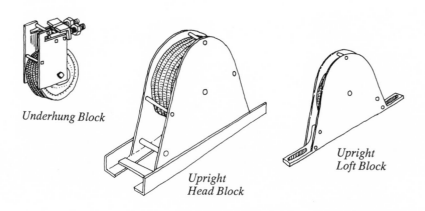

Underhung Block

*Upright
Head Block*

*Upright
Loft Block*

*Floor or
Deck Pulley*

Floor Mount Mule Block

*Underhung
Mule Block*

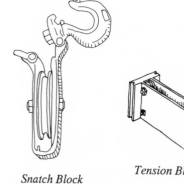

Snatch Block

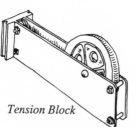

Tension Block

*Single   Double
Swivel Pulleys*

See also page 266 for diagram of a typical counterweight system.

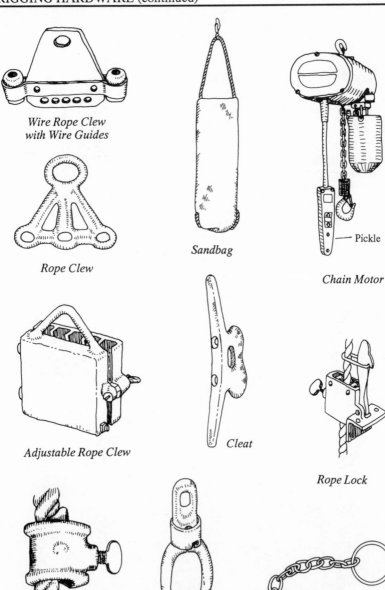

Wire Rope Clew
with Wire Guides

Rope Clew

Sandbag

Chain Motor

— Pickle

Adjustable Rope Clew

Cleat

Rope Lock

Knuckle Buster

Batten Clamp

Trim Chain

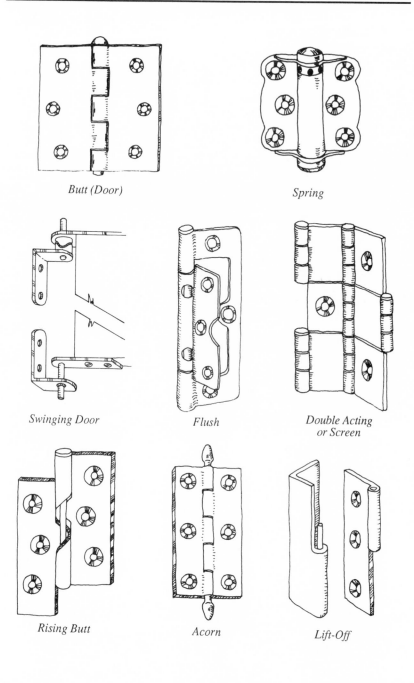

Butt (Door)

Spring

Swinging Door

Flush

Double Acting
or Screen

Rising Butt

Acorn

Lift-Off

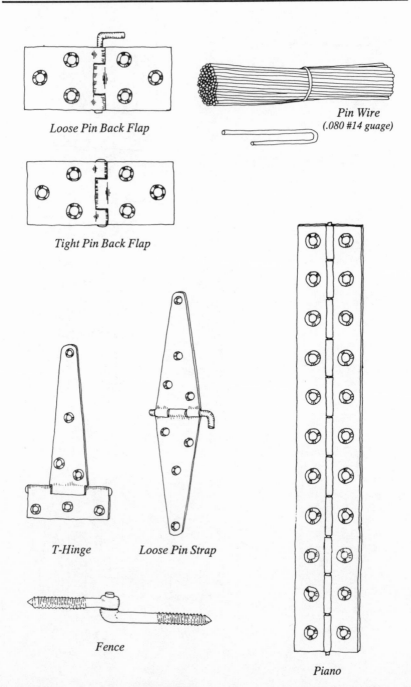

Loose Pin Back Flap

Pin Wire
(.080 #14 guage)

Tight Pin Back Flap

T-Hinge

Loose Pin Strap

Fence

Piano

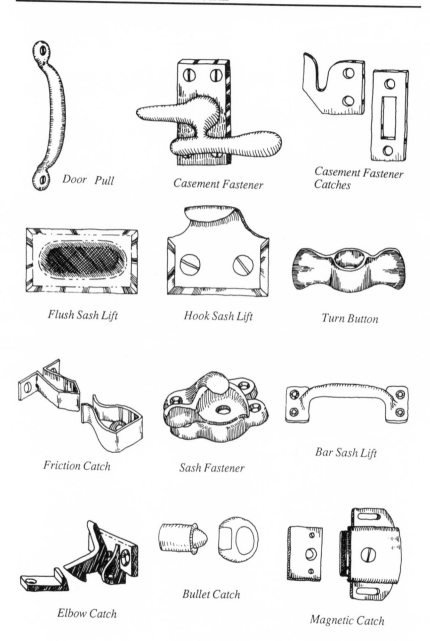

Door Pull

Casement Fastener

Casement Fastener Catches

Flush Sash Lift

Hook Sash Lift

Turn Button

Friction Catch

Sash Fastener

Bar Sash Lift

Elbow Catch

Bullet Catch

Magnetic Catch

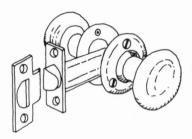

Tubular Rimset

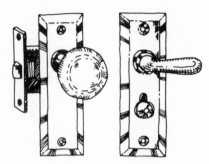

Screen Door Latch

Thumb Latch

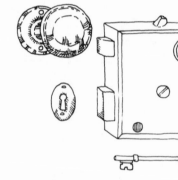

Rim Lockset

Hook and Eye

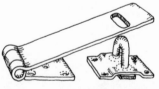

Safety Hasp

Barrel Bolt

Square Bolt

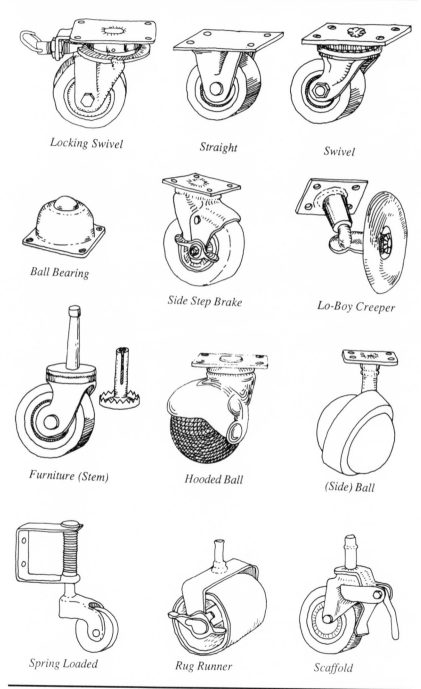

Locking Swivel

Straight

Swivel

Ball Bearing

Side Step Brake

Lo-Boy Creeper

Furniture (Stem)

Hooded Ball

(Side) Ball

Spring Loaded

Rug Runner

Scaffold

CASTER CHARACTERISTICS

Floor Surfaces	Asphalt	Brick, Ceramic Tile	Concrete	Terrazzo	Hardwood	Steel-Ribbed	Steel-Smooth	Carpet	Linoleum, Soft Tile	Wood Block
Metal Wheels*										
Cast Semi-Steel, Stainless Steel, Forged Steel	No	No	No*	No	No	No	OK	No	No	OK
Hard Wheels										
Polyolefin, Phenolic	OK	OK	Yes	No	Yes	No	OK	Yes	No	Yes
Solid Rubber, Hard Tread	OK	Yes	OK	No	Yes	No	OK	Yes	No	Yes
Nylon	OK	OK	Yes	OK	Yes	No	OK	Yes	OK	OK
Nylon Reinforced	OK	No	Yes	No	Yes	No	OK	Yes	No	Yes
Resilient Wheels										
Polyurethane	Yes	Yes	Yes	Yes	Yes	OK	Yes	Yes	OK	Yes
Semi-Pneumatic, Cushion Rubber, Pneumatic	Yes	Yes	Yes	Yes	Yes	OK	Yes	No	Yes	Yes
Cushion Neoprene	Yes	Yes	Yes	Yes	Yes	OK	Yes	OK	Yes	Yes
Hard Neoprene	OK	OK	OK	OK	OK	OK	OK	No	OK	OK

Floor Conditions	Floor Protection	Quiet Operation	Rolling Ease	Harsh Chemicals	Mild Chemicals (Wet)	Cold Below -20°F	Heat Above +160°F	Metal Chips, Large	Metal Chips, Small
Metal Wheels*									
Cast Semi Steel, Stainless Steel, Forged Steel	Low	No	High	Yes	Yes	Yes	Yes	No	Yes
Hard Wheels									
Polyolefin, Phenolic	Med	No	High	Yes	Yes	Yes	Yes	No	OK
Solid Rubber, Hard Tread	Med	No	High	Yes	Yes	Yes	No	No	OK
Nylon	High	Yes	Med	Yes	Yes	Yes	Yes	No	No
Nylon Reinforced	Med	No	High	Yes	Yes	Yes	Yes	No	Yes
Resilient Wheels									
Polyurethane	High	Yes	Med	No	Yes	Yes	No	Yes	Yes
Semi-Pneumatic, Cushion Rubber, Pneumatic	High	Yes	Low	No	No	No	No	OK	OK
Cushion Neoprene	High	Yes	Med	Yes	Yes	Yes	Yes	Yes	Yes
Hard Neoprene	Med	Yes	Med	Yes	Yes	Yes	Yes	No	No

* Metal wheels may harm concrete floors. Recommended for high capacity usage and/or extreme temperatures.

SNAPS, SWIVELS, HOOKS AND LINKS

Swivel Eye Snap

Rigid Strap Snap

*Double End Bolt Snap,
Double End Dog Clip*

Drapery Spring Snap

Chain Bolt Snap

*Swivel Bolt Snap,
Swivel Dog Clip*

Rigid Bolt Snap

Swivel Lead-Eye Snap

Lap Link

Shackle

Hammerlock

Missing Links

S-Hook

*Locking Link,
Quick Link*

*Carabiner
('biner)*

*Eye to Eye
Swivel*

*Eye to Jaw
Swivel*

Live End Pulley

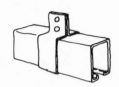

Track w/ Hanging Clamp

Dead End Pulley

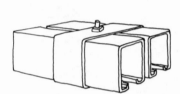

Track w/ Lap Clamp

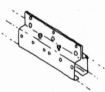

Splicing Clamp

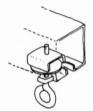

End Stop

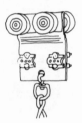

Master Carrier

Space Saver Carrier

Rubber Spacer

Single Carrier

Adjustable Floor Pulley

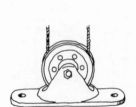

Floor Pulley

Tension Floor Pulley

GROMMETS

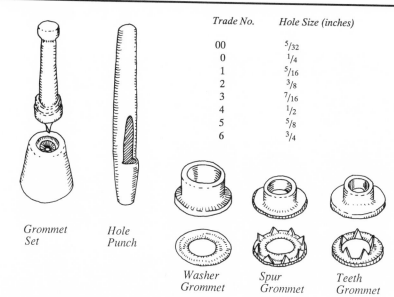

Trade No.	Hole Size (inches)
00	$5/32$
0	$1/4$
1	$5/16$
2	$3/8$
3	$7/16$
4	$1/2$
5	$5/8$
6	$3/4$

Grommet Set

Hole Punch

Washer Grommet

Spur Grommet

Teeth Grommet

ABRASIVE PAPERS AND CLOTHS

Description	Flint No.	Garnet No.	Garnet Grit	Aluminum Oxide No.	Aluminum Oxide Grit	Silicon Carbide Grit	Notes
Superfine	---	---	---	12/0	600	600	Wet sanding; produces high
	---	---	---	11/0	500	500	satin finish.
	---	---	---	10/0	400	400	
Very Fine	---	---	---	360	360	360	Wet sanding lacquer and
	---	---	---	9/0	320	320	varnish top coats.
	---	8/0	280	8/0	280	280	
Fine	5/0	7/0	240	7/0	240	240	Dry sanding of all finishing
	4/0	6/0	220	6/0	220	220	undercoats; these grades
	3/0	5/0	180	5/0	180	180	do not show sanding marks.
Medium	2/0	4/0	150	4/0	150	150	Final sanding of bare wood;
	1/0	3/0	120	3/0	120	120	smoothing old finishes;
	$1/2$	2/0	100	2/0	100	100	general wood sanding;
	1	1/0	80	1/0	80	80	sanding plaster patches.
Coarse	$1^1/2$	$1/2$	60	$1/2$	60	60	Rough wood sanding.
	2	1	50	1	50	50	
	$2^1/2$	$1^1/2$	40	$1^1/2$	40	40	
Very Coarse	3	2	36	2	36	36	Limited hand use; too coarse
	$3^1/2$	$2^1/2$	30	$2^1/2$	30	30	for pad sanders.
	4	3	24	3	24	24	

*External
Retaining Ring*

*Internal
Retaining Ring*

E-Clip

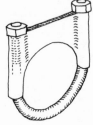

*U-Bolt Type
Pipe Clamp*

O-Ring

Conduit Clamps

**Hitch Pin or
Hairpin Cotter**

Pin Clip

Cotter Pin

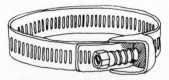

Worm Drive Hose Clamp

Compression Spring

Hose Clamp

Extension Spring

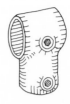

"Kee Klamp"

galvanized malleable iron
over 35 fitting configurations
available for $^3/_4$", $1^1/_4$", $1^1/_2$", 2" I.D. pipe

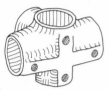

"Speed Rail®" (Hollaender)

(in-line railing system)
aluminum magnesium alloy
over 25 fitting configurations
available for $^3/_4$", 1", $1^1/_4$", $1^1/_2$" I.D. pipe

"Nu-Rail®" (Hollaender)

(offset railing system)
aluminum magnesium alloy
over 20 fitting configurations
available for $^3/_4$", 1", $1^1/_4$", $1^1/_2$", 2" I.D. pipe

"Rota Lock"
available for 1", $1^1/_4$", $1^1/_2$", 2" I.D. pipe

"Cheseborough"
available for $1^1/_4$", $1^1/_2$" I.D. pipe

ROPE FIBERS

Natural rope fibers come mainly from three plant sources.

Manila: The fibers of manila rope are derived from the leaves of the abaca plant. These leaves, which are harvested from the growing plants over several years, are stripped of their pulp leaving only the tough fibers. Manila fibers measure from three to eight feet in length and are the strongest natural rope fiber. The natural color varies from almost white to light brown.

Sisal: Sisal rope is derived from two plants – the agave sisalana, grown primarily in East Africa, Haiti and Brazil and the henequen plant, which is native to Mexico. The leaves of these plants, which resemble those of the century plant, reach lengths of up to four feet. The fibers are continuous from end to end and are white to almost yellow when processed.

Cotton: Cotton rope is the weakest natural fiber rope because the cotton fibers are very short. Cotton is grown in many semi-tropical areas and is naturally white in color.

Synthetic rope fibers are usually very long synthetic molecular chains made by rearranging the chemical structure of simpler compounds derived from coal, petroleum, natural gas, or agricultural residues.

Nylon: Filaments can be continuous in length, or cut into staple and spun into yarn. Nylon is a polyamide which is naturally pure white in color. It can be colored during manufacturing or the finished filaments can be fast dyed. Nylon can be cleaned with mild detergent.

Polyester: Filaments can be continuous in length, or cut into staple and spun into yarn. Polyester is naturally white. Coloring can be added during manufacturing, but the finished filaments are difficult to fast dye. Polyester is easily cleaned with mild detergent.

Polypropylene / Polyethylene: Filament length is limited only by the size of the take-up reel or bobbin. These two synthetic fibers are generically classed as polyolefins. They're naturally translucent in appearance and any color must be added during manufacturing. The finished filaments cannot be dyed. Both can easily be cleaned with mild detergent. Polyethylene rope has a slick, oily feel, while polypropylene has a smooth surface and is not slippery. Polypropylene is 5–10% stronger and slightly lighter than polyethylene.

Source: CG

APPROXIMATE SAFE WORKING LOADS OF
NEW 3-STRAND FIBER ROPE

Safety Factor = 5

Diameter (inches)	Manila (lbs.)	Sisal (lbs.)	Nylon (lbs.)	Polypropylene (lbs.)	Polyester (lbs.)	Polyethylene (lbs.)
$3/16$	100	75	200	150	200	150
$1/4$	120	90	300	250	300	250
$5/16$	200	---	500	400	500	350
$3/8$	270	200	700	500	700	500
$1/2$	530	400	1,250	830	1,200	800
$5/8$	880	---	2,000	1,300	1,900	1,050
$3/4$	1,080	810	2,800	1,700	2,400	1,500
$7/8$	1,540	---	3,800	2,200	3,400	2,100
1	1,800	1,350	4,800	2,900	4,200	2,500
$1^1/8$	2,400	---	6,300	3,750	5,600	3,300
$1^1/4$	2,700	---	7,200	4,200	6,300	3,700
$1^1/2$	3,700	---	10,200	6,000	8,900	5,300
$1^5/8$	4,500	---	12,400	7,300	10,800	6,500
$1^3/4$	5,300	---	15,000	8,700	12,900	7,900
2	6,200	---	17,900	10,400	15,200	9,500

Source: RM

RULES OF THUMB FOR DETERMINING
SAFE WORKING LOADS (S.W.L.) OF *USED* ROPE*

Manila: (20)
Change the rope diameter into eighths of an inch. Square the numerator and multiply by **20**.
Examples: (a) $1/2$ inch manila rope = $4/8$ inch diameter.
S.W.L **= 4^2 x 20 = 320 lbs.
(b) $5/8$ inch manila rope
S.W.L = 5^2 x 20 = 500 lbs.

Nylon: (60)
Change the rope diameter into eighths of an inch. Square the numerator and multiply by **60**.
Example: (a) $1/2$ inch nylon rope = $4/8$ inch diameter.
S.W.L = 4^2 x 60 = 960 lbs.

Polypropylene: (40)
Change the rope diameter into eighths of an inch. Square the numerator and multiply by **40**.
Example: (a) $1/2$ inch polypropylene rope = $4/8$ inch diameter.
S.W.L = 4^2 x 40 = 640 lbs.

Polyester: (60)
Change the rope diameter into eighths of an inch. Square the numerator and multiply by **60**.
Example: (a) $1/2$ inch polyester rope = $4/8$ inch diameter.
S.W.L = 4^2 x 60 = 960 lb.

Polyethylene: (35)
Change the rope diameter into eighths of an inch. Square the numerator and multiply by **35**.
Example: (a) 1 inch polyethylene rope = $8/8$ inch diameter.
S.W.L = 8^2 x 35 = 2240 lb.

*Since rope in the theatre is often very old, you will have to use judgement as to whether to use even these downgraded values for used rope. There should be no substitute for safety.

Source: RM

CHARACTERISTICS OF FIBER ROPE

	Manila	Sisal	Cotton	Nylon	Poly-ester	Poly-propylene	Poly-ethylene
Strength & Weight							
Wet Strength vs. Dry Strength	up to 120%	up to 120%	up to 120%	85–90%	100%	100%	105%
Shock load absorption ability	poor	poor	very poor	excellent	good	very good	fair
Strength vs. Weight Ratio	1.0	.75	.50	3.0	2.25	2.5	2.25
Able to float	no	no	no	no	no	yes	yes
Elongation							
Elongation at 20% of breaking strength	11%	11%	---	23%	17%	20%	22%
Elongation at 75% of breaking strength	19%	19%	---	42%	29%	37%	40%
Creep (extension under sustained load)	very low	very low	---	moderate	low	high	high
Degradation							
Surface abrasion resistance	good	fair	good	very good	best	good	fair
Internal abrasion resistance	good	good	good	excellent	best	good	good
Resistance to U.V. (sunlight)	good	good	good	good	excellent	good, black is best	good, black is best
Resistance to aging for properly stored rope	good	good	good	excellent	excellent	excellent	excellent
Effects of Temperature							
High temp. working limit	300°F	300°F	300°F	300°F	300°F	200°F	150°F
Melting point				480°F	482°F	330°F	285°F
Low temp. working limit	-100°F	-100°F	-100°F	-70°F	-70°F	-20°F	-100°F
Effects of Moisture							
Water absorption of individual fibers	up to 100% of weight	up to 100% of weight	up to 100% of weight	8.0 – 12.0%	1.0%	none	none
Resistance to rot and mildew	poor	very poor	very poor	excellent	excellent	excellent	excellent
Ability of rope to ease out smoothly over metal while under a load	excellent	good	good	poor	good	very poor	poor

Source: CG

WEIGHTS AND LENGTHS OF MANILA ROPE

Diameter (inches)	Pounds per Coil	Feet per Coil	Pounds per Foot
$^1/_4$	50	2500	.020
$^3/_8$	50	1220	.041
$^7/_{16}$	63	1200	.053
$^1/_2$	90	1200	.075
$^9/_{16}$	125	1200	.104
$^5/_8$	160	1200*	.133
$^3/_4$	200	1200*	.166

* $^5/_8$" and $^3/_4$" manila rope is also available in 600 foot coils.

SIZES OF BRAIDED WHITE COTTON CORD

Size (No.)	Diameter (inches)	Feet per Hank	Size (No.)	Diameter (inches)	Feet per Hank
4	$^1/_8$	48	8	$^1/_4$	100
$4^1/_2$	$^9/_{64}$	48	10	$^5/_{16}$	100
5	$^5/_{32}$	48	12	$^3/_8$	100
6	$^3/_{16}$	100			

Note: Cotton cord is available in sizes larger than $^3/_8$" ($^1/_2$" and $^5/_8$" are often used for curtain tracks), however it is not sized by numbers and is commonly referred to as "rope."

KNOT TERMINOLOGY

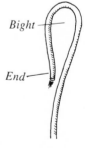

Bight

End

Standing
Part

Overhand
Loop

Underhand
Loop

100%
No knots or splices.

75%
*Rope strength decreases 25%
when a hitch is tied.*

85%
*A splice decreases rope
strength by 15%.*

50%
*Any kind of knot decreases
rope strength by 50%.*

50%
A bend used to tie two ropes together decreases overall rope strength by 50%.

50%
Overall rope strength is decreased by 50% when two ropes are linked in this fashion.

Source: RM

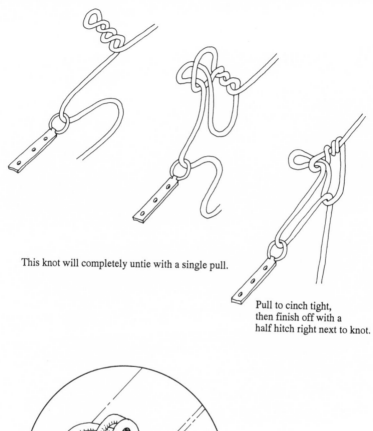

This knot will completely untie with a single pull.

Pull to cinch tight,
then finish off with a
half hitch right next to knot.

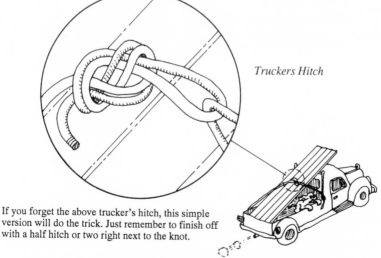

Truckers Hitch

If you forget the above trucker's hitch, this simple
version will do the trick. Just remember to finish off
with a half hitch or two right next to the knot.

BOWLINE KNOTS

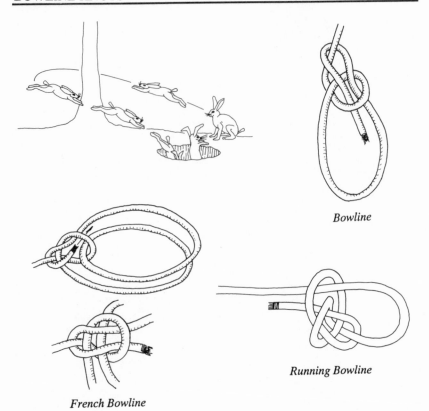

Bowline

French Bowline

Running Bowline

MISCELLANEOUS KNOTS

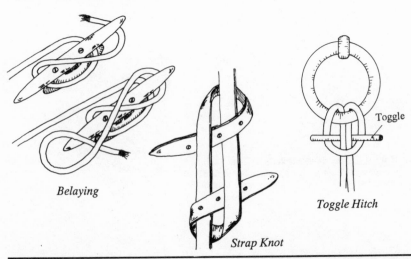

Belaying

Strap Knot

Toggle Hitch

Toggle

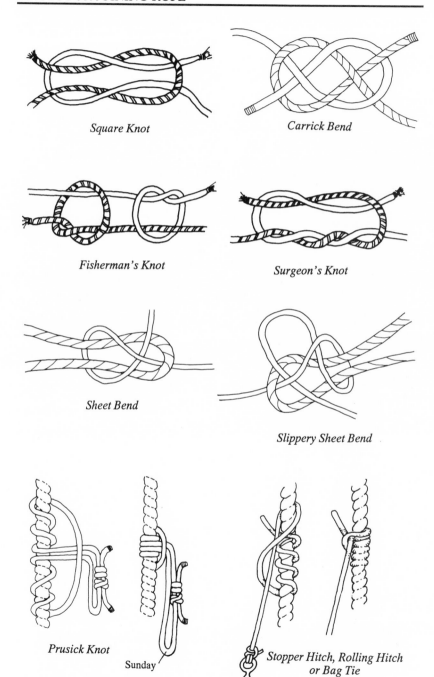

Square Knot

Carrick Bend

Fisherman's Knot

Surgeon's Knot

Sheet Bend

Slippery Sheet Bend

Prusick Knot

Sunday

Stopper Hitch, Rolling Hitch
or Bag Tie

Single Blackwall

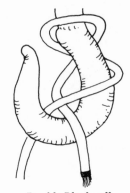

Double Blackwall

Cat's Paw

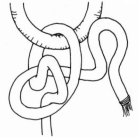
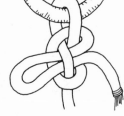

Mooring Hitch

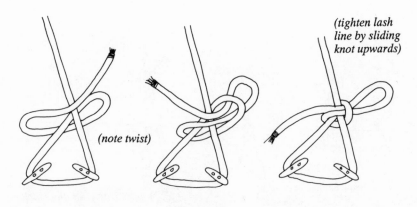

(note twist)

(tighten lash line by sliding knot upwards)

Lash Knot

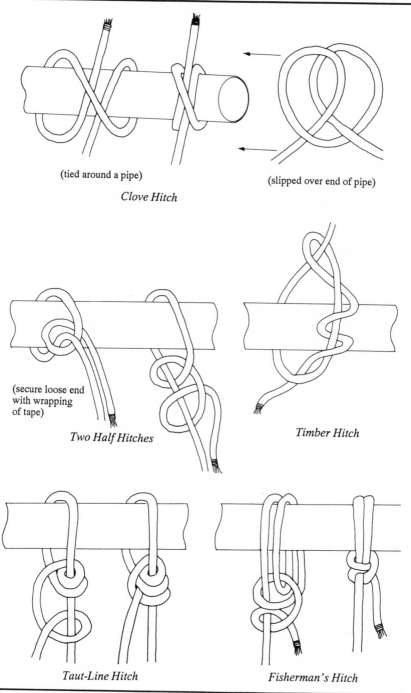

(tied around a pipe)

Clove Hitch

(slipped over end of pipe)

(secure loose end with wrapping of tape)

Two Half Hitches

Timber Hitch

Taut-Line Hitch

Fisherman's Hitch

Figure Eight Knot

Stevedore's Knot

Wall Knot

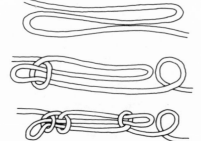

Sheepshank

Single Matthew Walker

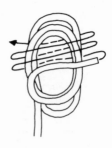
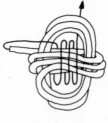

Monkey's Fist

EYE SPLICE

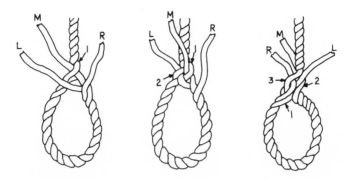

Unlay the rope end four or five turns. Tuck end M under strand 1.

Tuck end L over strand 1 and under strand 2.

Turn the rope over and tuck end R under strand 3 and over the next strand. Repeat this over and under movement with each end for several tucks.

END SPLICE

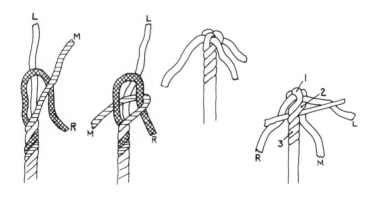

Unlay the rope end and make a crown knot as shown in the first three illustrations. Then tuck ends 1, 2 and 3 with the over and under movement. Finish by trimming the loose ends and smoothing the splice by rolling it underfoot.

LONG SPLICE

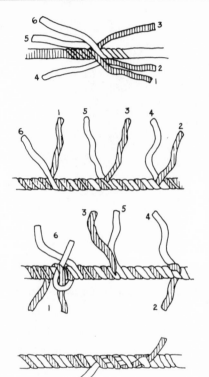

The long splice is characterized by its ability to run through a block without binding.

Begin the long splice by unlaying the strands of the rope ends about 15 turns. Butt the loosened ends together, alternating the strands and being careful to keep the strands untangled.

Unlay strand 4 several more turns and fill its place with its opposite strand, 2. Do the same with strands 1 and 6 in the opposite direction. Let strands 3 and 5 remain in the middle.

Tie strands 2 and 4 with an overhand knot. Then tuck each strand twice. The tuck goes over one, under the second and out between the second and third strands. After two tucks, taper off by gradually reducing the yarns in the strand. Repeat with strands 1 and 6, and 3 and 5.

Pound all the tucks into the rope, clip the ends and roll the splice underfoot to ensure that its finished diameter is no larger than the rest of the rope.

WHIPPING

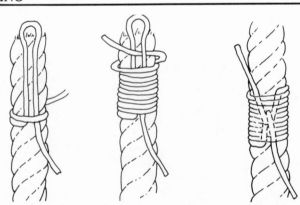

Lay a loop along the rope. Next, make a series of turns over the loop. The working end is finally stuck through the loop and the end pulled back out of sight. Both ends are trimmed. The whipping should be equal in width to the diameter of the rope.

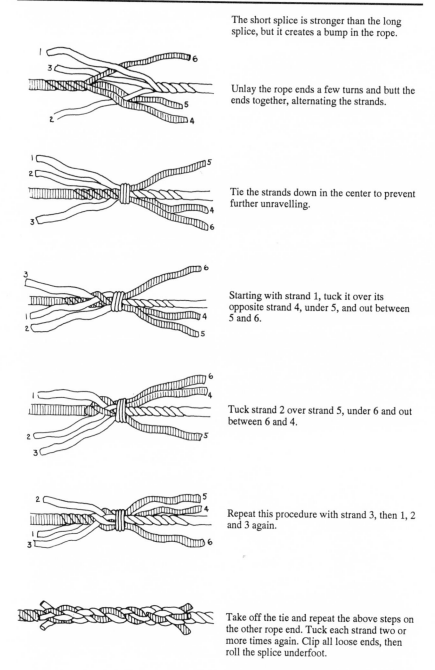

The short splice is stronger than the long splice, but it creates a bump in the rope.

Unlay the rope ends a few turns and butt the ends together, alternating the strands.

Tie the strands down in the center to prevent further unravelling.

Starting with strand 1, tuck it over its opposite strand 4, under 5, and out between 5 and 6.

Tuck strand 2 over strand 5, under 6 and out between 6 and 4.

Repeat this procedure with strand 3, then 1, 2 and 3 again.

Take off the tie and repeat the above steps on the other rope end. Tuck each strand two or more times again. Clip all loose ends, then roll the splice underfoot.

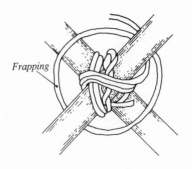

Frapping

Diagonal – Start with a timber hitch around both pieces. Tighten the hitch to draw the pieces together. Take three or four turns around one piece, then three or four around the second. The turns should be beside each other, not on top. Next, take two frapping turns around the lashing at the point where the pieces cross. End with a clove hitch around one of the pieces.

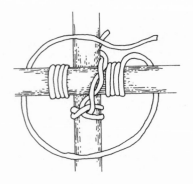

Square – Tie a clove hitch around the upright piece, directly below where the crosspiece will be. Tighten and twist the free and standing ends around each other. Next, wrap the rope behind the upright, down in front of the crosspiece, and around behind the upright. Repeat four times, keeping outside the previous turns on the crosspiece. Then make two or three frapping turns between the pieces and pull tight. Finish the lashing with a clove hitch on the crosspiece.

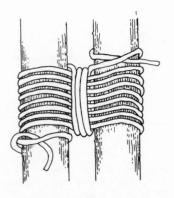

Shear – Tie a clove hitch around one piece. Make eight to ten wraps around both pieces. Then make two or three frapping turns between the pieces and pull tight. Finish with a clove hitch around the second piece.

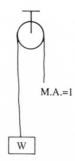

M.A.=1

Single Whip

$$\frac{P}{W} = \frac{10}{10} \ \mathbf{\frac{11}{10}}$$

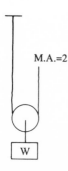

M.A.=2

Single Whip w/
Block at Weight

$$\frac{P}{W} = \frac{10}{20} \ \mathbf{\frac{11}{20}}$$

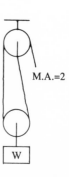

M.A.=2

Gun Tackle
Purchase

$$\frac{P}{W} = \frac{10}{20} \ \mathbf{\frac{12}{20}}$$

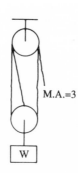

M.A.=3

Luff or Watch
Tackle

$$\frac{P}{W} = \frac{10}{30} \ \mathbf{\frac{13}{30}}$$

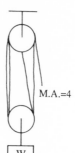

M.A.=4

Double Purchase or
Double Luff Tackle

$$\frac{P}{W} = \frac{10}{40} \ \mathbf{\frac{14}{40}}$$

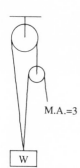

M.A.=3

Spanish Burton

$$\frac{P}{W} = \frac{10}{30} \ \mathbf{\frac{12}{30}}$$

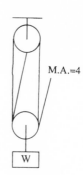

M.A.=4

Inverted Luff or
Inverted Watch Tackle

$$\frac{P}{W} = \frac{10}{40} \ \mathbf{\frac{13}{40}}$$

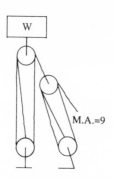

M.A.=9

Luff upon Luff

$$\frac{P}{W} = \frac{10}{90} \ \mathbf{\frac{16}{90}}$$

Note: W = Weight; M.A. = Mechanical Advantage; P = Pull Required. Ratios in bold type include friction at 10% loss per turn. See page 46 for illustrations of block and falls.

Wire Rope is designated and ordered by describing its eight characteristics:

1. Length: Measured in feet.

2. Diameter: Measured between the widest points. Most new rope measures slightly over its nominal size, e.g. $3/4$" rope is $1/32$" oversize.

3. Class: The number of strands and wires (n strands x n wires.). For example: **6 x 7** (Standard Coarse Rope), **6 x 19** (Standard Hoisting Rope), **7 x 19** (Aircraft Cable), and **6 x 36** (Extra Flexible Hoisting Rope).

4. Construction: The arrangement of the strands, the four following being the most common. **Ordinary**, where the wires are all the same size. **Seale**, where larger diameter wires are used on the outside of the strand and smaller wires are used on the inside of the strand. This provides flexibility and resists abrasion. **Warrington**, where alternate wires are large and small. This provides flexibility and abrasion resistance. **Filler**, where very small wires fill in the valleys between the outer and inner rows of wires. This provides good abrasion and fatigue resistance.

5. Preformed: A process where each strand is "pre-formed" to the helical shape it will assume in the finished rope.

6. Steel Types or Grades:
   EIPS: Extra Improved Plow Steel
   IPS: Improved Plow Steel
   PS: Plow Steel
   MPS: Mild Plow Steel

7. Core: The core can be made of fiber, cotton, asbestos, steel wire, etc. Wire (steel) cores can be composed of a multiple wire strand core (**WST**), or a small 6 x 7 independent wire rope core (**IWRC**). The IWRC is more flexible and resists crushing better than the WST. Steel core wire rope is $7^{1/2}\%$ stronger than fiber core rope.

8. Rope Lay: The direction of the rotation of the wires and strands in the rope:
   Right: Strands rotate clockwise around the core.
   Left: Strands rotate counter-clockwise around the core.
   Regular: Wire rotates around the core in the opposite direction to the rotation of the strands in the core.
   Lang: The wire and strands rotate in the same direction.

Aircraft cable is almost always used in theatrical rigging systems. This type of wire rope is 7 x 19, Seal, preformed, galvanized EIPS, IWRC, right regular lay.

Sources: UWP, WC, WREH

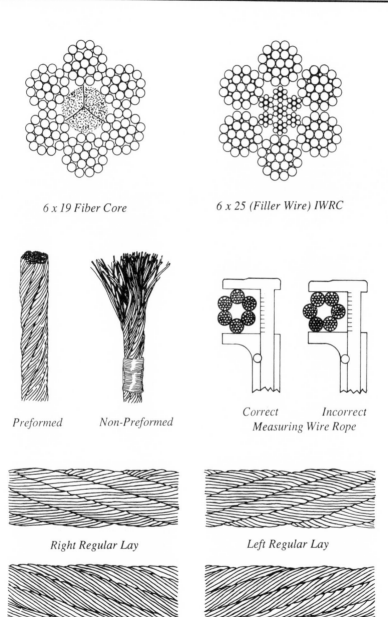

6 x 19 Fiber Core

6 x 25 (Filler Wire) IWRC

Preformed

Non-Preformed

Correct   Incorrect
Measuring Wire Rope

Right Regular Lay

Left Regular Lay

Right Lang Lay

Left Lang Lay

SAFE WORKING LOADS OF WIRE ROPE

Safety Factor = 5

6 x 19

Rope Diameter (inches)	---------Plow Steel---------		---Improved Plow Steel---	
	Fibre Core (lbs.)	Steel Core (lbs.)	Fiber Core (lbs.)	Steel Core (lbs.)
3/16	520	560	600	640
1/4	960	1040	1080	1160
5/16	1520	1550	1640	1760
3/8	2080	2320	2400	2560
7/16	2800	3000	3200	3440
1/2	3680	3920	4100	4500

7 x 19 Galvanized EIPS IWRC (Aircraft Cable) Safety Factor = 5

Size: (inches)	1/16	1/8	3/16	1/4	5/16	3/8	7/16	1/2
Working Load: (lbs.)	96	400	840	1400	1960	2880	3260	4560

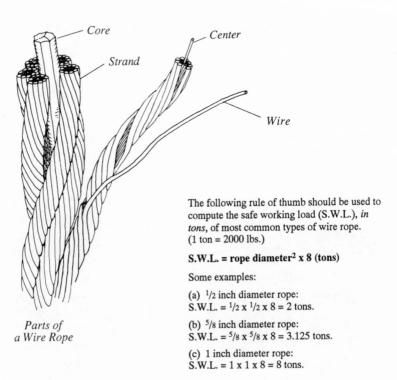

Core

Center

Strand

Wire

Parts of a Wire Rope

The following rule of thumb should be used to compute the safe working load (S.W.L.), *in tons*, of most common types of wire rope. (1 ton = 2000 lbs.)

S.W.L. = rope diameter^2 x 8 (tons)

Some examples:

(a) 1/2 inch diameter rope:
S.W.L. = 1/2 x 1/2 x 8 = 2 tons.

(b) 5/8 inch diameter rope:
S.W.L. = 5/8 x 5/8 x 8 = 3.125 tons.

(c) 1 inch diameter rope:
S.W.L. = 1 x 1 x 8 = 8 tons.

Source: RM, MH, WC

INSTALLATION OF WIRE ROPE CLIPS

Rope Diameter (inches)	Minimum No. of Clips	Amount of Rope Turn Back From Thimble (inches)	Torque in Foot-Pounds Unlubricated Bolts
1/8	2	3 1/4	4.5
3/16	2	3 3/4	7.5
1/4	2	4 3/4	15
5/16	2	5 1/2	30
3/8	2	6 1/2	45
7/16	2	7	65
1/2	3	11 1/2	65
9/16	3	12	95
5/8	3	12	95
3/4	4	18	130
7/8	4	19	225
1	5	26	225
1 1/8	6	34	225
1 1/4	6	37	360
1 3/8	7	44	360
1 1/2	7	48	360
1 5/8	7	51	430
1 3/4	7	53	590

U-Bolt

Saddle

Hex Nut

Saddle must always be against the live end. Remember: "Never saddle a dead horse."

Sources: C, CC, AB

INSTALLATION OF DOUBLE SADDLE CLIPS

Rope Diameter (Inches)	Minimum No. of Clips	Amount of Rope To Turn Back (Inches)	Torque in Foot-Pounds Unlubricated Bolts
3/16	2	4	30
1/4	2	4	30
5/16	2	5	30
3/8	2	5 1/2	45
7/16	2	6 1/2	65
1/2	3	11	65
9/16	3	12 3/4	130
5/8	3	13 1/2	130
3/4	3	16	225
7/8	4	26	225
1	5	37	225
1 1/8	5	41	360
1 1/4	6	55	360
1 3/8	6	62	500
1 1/2	6	66	500

Hex Nut

Saddle

Sources: C, CC, AB

NICOPRESS SLEEVES AND TOOLS

Nicopress Sleeve   *Thimble*

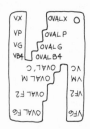

Go / No-Go Guage

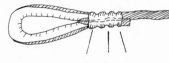

2   3   1
Note crimping order.

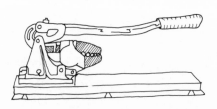

Swaging Tool

"Nicopress"
Compression Tool

SLINGS

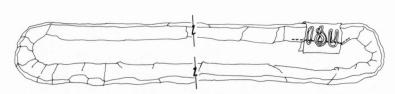

Roundsling

Sling or Basket

TURNBUCKLES

End Fitting Stock Diameter (inches)	S.W.L. Any Combination of Jaw End Fittings and Eye End Fittings (lbs.)	S.W.L. Any Turnbuckle w/ Hook End Fitting (lbs.)
1/4	500	400
5/16	800	700
3/8	1,200	1,000
1/2	2,200	1,500
5/8	3,500	2,250
3/4	5,200	3,000
7/8	7,200	4,000
1	10,000	5,000

Note: These safe working load figures refer only to turnbuckles made of weldless, forged alloy steel.

Sources: C, CC, AB

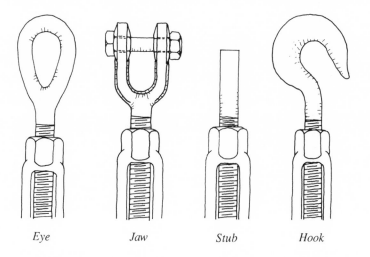

Eye   Jaw   Stub   Hook

ANCHOR SHACKLES

Nominal (Thread) Size	Safe Working Load	Dimensions (inches)		
		A	B	C
1/4"	800 lbs	1	1/2	5/16
3/8"	1,600 lbs	1 1/2	11/16	7/16
1/2"	2,800 lbs	2	7/8	5/8
5/8"	4,400 lbs	2 3/8	1 1/16	3/4
3/4"	6,400 lbs	2 7/8	1 1/4	7/8
1"	11,200 lbs	3 5/8	1 11/16	1 1/8

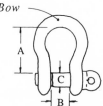

Bow

Note: Shackles are sized by the diameter at the bow, not the pin.

Sources: C, CC, AB

EYE, SHANK, & SWIVEL HOOKS

Throat Opening (inches)	S.W.L. (lbs.)	Throat Opening (inches)	S.W.L. (lbs.)
5/8	600	1 1/2	5,500
11/16	800	1 17/32	6,000
1	1,500	1 11/16	6,800
1 1/16	2,000	1 25/32	8,000
1 1/8	2,500	1 7/8	8,400
1 1/4	4,000	1 15/16	10,000
1 3/8	4,500	2 1/16	10,400
1 13/32	5,000		

Note: These safe working load figures refer only to hooks made of forged alloy steel.

Eye Snap Hook   *Swivel Snap Hook*   *Shank Snap Hook*

Sources: C, CC

CHAIN GRAB HOOKS

Throat Opening (inches)	For Size of Chain (inches)	S.W.L. (lbs.)
11/32	1/4	2,750
7/16	5/16	4,300
1/2	3/8	5,250
9/16	7/16	7,000
21/32	1/2	9,000
25/32	5/8	13,500
15/32	3/4	19,250
1 1/16	7/8	26,000
1 3/16	1	34,000

Note: These safe working load figures refer only to hooks made of forged alloy steel.

Clevis Grab Hook   *Eye Grab Hook*

Sources: C, CC

JACK CHAIN - Steel

Single

Double

Trade Size No.	Metal Thickness	Weight per 100'	Approx. S.W.L.
20	0.034"		3 lbs.
18	0.047"	2 lbs.	5 lbs.
16	0.062"	3 lbs.	10 lbs.
14	0.080"	5 lbs.	16 lbs.
12	0.105"	9 lbs.	29 lbs.
10	0.135"	14 lbs.	43 lbs.
8	0.162"	21 lbs.	60 lbs.
6	0.192"	28 lbs.	88 lbs.

Note: Double Jack Chain is available only in #16. Its weight per 100' is 4 lbs.

STEEL CHAIN - Straight & Twist

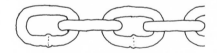

SAFETY OR PLUMBERS CHAIN

Trade Size	Metal Thickness	Approx. S.W.L.
00	0.018"	31 lbs.
0	0.023"	40 lbs.
1	0.028"	58 lbs.
2	0.028"	63 lbs.

SASH CHAIN - Steel

Trade Size	Metal Thickness	Approx. S.W.L.
8	0.035"	75 lbs.
25	0.042"	95 lbs.
30	0.028"	80 lbs.
35	0.035"	105 lbs.
40	0.042"	140 lbs.
45	0.050"	175 lbs.
50	0.062"	225 lbs.

BEAD CHAIN

Size	Links per Foot	Proof Test	Approx. S.W.L.
3/16"	12 1/2	1045 lbs.	520 lbs.
1/4"	12	1800 lbs.	900 lbs.
5/16"	10 3/4	2720 lbs.	1300 lbs.
3/8"	9 3/4	3720 lbs.	1860 lbs.

Sources: M, CC

Trade Size	Bead Diameter	Beads per inch	Approx. S.W.L.
2	0.082"	113	16 lbs.
3	3/32"	100	20 lbs.
6	1/8"	72	30 lbs.
8	5/32"	59	40 lbs.
10	3/16"	50	45 lbs.
13	1/4"	37	90 lbs.

MATERIALS

STEEL PIPE

The nominal dimension of steel pipe is not the actual dimension. You may have noticed that *none* of the dimensions of a 1¹/₂" pipe are really 1¹/₂". It used to be that the *inside* dimension of a pipe was its nominal dimension. If you measured the inside dimension (I.D.) of a 1¹/₂" pipe it was 1¹/₂". However, as the quality and strength of steel increased over the years, the manufacturers found they were able to decrease the thickness of the pipe walls (thereby saving some money) while still maintaining the same strength. But they had to keep the *outside* dimension (O.D.) the same due to existing threading and fixture standards, so the pipe's inside dimension was enlarged and the relationship between I.D. and nominal dimension was abandoned.

SCHEDULE # 4O PIPE SIZES

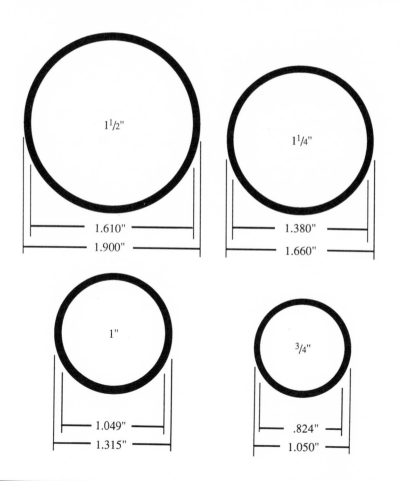

PIPE SIZES

Nominal Pipe Size	Outside Dia.	Schedule 40 Standard[1] (STD)		Schedule 80 Extra Strong[2] (XS)		(no schedule number) Double Extra Strong[3] (XXS)	
		Thickness	Lbs./Ft.	Thickness	Lbs./Ft.	Thickness	Lbs./Ft.
1/8"	.405	.068	.24	.095	.31	---	---
1/4"	.540	.088	.42	.119	.54	---	---
3/8"	.675	.091	.57	.126	.74	---	---
1/2"	.840	.109	.85	.147	1.09	.294	1.71
3/4"	1.050	.113	1.13	.154	1.47	.308	2.44
1"	1.315	.133	1.68	.179	2.17	.358	3.66
1 1/4"	1.660	.140	2.27	.191	3.00	.382	5.21
1 1/2"	1.900	.145	2.72	.200	3.63	.400	6.41
2"	2.375	.154	3.65	.218	5.02	.436	9.03
2 1/2"	2.875	.203	5.79	.276	7.66	.552	13.69
3"	3.500	.216	7.58	.300	10.25	.600	18.58
3 1/2"	4.000	.226	9.11	.318	12.50	---	---
4"	4.500	.237	10.79	.337	14.98	.674	27.54
5"	5.563	.258	14.62	.375	20.78	.750	38.55
6"	6.625	.280	18.97	.432	28.57	.864	53.16
8"	8.625	.322	28.55	.500	43.39	.875	72.42

1. Standard Pipe, when 10" or less in diameter, is the same as Schedule #40.
2. Extra Strong Pipe, when 8" or less in diameter, is the same as Schedule #80.
3. Double Extra Strong has no Schedule Number; it is always slightly larger than Schedule #160.
(Note: Most sizes are available in Black Iron (steel) or Galvanized (steel). Remember when ordering, most pipe has a weld seam running down the center which affects its inside dimension.)

Source: MH

PIPE RAILING FITTINGS

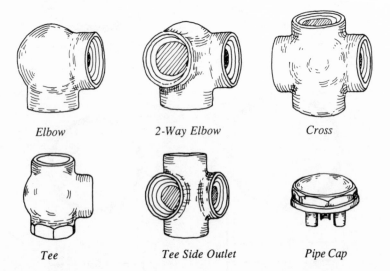

Elbow   2-Way Elbow   Cross

Tee   Tee Side Outlet   Pipe Cap

See also PIPE CLAMPS, page 83.

Lock Nut

Hex Bushing

Face Bushing

Sq. Head Plug

90° Elbow

45° Elbow

90° Street Elbow

45° Lateral

Coupling

Tee

Cross

Union

Shoulder Nipple

Hex Nipple

Close Nipple

Threaded Reducer

Reducing Adapter

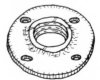

Hex Head Pipe Plug

Sq. Head Pipe Plug

Cap

Cap w/ Ring

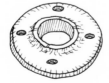

Threaded Flange

Slip-On Flange

Blind Flange

STOCK STEEL SHAPES

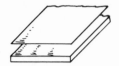
Sheet & Plate

Square Bar

Hex Bar

Shafting or Round Stock

Round Tubing

Square Tubing

Rectangular Tubing

Bulb Angle (Bulb)

Tee (T)

Zee (Z)

Crane Rail

SQUARE AND ROUND BARS

Size (inches)	Weight (lbs. per foot) □	Weight (lbs. per foot) ○	Area (sq. inches) □	Area (sq. inches) ○
1/8	.053	.042	.0156	.0123
1/4	.213	.167	.0625	.0491
3/8	.478	.376	.1406	.1105
1/2	.850	.668	.2500	.1963
3/4	1.913	1.502	.5625	.4418
1	3.400	2.670	1.0000	.7854
1 1/4	5.313	4.172	1.5625	1.2272
1 1/2	7.650	6.008	2.2500	1.7671
1 3/4	10.413	8.178	3.0625	2.4053
2	13.600	10.681	4.0000	3.1416
2 1/4	17.213	13.519	5.0625	3.9761
2 1/2	21.250	16.690	6.2500	4.9087
2 3/4	25.713	20.195	7.5625	5.9396
3	30.60	24.03	9.000	7.068
3 1/2	41.65	32.71	12.250	9.621
4	54.40	42.72	16.000	12.566
4 1/2	68.85	54.07	20.250	15.904

SQUARE AND RECTANGULAR STEEL TUBING

Size (inches)	Thickness (inches)	Gauge	Weight per Foot (lbs.)
1/2	.035	20	.215
1/2	.049	18	.290
1/2	.065	16	.364
5/8	.035	20	.275
5/8	.049	18	.373
5/8	.065	16	.475
3/4	.035	20	.334
3/4	.049	18	.456
3/4	.065	16	.585
7/8	.049	18	.540
7/8	.065	16	.696
7/8	.083	14	.865
1	.035	20	.453
1	.049	18	.623
1	.065	16	.806
1	.120	11	1.358
1 1/4	.049	18	.789
1 1/4	.065	16	1.027
1 1/4	.120	11	1.766
1 1/2	.049	18	.956
1 1/2	.065	16	1.248
1 1/2	.120	11	2.210
2	.049	18	1.289
2	.065	16	1.690
2	.120	11	2.940
2	.250	1/4	5.410
4	.120	11	6.220
4	.250	1/4	12.210
1 x 1 1/2	.065	16	1.027
1 x 1 1/2	.083	14	1.288
1 x 1 1/2	.120	11	1.766
1 x 2	.065	16	1.248
1 x 2	.083	14	1.570
1 x 2	.120	11	2.174

Note: Square and especially rectangular tubing are available in several other sizes. The ones listed here are most common for theatrical construction.

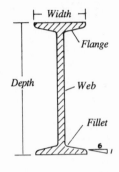

"S" is the section symbol for American Standard Beams (universally called I beams). S shapes are designated by their section letter, actual depth in inches, and nominal weight in pounds per foot. For example, S 5 x 14.75 indicates an S shape with a depth of 5 inches and a nominal weight of 14.75 pounds per foot.

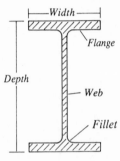

"W" is the section symbol for American Standard Wide Flange Beams. It may be compared to an S beam with extra wide flanges. W shapes are designated by their section letter, actual depth in inches, and nominal weight in pounds per foot. For example, W 18 x 35 indicates a W shape with a depth of 18 inches and a nominal weight of 35 pounds per foot.

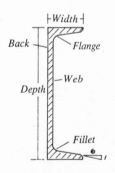

"C" is the symbol for American Standard Channels which may be compared to an S beam with the flanges missing from one side. C shapes are designated by their section letter, actual depth in inches, and nominal weight in pounds per foot. For example, C 3 x 6 indicates a C shape with a depth of 3 inches and a nominal weight of 6 pounds per foot.

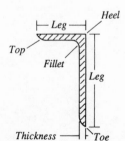

"L" is the symbol for American Standard Angles. L shapes are designated by their section letter, width of each leg, and thickness. For example, L 3 x 4 x $^1/_4$ indicates a L shape with one 3 inch leg and one 4 inch leg and a thickness of $^1/_4$ inch.

WIRE AND SHEET METAL GAUGES

Gauge Number	Manufacturers' Standard Gauge* for Steel Sheets (uncoated steel sheets and light plates)		USWG U.S. Steel Wire Gauge (steel wire except music wire)	AWG American or Brown & Sharpe Wire Gauge (non-ferrous sheets and wire)
	Weight (oz. per sq. ft.)	Approx. Thickness (inches)	Thickness (inches)	Thickness (inches)
7/0's	---	---	.4900	---
6/0's	---	---	.4615	.5800
5/0's	---	---	.4305	.5165
4/0's	---	---	.3938	.4600
3/0's	---	---	.3625	.4096
2/0's	---	---	.3310	.3648
1/0's	---	---	.3065	.3249
1	---	---	.2830	.2893
2	---	---	.2625	.2576
3	160	.2391	.2437	.2294
4	150	.2242	.2253	.2043
5	140	.2092	.2070	.1819
6	130	.1943	.1920	.1620
7	120	.1793	.1770	.1443
8	110	.1644	.1620	.1285
9	100	.1495	.1483	.1144
10	90	.1345	.1350	.1019
11	80	.1196	.1205	.0907
12	70	.1046	.1055	.0808
13	60	.0897	.0915	.0720
14	50	.0747	.0800	.0641
15	45	.0673	.0720	.0571
16	40	.0598	.0625	.0508
17	36	.0538	.0540	.0453
18	32	.0478	.0475	.0403
19	28	.0418	.0410	.0359
20	24	.0359	.0348	.0320
21	22	.0329	.0317	.0285
22	20	.0299	.0286	.0253
23	18	.0269	.0258	.0226
24	16	.0239	.0230	.0201
25	14	.0209	.0204	.0179
26	12	.0179	.0181	.0159
27	11	.0164	.0173	.0142
28	10	.0149	.0162	.0126
29	9	.0135	.0150	.0113
30	8	.0120	.0140	.01000
31	7	.0105	.0132	.00893
32	6.5	.0097	.0128	.00795
33	6	.0090	.0118	.00708

*Manufacturers' Standard Gauge is officially a weight gauge, in oz. per sq. ft. as tabulated. The approx. thickness shown is based on steel weighing 41.82 lbs. per square foot per inch of thickness and allowing an adjustment for average over-run in area and thickness. The now obsolete U.S. Standard Gauge is based on weights of wrought iron.

Source: MH

SHEET METAL SEAMS AND EDGES

Single Flange

Double Flange

Rolled Flange

Wired Edge

Lap Seam

Plain Flat Seam

Grooved Seam

Standing Seam

Single Hem

Double Hem

Single Seam

Double Seam

SHEET METAL DUCT FITTINGS

2-Piece 90° Elbow

2-Piece 45° Elbow

3-Piece 90° Elbow

4-Piece 90° Elbow

2-Piece 90° Square

2-Piece 45° Square

3-Piece 90° Square

ACTUAL GAUGE SIZES (U.S. Standard)

0 Gauge (.3065")

10 Gauge (.1345")

15 Gauge (.0673")

20 Gauge (.0359")

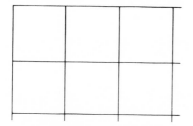

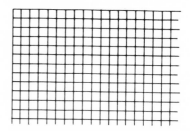

Steel Mesh: Welded 6" openings; $^5/_{32}$" or $^3/_{16}$" strands; 6' wide rolls.

Window Screen: Woven $^1/_{16}$" mesh; 24" to 48" wide rolls; also available in aluminum and plastic.

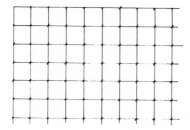

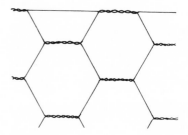

Rabbit Wire: (Hardware Cloth) Welded $^1/_4$" or $^1/_2$" openings.

Chicken Wire: (Poultry Netting) Large and small twisted mesh; 18" to 60" wide rolls.

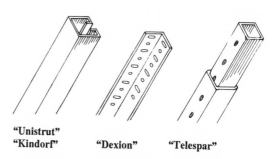

"Unistrut"
"Kindorf"   **"Dexion"**   **"Telespar"**

Perforated Strap: (Plumbers Tape) 20 gauge x $^3/_4$" with $^1/_4$" holes at $^1/_2$" spacings.

Available in various sizes up to 20' lengths.

Lumber Grading: Stick or board lumber is divided into two categories, *select* and *common. Select* is suitable for natural and painted finishes and is divided into the grades of A, B, C, D. *Common* lumber contains defects or blemishes which detract from the appearance of the finish but is suitable for general-utility and construction purposes. It is divided into five grades: 1, 2, 3, 4, and 5.

Select Grades:
Grade A - is practically free from defects.
Grade B - allows a few small defects or blemishes.
Grade C - allows a limited number of small defects or blemishes that can be covered with paint.
Grade D - allows any number of defects or blemishes which do not detract from the appearance of the finish especially when painted.
(Grades A & B are suitable for natural finishes; Grades C and D are suitable for painted finishes.)

Common Grades:
No. 1 - is sound and tight-knotted stock; size of defects and blemishes limited.
No. 2 - allows large and coarse defects; may be considered graintight lumber.
No. 3 - allows larger and coarser defects than No.2 and occasional knot holes.
No. 4 - allows the coarsest defects such as decay and holes.
No. 5 - is low-quality lumber; must hold together under ordinary handling.
(No. 1 and No. 2 are suitable without waste; No. 3 and No. 4 must allow for some waste; No. 5 is next to useless.)

BOARD FEET

Nominal Size	8'	10'	12'	14'	16'	18'	20'
1 x 4	2.66	3.33	4.00	4.66	5.33	6.00	6.66
1 x 6	4.00	5.00	6.00	7.00	8.00	9.00	10.00
1 x 8	5.33	6.66	8.00	9.33	10.66	12.00	13.33
1 x 12	8.00	10.00	12.00	14.00	16.00	18.00	20.00
$5/4$ x 4	3.33	4.17	5.00	5.83	6.66	7.50	8.33
$5/4$ x 6	5.00	6.25	7.50	8.75	10.00	11.25	12.50
$5/4$ x 8	6.66	8.33	10.00	11.66	13.33	15.00	16.66
$5/4$ x 10	8.33	10.41	12.50	14.58	16.66	18.75	20.83
$5/4$ x 12	10.00	12.50	15.00	17.50	20.00	22.50	25.00
2 x 4	5.33	6.66	8.00	9.33	10.66	12.00	13.33
2 x 6	8.00	10.00	12.00	14.00	16.00	18.00	20.00
2 x 8	10.66	13.33	16.00	18.66	21.33	24.00	26.66
2 x 10	13.33	16.66	20.00	23.33	26.66	30.00	33.33
2 x 12	16.00	20.00	24.00	28.00	32.00	36.00	40.00
4 x 4	10.66	13.33	16.00	18.66	21.33	24.00	26.66
4 x 6	16.00	20.00	24.00	28.00	32.00	36.00	40.00
6 x 6	24.00	30.00	36.00	42.00	48.00	54.00	60.00

One board foot equals 144 cu. inches (a piece of lumber 1"x 12"x 12" - nominal size). Board feet are always calculated using nominal dimensions. Therefore, a stick of lumber 1"x 8"x 10'-0 is considered to be $6^2/3$ board feet (1"x 8"x 120" = 960 cu. in. -- 960 + 144 = 6.66 cu. ft.), even though its actual dimensions are only $3/4$"x $7^1/2$" x 10'-0.

WEIGHTS OF WOODS

Species	--Lbs. per Cu. Ft.-- Green*	Airdry*	Species	--Lbs. per Cu. Ft.-- Green	Airdry
Alder, Red	46	28	Locust, Black	58	48
Ash, Black	52	34	Maple, Big Leaf	47	34
Aspen	43	26	Maple, Black	54	40
Balsa	9	7	Maple, Red	50	38
Basswood	42	26	Maple, Silver	45	33
Beech	54	45	Maple, Sugar	56	44
Birch	57	44	Oak, Red	64	44
Birch, Paper	50	38	Oak, White	63	47
Box	72	59	Pine, Lodgepole	39	29
Cedar, Eastern Red	37	33	Pine, Northern White	36	25
Cedar, White	28	22	Pine, Norway	42	34
Cedar, Western Red	27	23	Pine, Ponderosa	45	28
Cherry, Black	45	35	Pines, Southern Yellow:		
Chestnut	55	30	Loblolly	53	36
Cottonwood	49	28	Long Leaf	55	41
Cypress, Southern	51	32	Short Leaf	52	36
Douglas fir, Coast Region	38	34	Pine, Sugar	52	25
Douglas Fir, Rocky Mt.	35	30	Pine, Western White	35	27
Elm, American	54	35	Poplar, Yellow	38	28
Fir, Commercial White	46	27	Redwood	50	28
Gum	45	35	Spruce, Eastern	34	28
Hickory, Pecan	62	45	Sycamore	52	34
Hickory, True	63	51	Tamarack	47	37
Honey Locust	61	42	Walnut, Black	58	38
Larch, Western	48	36			

*Moisture contents: green timber = up to 50%; air dried timber = 15% to 20%.

METHODS OF SAWING LUMBER

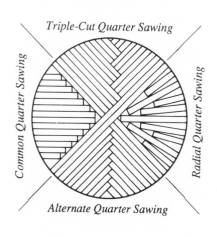

Triple-Cut Quarter Sawing

Common Quarter Sawing

Radial Quarter Sawing

Alternate Quarter Sawing

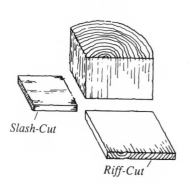

Slash-Cut

Riff-Cut

LUMBER SIZES AND WEIGHTS

Nominal Size	Actual Size (s4s)*	Area	Board Measure per linear	Weight of stick, in lbs. per linear foot**		
(inches)	(inches)	(sq. in.)	ft.	25 pcf	35 pcf	45 pcf
1 x 3	$3/4$ x $2^1/2$	1.875	.25	0.326	0.456	0.586
1 x 4	$3/4$ x $3^1/2$	2.625	.33	0.456	0.638	0.820
1 x 6	$3/4$ x $5^1/2$	4.125	.50	0.716	1.003	1.289
1 x 8	$3/4$ x $7^1/4$	5.438	.66	0.944	1.322	1.699
1 x 10	$3/4$ x $9^1/4$	6.938	.83	1.204	1.686	2.168
1 x 12	$3/4$ x $11^1/4$	8.438	1.00	1.465	2.051	2.637
$5/4$ x 4	$1^1/4$ x $3^1/2$	4.375	.42	.759	1.063	1.367
$5/4$ x 6	$1^1/4$ x $5^1/2$	6.875	.63	1.194	1.671	2.148
$5/4$ x 8	$1^1/4$ x $7^1/4$	9.063	.83	1.573	2.203	2.832
$5/4$ x 10	$1^1/4$ x $9^1/4$	11.563	1.04	2.007	2.810	3.613
$5/4$ x 12	$1^1/4$ x $11^1/4$	14.063	1.25	2.441	3.418	4.394
2 x 3	$1^1/2$ x $2^1/2$	3.750	.50	0.651	0.911	1.172
2 x 4	$1^1/2$ x $3^1/2$	5.250	.66	0.911	1.276	1.641
2 x 6	$1^1/2$ x $5^1/2$	8.250	1.00	1.432	2.005	2.578
2 x 8	$1^1/2$ x $7^1/4$	10.875	1.33	1.888	2.643	3.398
2 x 10	$1^1/2$ x $9^1/4$	13.875	1.66	2.409	3.372	4.336
2 x 12	$1^1/2$ x $11^1/4$	16.875	2.00	2.930	4.102	5.273
4 x 4	$3^1/2$ x $3^1/2$	12.250	1.33	2.127	2.977	3.828
4 x 6	$3^1/2$ x $5^1/2$	19.250	2.00	3.342	4.679	6.016
4 x 8	$3^1/2$ x $7^1/4$	25.375	2.66	4.405	6.168	7.930
6 x 6	$5^1/2$ x $5^1/2$	30.250	3.00	5.252	7.352	9.453
6 x 8	$5^1/2$ x $7^1/4$	41.250	4.00	7.161	10.026	12.891

* "s4s" is a standard abbreviation for "sanded four sides."
** Since wood varies in weight depending on what kind of wood it is (hard wood, soft wood) and how dry the wood is, three average weights are given: 25 lbs. per cubic foot, 35 lbs. per cubic foot, 45 lbs. per cubic foot. To determine the exact weight of a particular lumber, use the table, *WEIGHTS OF WOODS,* on page 112.

VENEER GRADES FOR SHEET MATERIALS

N   "Natural finish" veneer, all heartwood or sapwood; free of open defects.

A   Smooth and paintable with neatly made repairs; also used for natural finish in less demanding applications.

B   Solid surface veneer with circular repair plugs and tight knots.

C plgd.   Improved C veneer with splits limited to $1/8$" in width; knot holes and borer holes limited to $1/4$" by $1/2$".

C   Knotholes to 1", occasional knotholes $1/2$" larger permitted providing total width of all knots within a specified section does not exceed certain limits; limited splits permitted; minimum veneer permitted in exterior-type plywood.

D   Permits knots to $2^1/2$" larger under certain specified limits; limited splits permitted.

INTERIOR PLYWOOD

Grade	Face	Back	Inside	Width	Length	Thickness	Uses
	--Veneer Quality--			*-------Stock Sizes-------*			
A-A	A	A	D	3',4'	8'	1/4", 3/8" 1/2", 5/8" 3/4", 1"	Interior uses, such as cabinet doors, furniture, etc., where both sides will show.
A-B A-C	A A	B C	D D	3',4'	8'	1/4", 3/8" 1/2", 5/8" 3/4", 1"	High quality uses, where only one side will show.
A-D (Plypanel)	A	D	D	3',4'	8'	1/4", 3/8" 1/2", 5/8" 3/4", 1"	Uses include lesser quality wall paneling and cabinets. An all-purpose "good-one-side" sheet.
B-D	B	D	D	4'	8'	1/4",3/8" 1/2", 5/8" 3/4"	Can be used as a lower quality substitute for A-B if the panel is painted.
C-D (Plybase)	C	D	D	4'	8'	1/4", 3/8" 1/2", 5/8" 3/4"	Used for subfloors and as a base for tile, linoleum, and carpeting.

EXTERIOR PLYWOOD

Grade	Face	Back	Inside	Width	Length	Thickness	Uses
	--Veneer Quality--			*-------Stock Sizes-------*			
A-A	A	A	C	4'	8'	1/4", 3/8" 1/2", 5/8" 3/4", 1"	An expensive sheet used only where the appearance of both sides is critical.
A-B	A	B	C	4'	8'	1/4", 3/8" 1/2", 5/8" 3/4", 1"	Can be substituted for A-A if the appearance of the back side isn't critical.
A-C (Plyshield)	A	C	C	4'	8'	1/4", 3/8" 1/2", 5/8" 3/4", 1"	The most common exterior plywood. Used mainly where the back side doesn't show.
B-C (Utility)	B	C	C	4'	8'	1/4", 3/8" 1/2", 5/8" 3/4"	Used in inexpensive outdoor construction where the appearance is not important.
C-C (Underlayment)	C	C	C	4'	8'	1/4", 3/8" 1/2", 5/8" 3/4"	Used under linoleum and tile, especially in bathrooms and kitchens.
C-D (CDX)	C	D	D	4'	8'	5/16", 3/8 1/2", 5/8" 3/4"	A common, inexpensive exterior plywood. "X" denotes exterior glue.

Notes: Flame-proof or flame-retardant plywood is available in most grades. Interior plywood is unavailable in many areas. Exterior plywood is only water-resistant, "Marine Plywood" is water-proof. Some types of plywood are available in 4' x 10' and 5' x 10' sizes.

HARDWOOD PLYWOOD

| *Grade name** | *Uses* | *Sizes:* | *widths available from 24"to 48" in 6" multiples; lengths from 36" to 96", also 10' and 12' on order)* |

Custom grade — Expensive; reserved for cabinetwork or paneling where clear finishes are used. Veneers are selected for clear, uniform and matching grain.

Good grade (#1) — For fine natural and stained finishes on cabinets built-ins, paneling and furniture. Veneer has typical species grain markings, occasional small burls, pin knots and slight color streaks, but is smooth, tight and matched in grain where two pieces join. Comes in both good-one-side and good-two-sides grades. (Some mills identify as A grade or 1 grade.)

Sound grade (#2) — Veneers are not selected for color or appearance and may have sound, tight knots, small burls, patches, sapwood and mineral streaks.

Utility grade (#3) — For rough paint or natural finishes, such as for children's furniture, storage cabinets, shelves, playroom paneling. Has same defects as Sound Grade plus small splits not wider than $3/16$", rough grain and knotholes up to $3/4$".

Backing grade (#4) — Cheapest grade of hardwood plywood. Used where rustic paneling look is desired. Has knots, knotholes up to 2", splits and other defects that do not impair its strength.

*Grades established by the Hardwood Plywood Institute.

WALLBOARD ESTIMATING

					Length*						
Width*	8'	9'	10'	11'	12'	13'	14'	15'	16'	17'	18'
4'	224	244	264	284	304	324	344	364	384	404	424
5'	248	269	290	311	332	353	374	395	416	437	458
6'	272	294	316	338	360	382	404	426	448	470	492
7'	296	319	342	365	388	411	434	457	480	503	526
8'	320	344	368	392	416	440	464	488	512	536	560
9'	344	369	394	419	444	469	494	519	544	569	594
10'	368	394	420	446	472	498	524	550	576	602	628
11'	392	419	446	473	500	527	554	581	608	635	662
12'	416	444	472	500	528	556	584	612	640	668	696
13'	440	469	498	527	556	585	614	643	572	701	730
14'	464	494	524	554	584	614	644	674	704	734	764
15'	488	519	550	581	612	643	674	705	736	767	798
16'	512	544	576	608	640	672	704	736	768	800	832
17'	536	569	602	635	668	701	734	767	800	833	866
18'	560	594	628	662	696	730	764	798	832	866	900
19'	584	619	654	689	724	759	794	829	864	899	934
20'	608	644	680	716	752	788	824	860	896	932	968
21'	632	669	706	743	780	817	854	891	928	965	1002
22'	656	694	732	770	808	846	884	922	960	998	1036
23'	680	719	758	797	836	875	914	953	992	1031	1070

* Length and width of a room. This table shows the total surface area of the walls and ceiling (in square feet) of rooms with 8 foot ceilings; no allowance made for openings.

OTHER SHEET MATERIAL USED IN SCENERY CONSTRUCTION

Bending Lauan   Composition: 3 plies of Lauan (Phillipine Mahagony)
(Bending Board)   Sizes: 4' x 8' sheets, $^3/_8$" thick.
(Wiggle Wood)   Notes: The grain in all three plies runs the same direction.
Available with the grain running lengthwise (column), or
widthwise (barrel).

Compressed Paper   Composition: Compressed paper.
(Upson Board)   Sizes: 4' x 8' sheets; $^1/_8$", $^3/_{16}$" and $^1/_4$" thick.
(Easycurve)   Notes: White pebbled or smooth surface; good for curves; not
structural.

Corrugated Paper   Composition: Corrugated paper.
(Cardboard)   Sizes: Varies; $^5/_{32}$" and $^7/_{32}$" thick.
Notes: Economical.

Fiber Board   Composition: Compressed vegetable fibers.
(Homosote)   Sizes: 4' x 8' sheets, $^3/_8$", $^1/_2$", $^5/_8$" and $^3/_4$" thick
(Celotex)   Notes: Soft and flaky; good for sculptured surfaces and for
padding and sound deadening.

Gypsum Board   Composition: Gypsum faced with paper.
(Sheetrock)   Sizes: 4' wide, 8' to 16' long; $^1/_4$" to $^3/_4$" thick.
(GWB)   Notes: Heavy, brittle and fire-retardant. Also know as drywall and
wall board.

Hardboard-faced   Composition: Hardboard-faced plywood.
Plywood   Sizes: 4' x 8' sheets, $^1/_2$" to $^3/_4$" thick.
Notes: Combines smooth, paintable hardboard face with strength
of plywood backing for cabinet doors and counter tops.

Lauan Plywood   Composition: Phillipine Mahagony
Sizes: 4' x 8' sheets, $^1/_4$", $^1/_2$" and $^3/_4$" thick
4' x 10 sheets, $^1/_4$" thick, also paper covered
Notes: Tight grain; common skinning material for hardwall flats.

Oriented Strand   Composition: Long, narrow wood flakes, bonded in 3 to 5 layers.
Board   Sizes: 4' x 8' sheets; $^3/_8$", $^1/_2$", $^5/_8$" and $^3/_4$" thick
(OSB)   Notes: Because flakes in each layer are aligned in a direction 90º
from the adjacent layer, OSB has superior bending qualities
to its cousins, waferboard and particle board.

Overlaid   Composition: Plastic-faced exterior plywood.
Plywood   Sizes: 4' x 8' sheets, $^3/_8$" to $^3/_4$" thick.
Notes: Used for high-grade paint finishes that won't show grain,
for kitchen cabinets, and exterior siding.

Press Board   Composition: Compressed wood pulp
(Masonite)   Sizes: 4' x 8' sheets, $^1/_8$", $^1/_4$" and $^3/_8$" thick.
(Hardboard)   Notes: Available in tempered (dark brown, hard surface) and
untempered (light brown, softer surface); good for curved
surfaces and decking.

Particle Board   Composition: Wood chips, sawdust and bonding agent.
(Chip Board)   Sizes: 4' x 8' sheets: $^3/_8$", $^1/_2$" and $^3/_4$" thick.
Notes: Less expensive than plywood, but not as strong and the
edges tend to crumble.

Sign Board   Composition: Paper-covered plywood.
Sizes: 4' wide, 8' and 10' long; $^1/_2$" and $^3/_4$" thick.
Notes: Eliminates need for filling or priming before painting.

PROPERTIES OF COMMON WOODS

Wood	Color	Strength	Hardness	Sanding	Turning	Jointing
Ash	white to brown	high	medium	excellent	fair	good
Basswood	creamy white	low	soft	poor	poor	good
Birch	cream to brown	high	hard	fair	good	good
Cedar	red	medium	soft	good	fair	poor
Cherry	red to brown	high	medium	best	best	best
Chestnut	gray to brown	medium	soft	best	best	good
Cypress	cream to brown	medium	soft	fair	poor	good
Fir (Douglas)	cream to red	medium	soft	fair	poor	fair
Gum	cream to brown	medium	medium	fair	best	fair
Hickory	white to brown	high	hard	best	good	good
Mahogany	reddish brown	medium	medium	good	best	good
Maple	cream to brown	high	hard	good	good	fair
Oak (Red)	reddish brown	high	hard	best	good	best
Oak (White)	white to lt. brown	high	hard	best	good	best
Pine (White)	white to cream	low	soft	fair	good	good
Poplar	white to lt. brown	low	soft	poor	good	good
Redwood	red	medium	soft	poor	fair	good
Walnut	brown	high	medium	best	best	good

Wood	Base for Finishing	Resistance to Nail Splitting	Due to Weathering			
			Resistance to Decay	Amount of Shrinkage	Checking Conspicuous	Cupping Tendency
Ash	medium	poor	low	medium	yes	very high
Basswood	poor	good	low	high	yes	medium
Birch	good	poor	low	med. high	yes	very high
Cedar	good	poor	very high	low	no	low
Cherry	good	poor	medium	low	no	low
Chestnut	poor	medium	high	medium	yes	high
Cypress	poor	good	very high	med. low	no	low
Fir (Douglas)	poor	med. to poor	medium	medium	yes	medium
Gum	medium	medium	medium	medium	yes	very high
Hickory	good	poor	low	high	yes	very high
Mahogany	medium	good	high	med	yes	medium
Maple	good	poor	low	high	yes	very high
Oak (Red)	medium	medium	low	med. high	yes	very high
Oak (White)	medium	medium	high	med. high	yes	very high
Pine (White)	medium	good	medium	medium	yes	medium
Poplar	good	good	low	medium	no	high
Redwood	poor	good	very high	med. low	no	low
Walnut	medium	medium	high	medium	yes	high

Source: TD

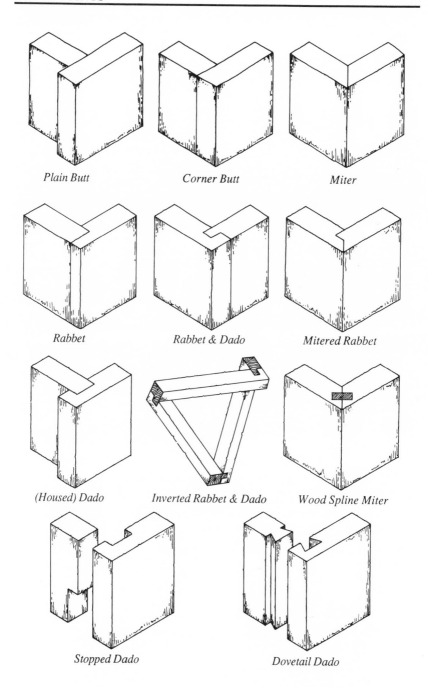

Plain Butt

Corner Butt

Miter

Rabbet

Rabbet & Dado

Mitered Rabbet

(Housed) Dado

Inverted Rabbet & Dado

Wood Spline Miter

Stopped Dado

Dovetail Dado

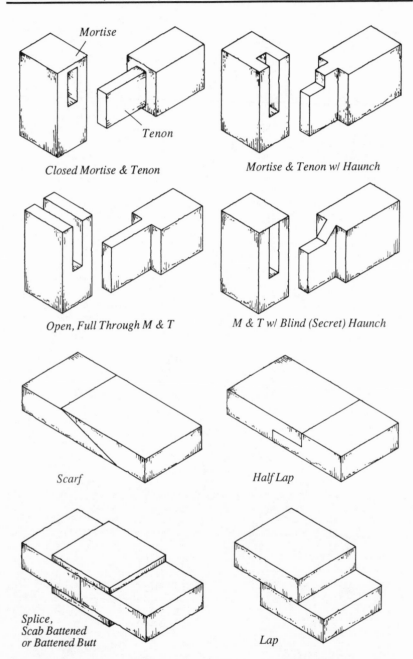

Closed Mortise & Tenon

Mortise & Tenon w/ Haunch

Open, Full Through M & T

M & T w/ Blind (Secret) Haunch

Scarf

Half Lap

Splice,
Scab Battened
or Battened Butt

Lap

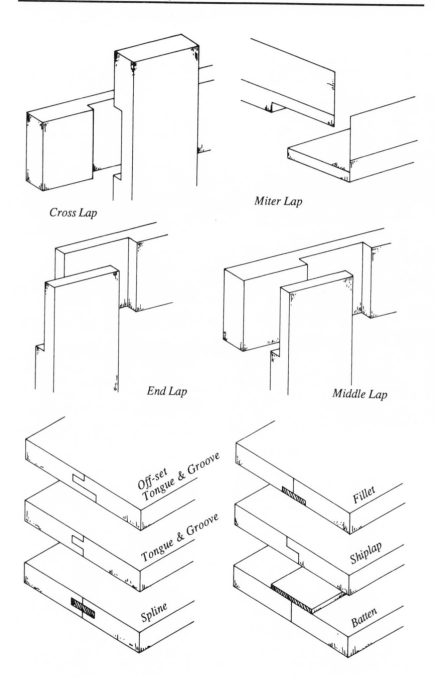

Cross Lap

Miter Lap

End Lap

Middle Lap

Off-set Tongue & Groove

Tongue & Groove

Spline

Fillet

Shiplap

Batten

WOOD JOINTS (continued)

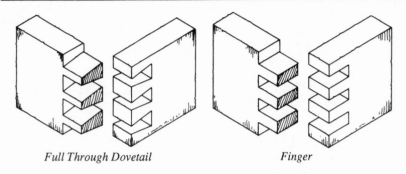

Full Through Dovetail   *Finger*

WOOD DEFECTS

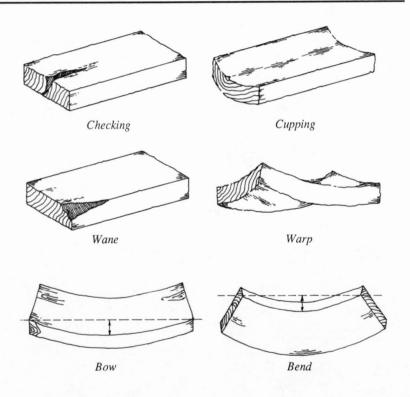

Checking   *Cupping*

Wane   *Warp*

Bow   *Bend*

Not Shown:

Shake: A lengthwise separation of the wood through the growth rings.

Decay: Disintegration of the wood due to fungi. Also called dote, rot or unsound wood.

TYPES OF PLASTIC

ABS (Acrylonitrile butadiene styrene)		(see *PROPERTIES OF PLASTIC PIPE* table)
Acetate	Sizes: Fire rating: Notes:	40" x 12' rolls, 3 to 10 mil. thick and single sheets of 24"x 40". Varies; slow to fast burning. Clear, heavy-weight plastic used for drafting, stencils, glass substitute, etc.; attach with tape or staples.
Acrylic	Sizes: Fire rating: Notes:	4' x 8' sheets; $1/8$" to 1" thick; also available in rods, bars and extruded shapes. Slow burning to flame retardant. *Plexiglass* is Rohm & Haas' trade name; *Lucite* is DuPont's trade name; *Acrylite* is American Cyanamid's trade name; all are available in clear, frost, white, colors, translucent, opaque, semi-opaque, and transparent; can be weight-bearing in larger thicknesses; see also *Polycarbonate*.
CPVC (Chlorinated polyvinylchloride)		(see *PROPERTIES OF PLASTIC PIPE* table)
Fluoroethylene (Teflon)	Sizes: Fire rating: Notes:	Bars and sheets. Will not burn. Low friction and high strength; good resistance to chemicals.
Polyamides (Nylon)	Sizes: Fire rating: Notes:	Bars, sheets and fabrics. Slow burning to self-extinguishing. Very strong; good for casters and bearings.
PB (Polybutylene)		(see *PROPERTIES OF PLASTIC PIPE* table)
Polycarbonate	Sizes: Fire rating: Notes:	Sheets, rods and bars; sizes same as acrylics. Slow burning, self-extinguishing or flame retardant. Similar to acrylic but highly resistant to impact; sold under the trade name *Lexan*
PE (Polyethylene)	Sizes: Fire rating: Notes:	36" to 20' wide, rolls up to 100', 2 to 10 mil. thick; also pipe and extruded shapes. Varies; slow to fast burning. Available in clear or black; used for drop-cloths, etc.; attach with clear polyethylene tape or staples. (see *PROPERTIES OF PLASTIC PIPE* table)
Low Density PE (Ethafoam)	Sizes: Fire rating: Notes:	Available in sheets and rods from $1/4$" to 6"; sizes under 1" are available in 1000' rolls. Flammable. Flexible; should be covered with cheesecloth or muslin before painting; do not use with rubber cement.
Polyester **casting resin**	Sizes: Fire rating: Notes:	Liquid with catalyst. Slow burning, self-extinguishing or can be bought flame retardant. Used for stained glass, fake jewels, etc.; can be laminated with fiberglass to make strong forms.

PP (Polypropylene)		(see *PROPERTIES OF PLASTIC PIPE* table)
Polyurethane	Sizes:	1" to 6" thick, up to 76" wide and 80" long.
	Fire rating:	Flammable; fumes are toxic!
	Notes:	Mattress and pillow foam; glue with contact cement.
Polyurethane Foam	Sizes:	Liquid, pints to 55 gallon drums.
	Fire rating:	Flammable; fumes are toxic!
	Notes:	Two-part liquid which when mixed expands many times its volume to a hard, styrofoam-like material; also called *Duo-Foam*.
PVC (Polyvinylchloride)	Sizes:	Pipe ($^1/8$" to 12"+); also rods and sheets.
	Fire rating:	Slow burning to self extinguishing.
	Notes:	Good for vacuum-forming stock; also easily formed with heat gun. (see *PROPERTIES OF PLASTIC PIPE* table)
Polystyrene (Styrofoam)	Sizes:	$^1/2$", $^3/4$", 1", $1^1/2$", 2", 3" thick in 4' x 8' sheets or blocks up to 16"x 6"x 9' or 14"x 6"x 8'.
	Fire rating:	Blue polystyrene is flame retardant and self-extinguishing; white polystyrene is fire retardant and not self-extinguishing.
	Notes:	Rigid, lightweight; a good adhesive for both is Mastic #11 (Dow Chemical Corp.); other choices are contact cement and white glue; *Styrofoam* is a DuPont trade name.
SR (Styrene rubber plastic)		(see *PROPERTIES OF PLASTIC PIPE* table)
Vinyl	Sizes:	36" and 48" widths in rolls up to 100' long, typically 4 mil. thick.
	Fire rating:	Varies; slow to fast burning.
	Notes:	Clear; attach with tape or staples.

Source: MH

PROPERTIES OF PLASTIC PIPE

Type of Plastic	Properties	Joining Methods
ABS (Acrylonitrile butadiene styrene)	Rigid; high impact strength.	Solvent cement; threading; transition fitting.
PE (Polyethylene)	Flexible; high impact strength.	Heat fusion; insert and transition fitting.
PVC (Polyvinylchloride)	Rigid; high impact and tensile strength; fire self-extinguishing.	Solvent cement; elastometric seal; mechanical coupling; transition fitting.
CPVC (Chlorinated polyvinylchloride)	Rigid; high impact and tensile strength; fire self-extinguishing.	Solvent cement; threading; mechanical coupling; transition fitting.

PROPERTIES OF PLASTIC PIPE (continued)

Type of Plastic	Properties	Joining Methods
PB (Polybutylene)	Flexible.	Insert fitting; heat fusion; transition fitting.
PP (Polypropylene)	Rigid; very light; high impact strength.	Mechanical coupling; heat fusion; threading.
SR (Styrene rubber plastic)	Rigid; fair impact strength.	Solvent cement; transition fitting; elastometric seal.

DIMENSIONS AND WEIGHTS OF THERMOPLASTIC PIPE

Nominal Pipe Size	Outside Diameter	----Schedule 40----		----Schedule 80----	
		Thickness	Wt./Ft.*	Thickness	Wt./Ft.*
1/8	.405	.072	.032	.101	.042
1/4	.540	.093	.057	.126	.071
3/8	.675	.096	.076	.134	.099
1/2	.840	.116	.114	.156	.145
3/4	1.050	.120	.152	.163	.197
1	1.315	.141	.225	.190	.291
1 1/4	1.660	.148	.305	.202	.401
1 1/2	1.900	.154	.366	.212	.487
2	2.375	.163	.491	.231	.674
2 1/2	2.875	.215	.779	.293	1.03
3	3.500	.229	1.02	.318	1.38
3 1/2	4.000	.240	1.23	.337	1.68
4	4.500	.251	1.45	.357	2.01
5	5.563	.273	1.97	.398	2.80
6	6.625	.297	2.56	.458	3.85
8	8.625	.341	3.85	.530	5.84
10	10.750	.387	5.46	.629	8.67
12	12.750	.430	7.22	.728	11.92

* Based on density of 1.00 g/cm³.

Note: To calculate weights per foot of specific types of plastic pipe, use the following approximate density multipliers: ABS = 1.06; PE = 0.945; PVC = 1.37; CPVC = 1.55; PB = 0.91; PP = 0.91; SR = 1.05.

Source: MH

PAINT FORMULAS

Color	Binder	Formula
Dry Pigment	Liquid flexible glue	1 part liquid flex glue 8 parts water
	Latex or vinyl	1 part latex or vinyl 4 parts water
	White glue (synthetic resin)	1 part white glue 10 parts water
	Animal glue	(See glue formulas on page 110.)
Aniline Dye	Concentrated dye without binder	1 teaspoon powdered dye into 1 qt. boiling water, while stirring or $1/2$ cup denatured alcohol, then dilute with hot water
	Clear vinyl	1 part vinyl 8 parts water with dye
	For transparent painting on glass	3 parts vinyl 1 part water with dye
	Heavy starch*	Dissolve 1 lb. box "Argo" gloss starch in $1/2$ gal. cold water, pour into 1 gal. boiling water
Bronzing Powder	Vinyl	1 part water 2 parts clear gloss vinyl

* Glue size or clear vinyl can be added.

PAPERS

Type	Size	Use	Notes
Brown Kraft paper	18" to 8' wide rolls	Pounces; layout; covering floors; wrapping drops and scenery; mixing paints.	Can "alligator" under drops if they're not floated after sizing.
Grey Bogus paper	58" wide rolls	Heavy weight; absorbs water under drops being painted; packing.	More expensive than brown kraft paper.
Wax paper	Up to 48" wide rolls	Can be used under drops and scrims to keep them from sticking to floor while painting.	Usually doesn't stick, but when it does...!
Tracing paper	12" to 42" rolls, also pads	Transferring drawings.	Yellow or white
Stencil paper	3' and 4' wide rolls Sheets: 18" x 24" 24" x 36"	Stencilling.	Should be shellacked on both sides after cutting for extra strength.

BINDERS, SEALANTS AND CLEAR MEDIA

Type	Form	Solvent	Drying time	Coverage sq. ft./gal.	Notes
Vinyl	Liquid	Water	30 min	300-500	Use with dye, bronzing powder, dry pigment; dries cloudy if temp. is too cold.
Acrylic	Liquid	Water	1 hour	350-400	Fabulon (plastic resin), Rhoplex, Rosco brands.
Shellac[1]	Liquid	Denatured alcohol	Allow 2 hrs. for 2nd coat	500[2]	Transparent glaze; use with aniline dyes or tints; a good preservative.
Varnish	Liquid	Mineral spirits	High gl.: 30 min.; others: 1-2 hrs.[3]; hard: 10-12 hrs.	400-500	Durable for floors, woodwork.
Polyurethane	Liquid	Mineral spirits	Touch: 3 hrs.; 2nd coat: 6 hrs.	500	Extremely durable; good for floors.
Polyurethane	Liquid	Water	Touch: 15-30 mins.; 2nd coat: 1-2 hrs.	400-600	Water clean-up.
Glaze Coat ("McCloskeys")	Liquid	Mineral; spirits	Touch: 8 hrs.[4]; Topcoat: 24-48 hrs.	400	Drys with slight sheen; good for translucent glazes; longer drying time means it's easier to work with.
Glaze Coat	Liquid	Water	Touch: 1 hr.; Topcoat: 16 hrs.	500	Water clean-up. Made by Pratt & Lambert.
Lacquer	Liquid	Lacquer thinner[5]	Fast	Varies	Good for non-porous surfaces; usually sprayed; always use respirator.
Glutoline (wallpaper paste)	Powder	Water	Varies	Varies	Mixed with tints; used for translucent glazes; can be washed off. "Tecknabond" is a popular brand.
Starch	Powder	Water	Used to retard drying time of caseins and dyes	100	Used with aniline dyes for painting translucent drops.

1. Available in "orange" and "clear" and the following cuts; 5 lb. (42.5% shellac solids - 57.5% denatured alchohol), 4 lb. (37.1% shellac solids - 62.9% denatured alchohol), and 3 lb. (30.7% shellac solids - 69.3% denatured alchohol).
2. Depending on cut and surface.
3. Available in "dust free" 1 hour drying version.
4. Tints and oils accelerate drying; acrylics retard drying.
5. Water-based (non-toxic) lacquer available. Similar drying time and durability.

THINNERS AND SOLVENTS

Solvent Class		TLV[1] (ppm)	FP[2] (°F)	VP[3] (mm Hg)
Alcohols				
Ethanol	Ethyl or grain alcohol with 6% water added; the least toxic solvent in the alcohol class; taxed as an alcoholic beverage. Denatured alcohol is ethyl or grain alcohol with various materials added to render it useless for beverages; not taxed.	1000	55	43
Methanol	Wood or methyl alcohol; very pure, only 1% water. Less expensive than ethyl alcohol but very poisonous if taken internally. Use ethanol when possible.	200	52	97
Isopropyl (rubbing alcohol)	Rubbing alcohol is denatured alcohol with ingredients that are okay for skin contact, but not good for paint thinning. Can be up to 25% water.	400	53	33
N-propyl		200	59	15
Aliphatic Hydrocarbons				
N-hexane	Do not use; extremely flammable.	50	-7	124
Heptane	Good substitute for n-hexane.	400	25	40
Benzine	May contain hexanes, pentanes and/or VM&P naptha. Use mineral spirits when possible.	100	varies	varies
Petroleum Naptha	May contain benzene.	100	-50	40
Gasoline	Do not use. May contain benzene and/or lead; extremely flammable.	300	100-150	40
VM&P Naptha	One of the least toxic in this class.	300	20-55	2-20
Mineral Spirits	Also called "odorless" paint thinner.	200	86-105	0.8
Kerosene	Lowest grade of thinner; not recommended.	none	65-100	varies
Aromatic Hydrocarbons				
Benzene (benzol)	Do not use; cancer agent!	10	12	75
Toluene (toluol)	Try to avoid.	100	40	22
Xylene (xylol)	Try to avoid.	100	81	9
Styrene (vinyl benzene)	Try to avoid.	50	90	4.5
Chlorinated Hydrocarbons				
Carbon Tetrachloride	Do not use; suspected cancer agent.	5	none	91

THINNERS AND SOLVENTS (continued)

Solvent Class		TLV[1] (ppm)	FP[2] (°F)	VP[3] (mm Hg)
Esters				
Methyl Acetate	Extremely flammable.	200	14	173
Ethyl Acetate	Least toxic in class.	400	24	76
Isopropyl Acetate		250	40	43
Amyl Acetate		100	77	4
Ketones				
Acetone	Least toxic in class; extremely flammable.	750	1.4	266
Methyl Ethyl Ketone (MEK)		200	21	70
Methyl Isobutyl Ketone (MBK)		50	73	15
Others				
Turpentine	Derived from pine tree sap. Wood turpentine is derived from pine tree stumps and scraps and has an obnoxious odor. Use mineral spirits when possible.	100	95	5

1. Threshold Limit Value: set by American Conference of Governmental Industry Hygienists (ACGIH) 1984-85.
2. Flash Point: in degrees Fahrenheit. The lower a solvent's flash point, the lower the temperature at which its vapors can ignite in the presence of a spark or flame. Solvents such as acetone and hexane, whose flash points are below room temperature, are especially dangerous.
3. Vapor Pressure. The higher a solvent's vapor pressure, the more quickly it can convert from a liquid to a vapor (evaporate). Solvents with high vapor pressure are dangerous because they are flammable and their vapors ignite readily.

Adapted from COH2

NOTE: All solvents are dangerous! Avoid skin contact and breathing vapors.

PAINTS AND DYES

Type	Form	Solvent (Thinner)	Drying[1] Time	Coverage[2] sq. ft./gal.	Notes
Latex	Liquid or paste	Water	30-45 min.	400	
Casein	Paste	Water	40 min.	Varies	Brilliant colors.
Vinyl (Flo Paint)	Liquid	Water	30 min.	300-400	Available in clear flat and gloss as well as colors.
Acrylic	Heavy liquid or paste	Water	Varies	350-400	Good on glass, foam, plexi, leather, metal, etc.
Shellac Based (Enamelac, BIN, Black Shellac)	Liquid	Denatured alcohol	Touch: 20 min. Final: 45 min.	475	Good primer; for color, add tint, dye, or dry pigment.
Oil (Enamel, Alkyd)	Liquid	Mineral spirits, turpentine	Touch: 3-4 hrs. Final: 5-7 days	500	Good for metal, outdoors, floors etc.; very tough.
Japan colors	Paste	Mineral spirits	Varies	Not applicable	Brilliant colors, good for tinting oils.
Dry pigment[3]	Powder	Depends on binder[4]	Depends on binder[4]	Not applicable	Wide variety of colors.
Aniline dyes[3]	Powder or crystal	Depends on binder[4]	Depends on binder[4]	Not applicable	Brilliant translucent colors.
Tinting colors[3]	Liquid or paste	Depends on binder[4]	Depends on binder[4]	Not applicable	Use no more than $1/2$ pint per gallon of paint.
"Krylon"	Spray	Acetone	5 min.	Not applicable	Good for metal; always use with respirator.

1. Drying time will vary greatly depending on atmospheric conditions.
2. Coverage varies depending on surface material and condition.
3. Must be used with binders.
4. Refer to *BINDERS, SEALANTS AND CLEAR MEDIA* table on page 135.

Caution: Paints containing lead are highly toxic and should not be sprayed or sanded.

FORMULAS: GLUE, SIZE AND MISC.

Material	Use	Formula
Starch	Primer; best for translucent muslin drops	Dissolve 1 lb. box "Argo" gloss starch in $1/2$ gal. cold water; pour into 3 gals. boiling water; stir, let cool, strain well. Allow 10 gal. starch per 1000 sq. ft. of fabric.
Methocel	Binder, primer for dyes, translucents	Concentrate: 1 part methocel powder 10 parts water
Animal glue (Gelatin glue)	Dissolved glue (concentrated)	Start with 1 part dry glue to 1 part cold water; soak 1 hour; heat in double boiler until dissolved.
	Priming size	1 part dissolved glue (as above) to 8-10 parts hot water.
	Priming paint	1 part priming size and 1 part dry whiting.
	Working size (for dry pigment binder)	1 part priming size and 2 parts water.
	Size water (for spraying)	1 part size to 4 parts water.
Liquid flexible glue (Flex glue)	Dissolved glue	Soak 1 slab (8 lb.) flex glue in 2 qts. cold water for 1 hour; then heat in double boiler until dissolved.
	Working size	Mix above with 8 parts hot water.
White Glue	Priming size	1 part glue to 10 parts water.
Wheat paste	Wallpaper paste	1 lb. dry powdered wheat paste to $2^{1/2}$ qt. cold water.
Glutoline	Wallpaper paste, glazing	Follow directions on box. Covers 1350-1950 sq. ft. per lb. for wallpapering.
Canvas gluing dope	Gluing muslin and canvas to wood without stains	1 part hot animal glue concentrate 1 part hot water 2 parts dry whiting
Scenic dope	Texture	1 part hot animal glue concentrate or white glue to 2 - 4 parts hot water to 2 - 4 parts dry whiting. Proportions depend on consistency desired.
Flame retardant solution	To be sprayed on back of drops *after* painting	10 lbs. ammonium sulfamate (a DuPont product) in 5 gals. warm water; or, 4 lbs. borax, 4 lbs. sal ammoniac in 3 gals. warm water.

ADHESIVES

Animal glue
    Form: Flake or ground.
    Composition: Animal skin, hide sinew and bones.
    Thinner: Water.
    Notes: Must be melted by heating in a double boiler;
    (see page 139 for formulas).

Casein
    Form: Powder.
    Composition: Milk proteins.
    Thinner: Water.
    Notes: Dries slowly; inexpensive but not good for exterior use.

Contact cement
    Form: Liquid (1 oz. to 5 gal.).
    Thinner: Contact cement thinner.
    Notes: For non-porous surfaces (masonite, some plastics, glass, etc.); not for styrofoam. Available in flammable (good) and non-flammable (not so good); use with a respirator!

"Fastbond 30NF" (3M)
    Form: Liquid (1 qt. to 55 gal.).
    Composition: Non-flammable contact cement.
    Thinner: None.
    Notes: Contains toluene. Excellent for polystyrene. Dries in 30 min. to 4 hrs. "Wait until the green glue turns blue."

"Hot melt" glue
    Form: Cartridges or coils.
    Composition: Rubber based polymer; 100% binder.
    Thinner: None.
    Notes: Extruded from hot melt gun; good for almost any small job where strength is not important.

Latex
    Form: Liquid (1 qt. to 55 gallon drums).
    Thinner: Water.
    Composition: Latex (synthetic rubber).
    Notes: Used where flexibility is called for: cloth, drops, foam. Should not be clamped.

Mastic #11 (Dow)
    Form: Thick paste (5 gal. cans).
    Composition: Rubber based, solvent dispersed.
    Thinner: Mineral spirits.
    Notes: Good for polystyrene.

"Phlexglue"
    Form: Liquid (1 gal. cans and 55 gallon drums).
    Composition: Vinyl acrylic.
    Thinner: Water.
    Notes: Remains very flexible after drying; glossy finish.

"Super Glue"
    Form: Liquid; 1 or 2 part (small quantities).
    Composition: Cyanoacrylate Ester.
    Notes: Acetone is a solvent for some brands.

Wheat paste
    Form: Powder (1 to 5 lb. bags).
    Composition: Unrefined flour and rat poison.
    Thinner: Water.
    Notes: For wallpaper and other paper glueing.

White glue ("Elmers")
    Form: Liquid (2 oz. to 55 gallon drums).
    Composition: Polyvinyl acetate.
    Thinner: Water.

Yellow glue
    Form: Liquid (2 oz. to 55 gal drums)
    Composition: Aliphatic resin
    Thinner: Water
    Notes: Mainly used for wood. Dries in 45 min. to 2 hrs.

SCENIC FABRICS

Muslin
Widths: 40", 45", 60", 72", 76", 80", 90", 108", 120", 144", 16'-5", 19', 25', 33', 40'.
Weights: #114, #128, #140.
Colors: Off white, bleached, sky-blue, dark blue, light gray, dark gray.
Notes: Can be purchased fire-proofed. Weights are designations of thread counts. For example, #140 count muslin has 70 vertical threads and 70 horizontal threads per sq. inch. When fire-proofing muslin, remember shrinkage will reduce the width by 5 to 10%.

Duck
Widths: 36" to 69".
Weights: 5 oz. to 8 oz. (per square yard).
Colors: Off white and colors.
Notes: Can be fire-proofed. Duck and canvas are often used interchangeably, or called duck canvas or canvas duck.

Canvas
Widths: 36" to 185".
Weights: 7, 9, 12, 15, 16, & 21 oz. (per square yard).
Colors: Off white and colors.
Notes: Can be fire-proofed. Ground cloth canvas is commonly ordered by number designations: #12 is 12 oz., #10 is 15 oz., #8 is 21 oz.

Velour
Widths: 45" to 54" (54" is standard).
Weights: 12, 16, 19, 21, 25, and 32 oz. (per yard @ 54" width)
Colors: All.
Notes: Can be purchased fire-proofed or fabric can be made of "Trevira polyester" which is inherently fire retardant. 21 oz. is average for scenic velour, 25 oz. is typical for stage draperies. Always note direction of nap.

Velveteen
Widths: 45" to 48" wide.
Colors: All.
Notes: Can be purchased fire-proofed. A light-weight velour of napped cotton.

Duvetyne
Widths: 36" to 118".
Colors: All.
Notes: Sometimes called commando cloth, duvetyne is a light-weight, less expensive substitute for velour. Available with nap on both sides, called "double-faced."

Burlap
Widths: 48" to 72".
Weights: $7^1/_2$ oz. and 10 oz.
Colors: Natural and colors.
Notes: Cannot be purchased fire-proofed.

Erosion Cloth
Widths: 48" wide.
Colors: Natural.
Notes: A very open weave burlap, used for textural effects.

Cheesecloth
Widths: 36" wide.
Colors: White.
Notes: Commonly used for straining paint and for covering foam and plastic.

Sharkstooth Scrim   Widths: 36 inches to 36 feet.
                     Bolts: 100 yards.
                     Colors: White, black, grey and blue.
                     Notes: Can be purchased fire-proofed.

Leno Filled Scrim: Widths: 14'-6" or 31'
                     Colors: White, grey, blue.
                     Notes: Similar to Sharkstooth, but the weave is much closer,
                                thereby making the fabric opaque.

Bobbinet   Widths: Up tp 31'.
                     Colors: Natural, white and black.
                     Notes: Light-weight cotton gauze with hexagonal weave; $1/8$" to
                                $3/16$" openings. Used for windows (black) and in front of
                                cycs or sky drops (white) to increase illusion of distance.

Scenic Netting   Widths: Up to 30'.
                     Colors: White and black.
                     Notes: Open net, 1" squares, used as support for cut drops.
                                Available in cotton (can be dyed) or nylon.

Opera Netting   Widths: Up to 29'.
                     Colors: White and black.
                     Notes: Similar to sharkstooth, but with a much more open weave.

Theatrical Gauze   Widths: 66"/70".
                     Colors: Natural and off-white.
                     Notes: Made of linen, sometimes called Linen Gauze.

Square Guaze   Widths: 35'
                     Colors: White and black.
                     Notes: Cotton net with $1/8$" weave.

Sharkstooth Scrim

Leno Filled Scrim

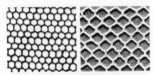

Bobbinet (two sizes)

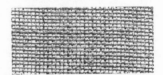

Theatrical Gauze

Fine Gauze

Square Gauze

BURN TESTS

Type of Fibers	Burning/ Melting Characteristics	Residue	Odor
Acetate Triacetate: acrilan, arnel, creslan, orlon	Not self-extinguishing; burns and melts; shrinks from flame.	Dark, hard, solid bead.	Combination of burning paper and vinegar.
Acrylic	Burns and melts; gives off black smoke; shrinks from flame.	Hard, irregular shape bead.	Boiled fish.
Cellulosic: cotton, flax, hemp, rayon, jute, etc.	Not self-extinguishing; burns and chars.	Fine, feathery, grey ash.	Burning paper, leaves or wood.
Glass, asbestos	Does not burn.		
Nylon	Self-extinguishing; burns and melts; shrinks from flame; flaming usually caused by finish; drops of melted fiber may fall.	Hard, cream-colored bead; if fibers are overheated, bead will become dark.	Celery.
Olefin	Self-extinguishing; burns and melts; shrinks from flame; flame with black smoke.	Hard, tan-colored bead.	Chemical.
Polyester	Self-extinguishing; burns and melts; shrinks from flame; flame gives off black smoke; drops of melted fiber may fall.	Hard, cream-colored bead; if fibers are overheated, bead will become dark.	Sweet chemical.
Silk	Self-extinguishing; burns briefly and chars; shrinks from flame.	Black, hollow irregular bead which crushes easily to a gritty black powder.	Charred or burning meat.
Spandex	Self-extinguishing; melts and burns.	Soft, black ash.	Chemical.
Vinyl	Self-extinguishing; burns and melts; shrinks from flame.	Hard, tan bead.	Paraffin-like or chemical.
Vinyon	Self-extinguishing; burns and melts; shrinks from flame.	Hard, black, irregular bead.	Acrid.
Wool, mohair, alpaca, cashmere	Self-extinguishing; burns briefly and chars; shrinks from flame.	Black, hollow irregular bead which crushes easily to a gritty black powder.	Strong odor of burning hair or chicken feathers.

FABRIC TERMS AND DEFINITIONS

Batiste:	A sheer, plain weave, finely woven cotton or cotton blend fabric.
Banjo Cloth:	Textured synthetic blend fabric. Commonly used for trade show drapes.
Beaver:	An overcoating cloth, heavily milled, with one face sheared and a nap raised finish; soft to handle. Woven from fine grade wool.
Bengaline:	A heavy-ribbed silk having the appearance of "grosgrain." Silk warp with worsted filling or cotton filling. Often used for draperies.
Bobbinet:	Light-weight cotton gauze with hexagonal weave. (see also page 142)
Bouclé:	A kind of yarn having a loose thread that gives the cloth made from it a tufted or knotted texture. The term is also used to describe the fabric. A popular bouclé is known as "poodle fabric."
Broadcloth:	A closely woven cotton or cotton-blend fabric with a fine, ribbed texture.
Brocade:	A satin-weave fabric using multicolored yarns. Pattern is usually woven into fabric with background and pattern having different textures.
Buckram:	A coarse cotton fabric sized with starch, primarily used in millinery. Usually only white and black.
Burlap:	Coarse texture, stiff, rough, and scratchy. (see also page 141)
Calico:	A term applied to any plain cotton heavier than muslin. Also describes a distinctive print on cotton.
Cambric:	A very fine white linen from Cambria, France. Used for collars, handkerchiefs, cloth napkins, etc. Also a cotton linen combination.
Canvas:	Technically, an open mesh fabric, usually of linen. Commonly used to denote heavy cotton scenic fabric. (see also page 141)
Cashmere:	Wool of the Cashmere goat, often woven with a mixture of cotton or cotton and wool weft.
Challis:	Named after the American Indian term "shalee," meaning soft, this is an extremely soft, plain or twill weave fabric with a faintly ribbed texture. Woven from fine wool or cotton thread.
Charmeuse:	A light-weight, rich looking satin weave with a dull back; well adapted to draping. May be described as a very soft satin with a subdued luster, due to the spun silk filling. Often used in 1930's underwear.
Cheesecloth:	Originally used for wrapping cheese. Thin, loosely woven cotton material, made from coarse yarns. When dyed called bunting. Is also called gauze, which should not be confused with Scenic Gauze. (see also page 142)
Chenille:	This fancy weft is made by first weaving a fabric on an ordinary loom which has a gauze mounting, and then cutting the material into strips. These strips are used as weft threads in shawls, tablecovers, and robes.
Chiffon:	A sheer voile fabric with a dull finish. Can be silk or synthetic, made of fine, hard-twisted yarns.
China Silk:	A soft, light-weight, extremely thin silk. The most inexpensive of silks.
Chincha:	Light-weight natural cotton. Heavier than gauze, lighter than muslin.
Chintz:	Plural for "chint," the Eastern name for printed cotton. Originally any printed cotton fabric. Now a drapery fabric with a glossy finish.

FABRIC TERMS AND DEFINITIONS (continued)

Cotton: Of the cotton plant, and woven in many thicknesses and qualities.

Corduroy: Usually cotton or cotton-blend fabric. The pile of this fabric is woven to form ridges called wales. Wide wale, narrow wale, and pin wale (very narrow wale) are available.

Coutil: French *fil de coutil* drill. Tough, firm variety of drill used for corsets. A variety of effects produced by weave which varies from twill to herringbone or reverse twist to many fancy stripes and figures.

Crepe: Soft, draping quality with some sheen. Made of silk, rayon, nylon, dacron, and other synthetics.

Crepe de Chine: A very soft silk crepe with a fine crinkled effect; easy to drape; used today mostly for blouses.

Damask: A fabric woven in geometrical or floral patterns. The designs are produced on a jacquard loom by interchanging the warp and weft threads in satin and twill weaves. The design appears on both sides of the fabric. The reflection of light on the material is what brings out the pattern.

Denim: An extremely sturdy twill-weave fabric of cotton or cotton blend with a solid color warp and a white filling yarn. Heavy, durable, with a rough texture, and yet launders well. From the French town of Nimes; originally called *serge de Nimes*.

Double Knit: A weft-knit fabric made on a machine that uses two sets of needles. The result is a fabric that looks the same on both sides.

Drill: A coarse linen or cotton cloth with a diagonal weave.

Duck: So called because it sheds water; a heavy, close, cotton fabric. The term is often used interchangeably with heavy canvas. (see also page 141)

Duvetyne: A light weight, less expensive substitute for velour. Sometimes called "commando cloth."

Erosion Cloth: A very open weave burlap, used for textural effects. (see also page 141)

Eyelash Cloth: A metallic cloth with cut loops.

Faille: A light-weight fabric of silk, polyester, or rayon, woven in a variation of a plain weave that has a slightly ribbed effect.

Felt: A fabric which is pressed rather than woven. Usually made from cotton, wool, or rayon.

Flannel: Any smooth-surfaced fabric with a slight nap to it concealing the weave. Usually wool, a wool blend, or cotton.

Foulard: A twill weave of a light-weight silk or rayon; usually a patterned fabric. From the French, meaning *silk handkerchief*.

Gabardine: A compact twill weave of wool, wool blend, cotton, cotton blend, or synthetics such as polyester and rayon.

Georgette: A semi-transparent material with a crepe weave. Woven from either silk or fine Egyptian cotton yarns. Now usually synthetic.

Gossamer: A very thin, soft, filmy cloth.

Grosgrain: A sturdy silk with a corded weft, giving a firm ribbed appearance. The corded weft thread can be of cotton or silk. Also refers to ribbons woven in the same manner. Now usually synthetic.

Harris Tweed:	A trademarked woolen material spun, dyed, and woven by hand by islanders in Harris and other islands of the Outer Hebredies, Scotland.
Herringbone:	A distinct woolen twill weave in which a zigzag effect is created by alternating the direction of the twill.
Homespun:	A coarse cloth of tweed character. The yarn is spun and then woven in the home.
Hopsacking:	A basket weave of wool, cotton, or other fabrics, copied from the burlap sacks of hops pickers; rough texture.
Horsehair:	This term is used to describe both a millinery unwoven net used to stiffen draped hats, and to describe a fine nylon net.
Jacquard:	An intricately knitted or woven fabric with a raised motif of figures. Damasks, tapestries, brocades and all cloths with elaborate figures require the Jacquard loom.
Jean:	A twilled cotton dyed or bleached and used for trousers.
Jersey:	A weft-knitted fabric with a plain, not a rib, stitch; may be of a variety of materials, including wool, cotton, acrylic, silk, polyester, rayon. Noted for its drape and movement.
Jute:	Natural fiber taken from the jute plant and used by man since prehistoric times.
Lace:	A delicate openwork fabric or network made of linen, silk, cotton, or other fibers.
Lamé:	A fabric made with metallic threads.
Linen:	The yarn is made from the flax plant. Woven in many qualities, it is strong and endurable. Can be bleached a pure white.
Madras:	First made in Madras, India, for sailors' headdresses. Soft, cotton fabric, usually a woven print.
Marquisette:	An open, loose fabric of leno or gauze-weave construction. Often incorrectly applied to scrim and voile which have a plain weave. Marquisette comes woven from cotton, silk, rayon, and wool, as well as synthetics.
Metallic Fabrics:	Many types of metallic fabrics are available. Usually metallic threads are woven into the fabric. Silver, gold, and copper are most popular. Lame is one form of metallic fabric.
Mohair:	A fine fabric from the hair of the Angora goat.
Moire:	A term referring to the watered effect given to fabrics by the pressure of engraved rollers which displace and flatten the threads. Usually processed on the silk grosgrain, or synthetic fabrics. Heavy washing destroys the effect, although careful washing in lukewarm water with a mild soap and no bleach is OK.
Monks Cloth:	A heavy cotton cloth with a basket weave.
Muslin:	A plain weave cotton fabric of varying fineness. Either bleached or unbleached. Dyes easily.
Net:	A stiff fabric woven to form an open pattern or meshwork; usually nylon or cotton. (see also Scenic and Opera Netting, page 142)

Noils:	Short fibers which come from the combing process in preparing yarns as for worsted. Short wool fibers are wool noils. There are silk noils, cotton noils, and rayon noils.
Nylon:	The generic name for manufactured fiber in which the fiber-forming substance is any long chain synthetic polamide having a recurring amide group as an integral part of the polymer chain.
Organdy:	A stiff, semi-transparent fabric made of cotton, silk, nylon, and other synthetics. Has a starched or permanently stiff, starchless finish.
Osnaburg:	A coarse, heavy cloth, originally of linen, now of cotton.
Oxford Cloth:	A modified basket weave of cotton or cotton-polyester blend. May be all white or may have a colored warp and a white filling yarn.
Panne:	A light-weight velvet with *laid* or flattened pile.
Paisley:	Designs, printed or woven, which imitate patterns in Paisley shawls.
Patent Vinyl:	Also known as patent leather, a very shiny, usually colorful or black.
Peau de Soie:	French for *skin of silk.* Strong, firm, leather-like, fabric with dull satiny surface. Woven like grosgrain but with the rib so fine that it produces a smooth twill surface.
Pellon:	A stiff, non-woven, pressed fabric.
Percale:	A closely woven cotton fabric without gloss; bleached, dyed or printed.
Pima:	A good quality, dense cotton.
Pique:	A firm fabric woven with a raised rib. Usually of cotton.
Point d'Esprit:	A white cotton net with small dots scattered over the surface for a snowflake effect.
Polished Cotton:	A cotton fabric woven so as to give it a satin surface. Can be soft or stiff. Permanent sheen creates "silky" effect. Also available in rayon and nylon.
Polyester:	A generic name for a manufactured fiber in which that fiber-forming substance is any long chain synthetic polymer composed of at least 85 percent by weight of an ester of a dihydric alcohol and terephthalic acid. Wrinkle resistant, permanent press, superior to nylon, resistant to sun degradation.
Pongee:	A light-weight, natural-colored, textile, usually of silk with an irregular texture in a plain weave.
Poplin:	A tight plain weave material with a ribbed or corded texture of wool, cotton, silk, polyester or fiber blends. Often given special finishes – water-repellent, fire-retardant, mildew-proof, etc.
Rayon:	The generic name for a manufactured fiber composed of regenerated cellulose, as well as manufactured fibers composed of regenerated cellulose in which substituents have replaced not more than 15 percent of the hydrogens of the hydroxyl groups. It is often referred to as artificial silk.
Repp:	A fabric with a finely ribbed surface, the ribs running transversely. Also spelled Rep.
Ripstop:	A fabric usually made of nylon, with heavier threads woven in every quarter inch or so, which have the effect of stopping the fabric from ripping.
Sateen:	A cotton material with a satin surface, often used for linings. Also referred to as cotton-back satin.

FABRIC TERMS AND DEFINITIONS (continued)

Satin: A silk, cotton, rayon, or acetate fabric, often thick in texture, with glossy face and dull back. Also describes a weaving technique.

Scrim: Generic term for open weave fabrics used as backdrops and transluscent drops. Types of scrim include sharkstooth, filled sharkstooth, bobbinette and gauze.

Seersucker: A cotton or cotton blend fabric with a puckered finish created by alternately loosening and tightening warp yarns. Usually with a stripe, check or plaid pattern.

Serge: A twill-weave, smooth-surfaced, fabric made of a smooth, sturdy worsted yarn of wool, cotton, or fiber blend. Usually dark blue in color.

Shantung: A plain-weave silk with an irregular nubby texture. It gets its name from Shantung, China where the weave originated.

Sharkskin: A smooth surfaced material made of a twill weave of two tones of yarn; usually with a faint luster. Used in worsted wool for suits and topcoats, in acetate and triacetate for sportswear.

Silesia: Originally made in Silesia, a province of Prussia. Closely woven, light-weight, smoothly finished cotton fabric. Used in linings, trouser pockets.

Silk: Produced from the silkworm cocoons. The filaments are drawn off in pairs and twisted together, using as many as ten or twelve pairs to make one thread. Its characteristics are strength, luster, and elasticity.

Spandex: A synthethic fabric whose ability to stretch and recover is similar to rubber.

Sparkle Sheer: A nylon blend sheer fabric with iridescent qualities.

Taffeta: A fine, plain-weave, somewhat stiff fabric of silk, rayon, or many other synthetic fibers. It has a smooth surface, a moderate amount of sheen and is available in several degrees of stiffness.

Terry Cloth: A pile fabric (usually cotton) in which the loops are uncut.

Tricot: A warp-knitted fabric using a rib stitch and usually made with synthetics such as nylon and polyester, and man-made fibers, such as rayon.

Tulle: A gossamer net fabric made of silk, cotton or synthetic yarns.

Tweed: A cloth woven from soft woolen yarns. Originally made by the banks of the river Tweed. It is open and elastic in texture and of a plain or twilled weave.

Twill: A weaving technique resulting in a strong diagonal design. Also a general name for any fabric with a distinct diagonal cord in its texture. Some examples of fabrics in twill weave include wools – broadcloth, cashmere, tweed, herringbone; cottons – coutil, denim, drill, gabardine, jean, khaki, ticking.

Velvet: A closely-woven fabric with a short dense pile on the upper surface.

Chiffon Velvet: A light-weight velvet, its pile laid flat by pressing.

Millinery Velvet: Also called *Lyons velvet*, it is generally silk and has a deep, erect pile.

Cotton Velvet: It is generally woven entirely of cotton fiber, but there can be cotton-back velvet, with a cotton back and a silk pile.

Rayon Velvet: Made entirely from rayon.

Velveteen: Same as Cotton Velvet.

FABRIC TERMS AND DEFINITIONS (continued)

Velour:	A napped fabric (cotton or cotton blend), heavier than corduroy or velveteen.
Vicuna:	The wool made from the wild ruminant of the Andes.
Viella Flannel:	Tradename fabric made in England. Cotton and wool in equal amounts mixed before spinning; twill weave.
Vinyl:	A plastic derived from ethylene.
Voile:	A semi-transparent fabric, much like heavy veiling. (see also cotton chifon)
Warp:	The set of yarns running lengthwise in a piece of cloth which form the basic structure of the fabric.
Weft or Woof:	The threads that cross the warp; the filling. Sometimes called "woof."
Woolen:	A fabric term used to describe garments made of coarse wool fibers (hair obtained from the fleece of sheep) that give the fabric a fuzzy nap. Tweed is a typical woolen fabric.
Worsted:	A general term for yarns that are tightly twisted and extremely smooth. It is also used to describe fabrics made from these yarns and is used to differentiate smooth textured wool suits from the shaggier woolens (above).

RESILIENT FLOORING

Type	Components	Sizes	Thickness
Vinyl sheet	Vinyl resins	6' wide	.065" - .095"
Vinyl tile (VCT)	Vinyl resins	9"x 9", 12"x 12"	$1/16"$, $3/32"$, $1/8"$
Cork tile	Raw cork and resins	9"x 9"	$1/8"$, $3/16"$, $1/4"$
Cork tile with vinyl coating	Raw cork and vinyl resins	9"x 9", 12"x 12"	$1/8"$, $3/16"$
Rubber tile	Rubber compound	9" x 9", 12"x 12"	$3/32"$, $1/8"$, $3/16"$
Linoleum (sheet and tile)	Cork, wood, and oleoresins	6' wide or 9" x 9"	$1/8"$
Asphalt tile	Asphalt compounds and resins	9"x 9"	$1/8"$, $3/16"$

FLOOR TILE ESTIMATING

Square Feet	--Number of Tiles Needed--			Square Feet	--Number of Tiles Needed--		
	9"x 9"	12"x 12"	9"x 18"		9"x 9"	12"x 12"	9"x 18"
1	2	1	1	60	107	60	54
2	4	2	2	70	125	70	63
3	6	3	3	80	143	80	72
4	8	4	4	90	160	90	80
5	9	5	5	100	178	100	90
6	11	6	6	200	356	200	178
7	13	7	7	300	534	300	267
8	15	8	8	400	712	400	356
9	16	9	8	500	890	500	445
10	18	10	9	600	1068	600	534
20	36	20	18	700	1246	700	623
30	54	30	27	800	1424	800	712
40	72	40	36	900	1602	900	801
50	89	50	45	1000	1780	1000	890

Tile waste allowance:

1	to	50 sq. ft:	allow 14%
50	to	100 sq. ft:	allow 10%
100	to	200 sq. ft:	allow 8%

200	to	300 sq. ft:	allow 7%
300	to	1000 sq. ft:	allow 5%
	over	1000 sq. ft:	allow 3%

CERAMIC TILE

Type	Thickness	Sizes
Glazed wall tile	5/16"	4 1/4" x 4 1/4" 4 1/4" x 6" 6" x 6"
Ceramic mosaic tile	1/4"	1" x 1" 1" x 2" 2" x 2"
Quarry tile and pavers	1/2", 3/4"	2 3/4" x 6" 4" x 4" 4" x 6" 6" x 6" 6" x 9" 9" x 9"

TYPES OF GLASS

Sheet glass: The two surfaces are never parallel and never distortion-free.
Thicknesses: 1/16" to 7/16".
Maximum sizes:

single strength:	3/32" thick	40" x 50"
double strength:	1/8" thick	60" x 80"
high strength:	3/16" thick	120" x 84"
	1/4" thick	120" x 84"
	3/8" thick	60" x 84"
	7/16" thick	60" x 84"

Float glass: Better quality than sheet glass and has less distortion.
Thicknesses: 1/8", 3/16", 1/4".
Maximum size: 122" x 200"

Plate glass: Better quality; provides clear, undistorted vision.
Thicknesses: 1/8" to 1"
Maximum sizes:

1/8" thick	130" x 80"
1/4" thick	130" x 240"
3/8" thick	125" x 281"
1/2" thick	125" x 281"

INSULATING PROPERTIES OF MATERIALS

Material[1]			*(r) Value*[2]
Wood	Plywood		1.25
	Hardwood		.91
	Softwood		1.25
	Solid core door: $1^3/4$"		1.96
Masonry	Common brick		.20
	Concrete block: 8"		1.11
	Block with light-weight aggregate: 8"		2.00
Concrete	Cement mortar		.20
	With light-weight aggregate		.59
	Stucco		.20
	Sand, gravel, stone aggregate		.11
Metal	Aluminum		.0007
	Steel		.0032
	Copper		.0004
Plaster			.20
Gypsum	Gypsum or plaster board: $5/8$"		.39
	Gypsum or plaster board: $1/2$"		.32
Finish flooring	Carpet		2.08
	Cork: $1/8$"		.28
	Vinyl tile		.05
Roofing	Asphalt shingle		.44
	Wood shingle		.87
	Slate		.05
	Built-up roof		.33
Glass	Single thickness		.88
Insulation materials	Batt:	Mineral wool	3.12
	Loose fill:	Mineral wool	3.70
		Perlite	2.78
	Boards:	Expanded polystyrene	4.00
		Mineral fiber board	2.94
		Glass fiber	4.17
Air space[3]	Between non-reflective surfaces		1.34
	Between a reflective and a non-reflective surface		4.64

1. Per 1" of thickness, unless otherwise indicated. Contact manufacturers for more detailed information.
2. (r) = rate of heat flowing through a homogeneous material one inch thick measured by the temperature difference in degrees (F) between the two exposed faces required to cause one British Thermal Unit (BTU) to flow through one square foot per hour. [1 ft^2 h deg. F/BTU in.= 6.933 m°C/W (meter degree Celsius per watt)].
3. Value does not increase significantly for thicknesses above $3/4$".

AVERAGE WEIGHTS OF MATERIALS - Per Cubic Foot (lb/ft³)

Material	Lb/Ft³	Material	Lb/Ft³
Alcohol	50	Salt, common	48
Aluminum	169	Sand, dry	100
Asbestos	150	Sand, wet	125
Brick, common	112	Silver	650-657
Brick, fire	143	Slate	175
Brick, hard	125	Snow (see water)	
Brickwork, in mortar	100	Soapstone	168
Brickwork, in cement	112	Stainless steel	510
Cement, Portland (set)	193	Steel	489
Chalk	143	Stone, plain	144
Charcoal	25	Sulphur	125
Coal, anthracite	94	Tar	64-75
Coal, bituminous	81	Tile	112
Concrete (average density)	137	Tin	455
Copper	555	Turpentine	54
Cork	15	Vermiculite	25-60
Earth, dry	65-88	Water	62.5
Earth, moist	95-135	Ice	56
Emery	249	Snow, fresh	5-12
Gasoline	44	Snow, wet, compact	15-20
Glass, common	150-175	Zinc	443
Glass, flint	180-370		
Gold	1204		
Granite	165-172		
Gravel, damp,	82-125		
Gravel, dry	90-145	**Gases**	
Gypsum	145-150		
Ice	56	Acetylene	.0732
Iron, cast gray	439-445	Air	.0807
Iron, wrought	487-493	Ammonia	.04813
Iron slag	168	Butane, iso	.1669
Ivory	114-120	Carbon dioxide	.123
Kerosene	50	Carbon monoxide	.07806
Lead	687	Chlorine	.2006
Leather	59	Ether vapor	.2088
Lime	53-75	Ethylene	.07868
Limestone	162	Helium	.01114
Magnesium	109	Hydrogen	.00561
Marble	160-177	Mercury vapor	.56013
Masonry	150	Methane	.04475
Mica	175	Nitrogen	.07807
Mortar	94	Oxygen	.08921
Nickel	549	Propane	.1254
Paper	58	Sulfur dioxide	.1827
Paraffin	54-57	Water vapor	.05028
Phenolic plastic, cast	79-82		
Platinum	1334		
Plaster of Paris	112		
Plastic, styrene	66		
Plastic, vinyl	87	(See also page 160 for other metals.)	
Polyethylene	57		
Quartz	162		

(See also page 160 for other metals.)

Sources: BCI, MH

AVERAGE WEIGHTS OF MATERIALS - Per Square Foot (lb/ft^2)

Material	Lb./Ft.^{2}
Concrete	
Reinforced (per 1" of thickness):	
stone	12.5
slag	11.5
light-weight	6-10
Plain (per 1" of thickness):	
stone	12
slag	11
light-weight	3-9
Glass	
Sheet:	
1/8"	1.60
1/4"	3.25
Wire: 1/4"	3.50
Steel	
Mild steel plates:	
3/16"	7.65
1/4"	10.21
5/16"	12.75
Walls and Partitions	
Brick (per 4" of thickness)	35
Concrete block:	
stone & gravel aggregate:	
4" thick	34
6" thick	50
8" thick	58
12" thick	90
light-weight aggregate:	
4" thick	22
6" thick	31
8" thick	38
12" thick	55
Glass block, 4" thick	18
Gypsum board, 1/2" thick	2
Metal lath	0.5
Metal studs, w/ lath & plaster	18
Plaster (per 1" of thickness):	
cement	10
gypsum	5
Plywood:	
1/8"	.42
1/4"	.80
1/2"	1.52
3/4"	2.25
1"	3.00

Material	Lb./Ft.^{2}
Walls and Partitions (continued)	
Stone:	
granite, 4"	59
limestone, 6"	55
marble, 1"	13
sandstone, 4"	49
slate, 1"	14
Tile:	
ceramic mosaic, 1/4"	2.5
structural clay, 4"	18
6"	28
10"	40
Wood studs:	
2 x 4 w/ lath & plaster	16
Flooring	
Marble, 1"	13
Terrazzo, 1"	13
Tile, 3/4" ceramic or quarry	10
Wood:	
hardwood, 25/32"	4
softwood, 3/4"	2.5
woodblock, 3"	15
Vinyl tile, 1/8"	1.33
Ceilings	
Acoustical fiber tile, 3/4"	1
Acoustic plaster:	
on gypsum, lath base	10
Channel suspended system	1
Roofing	
Built-up (5-ply felt & gravel)	6
Corrugated iron (galvanized)	1.5
Fiberglass	0.5
Lead, 1/8"	8
Shingles:	
asphalt	3
asbestos cement	3
slate, 1/4"	10
wood	2
Tile:	
cement tile	16
clay tile	14

Sources: BCI, MH

AVERAGE WEIGHTS OF SHEET MATERIALS

	-------Pounds per-------			-------Pounds per-------	
	Sq. Ft.	4' x 8' Sheet		Sq. Ft.	4' x 8' Sheet
Plywood			Particle Board / Press Board		
1/8"	.42	13	1/4"	.75	24
1/4"	.80	26	1/2"	1.94	62
1/2"	1.52	49	3/4"	2.99	96
3/4"	2.20	70			
1"	3.00	96	Homosote / Soundboard		
			1/2"	1.00	32
Masonite					
1/8"	.59	19	Acrylic		
1/4"	1.19	38	1/8"	.74	24
			3/16"	1.11	36
Gypsum			1/4"	1.48	48
3/8"	1.5	48	3/8"	2.22	71
1/2"	2	64	1/2"	2.96	95

AVERAGE WEIGHTS OF BOARD LUMBER

	Per 1' *	Per 8'	Per 12'	Per 16'
1 x 3, pine	0.326	2.60	3.91	5.21
1 x 6, pine	0.716	5.73	8.59	11.46
1 x 12, pine	1.465	11.72	17.58	23.44
5/4 x 3, pine	0.543	4.34	6.51	8.68
5/4 x 6, pine	1.194	9.55	14.32	19.10
5/4 x 12, pine	2.441	19.53	29.30	39.06
2 x 4, fir	0.911	7.29	10.94	14.58
4 x 4, fir	2.130	17.01	25.52	34.03

* At 25 lbs. per cubic foot (.1736 lbs. per cubic inch).

AVERAGE WEIGHTS OF LIGHTING INSTRUMENTS

Lighting Instruments
  6" fresnel   6 - 8 lbs
  8" fresnel   13 - 16 lbs
  6" x 9" ERS   12 - 16 lbs

"Hanging weight" = 25 lbs.
(Average weight per instrument, with cable, on a 60' batten.)

AVERAGE WEIGHTS OF BEVERAGES

6-pack, cans   5 lbs
6-pack, bottles   8.6 lbs
keg   140 lbs

Note: The beer dispenser known as a "keg" is actually a "half-keg" and there are approx. 250 glasses in a half-keg. There is also half size keg called a "quarter-keg."

For additional references to weights of materials, see the following pages: p. 50 (nails), p. 87 (rope), p. 112 (pipe), p. 114 (steel bars), p. 121 (wood), p. 133 (plastic pipe), p. 160 (metals).

THE ELEMENTS

Name	Symbol	Atomic Number	Atomic[1] Weight	Name	Symbol	Atomic Number	Atomic[1] Weight
Actinium	Ac	89	227	Molybdenum	Mo	42	95.95
Aluminum	Al	13	26.97	Neodymium	Nd	60	144.27
Americium	Am	95	(241)	Neon	Ne	10	20.183
Antimony	Sb	51	121.76	Neptunium	Np	93	(237)
Argon	A	18	39.944	Nickel	Ni	28	58.69
Arsenic	As	33	74.91	Niobium	Nb	41	92.91
Astatine	At	85	(210)	Nitrogen	N	7	14.008
Barium	Ba	56	137.36	Osmium	Os	76	190.2
Berkelium	Bk	97		Oxygen	O	8	16.00
Beryllium	Be	4	9.013	Palladium	Pd	46	106.7
Bismuth	Bi	83	209.00	Phosphorus	P	15	30.98
Boron	B	5	10.82	Platinum	Pt	78	195.23
Bromine	Br	35	79.916	Plutonium	Pu	94	(239)
Cadmium	Cd	48	112.41	Polonium	Po	84	210
Calcium	Ca	20	40.08	Potassium	K	19	39.096
Californium	Cf	98	(248)	Praseodymium	Pr	59	140.92
Carbon	C	6	12.011	Promethium	Pm	61	(147)
Cerium	Ce	58	140.13	Proactinium	Pa	91	231
Cesium	Cs	55	132.91	Radium	Ra	88	226.05
Chlorine	Cl	17	35.457	Radon	Rn	86	222
Chromium	Cr	24	52.01	Rhenium	Re	75	186.31
Cobalt	Co	27	58.94	Rhodium	Rh	45	102.91
Columbium[2]				Rubidium	Rb	37	85.48
Copper	Cu	29	63.54	Ruthenium	Ru	44	101.1
Curium	Cm	96	(245)	Samarium	Sm	62	150.43
Dysprosium	Dy	66	162.46	Scandium	Sc	21	45.10
Erbium	Er	68	167.2	Selenium	Se	34	78.96
Europium	Eu	63	152.0	Silicon	Si	14	28.06
Fluorine	F	9	19.00	Silver	Ag	47	107.88
Francium	Fr	87	(223)	Sodium	Na	11	22.991
Gadolinium	Gd	64	156.9	Strontium	Sr	38	87.63
Gallium	Ga	31	69.72	Sulphur	S	16	32.066
Germanium	Ge	32	72.60	Tantalum	Ta	73	180.95
Gold	Au	79	197.0	Technetium	Tc	43	(99)
Hafnium	Hf	72	178.6	Tellurium	Te	52	127.61
Helium	He	2	4.003	Terbium	Tb	65	158.93
Holmium	Ho	67	164.94	Thallium	Tl	81	204.39
Hydrogen	H	1	1.008	Thorium	Th	90	232.05
Indium	In	49	114.76	Thulium	Tm	69	168.94
Iodine	I	53	126.92	Tin	Sn	50	118.70
Iridium	Ir	77	192.2	Titanium	Ti	22	47.90
Iron	Fe	26	55.85	Tungsten[3]			
Krypton	Kr	36	83.7	Uranium	U	92	238.07
Lanthanum	La	57	138.92	Vanadium	V	23	50.95
Lead	Pb	82	207.21	Wolfram	W	74	183.92
Lithium	Li	3	6.94	Xenon	Xe	54	131.3
Lutetium	Lu	71	174.99	Ytterbium	Yb	70	173.04
Magnesium	Mg	12	24.32	Yttrium	Y	39	88.92
Manganese	Mn	25	54.94	Zinc	Zn	30	65.38
Mercury	Hg	80	200.61	Zirconium	Zr	40	91.22

1. International Atomic Weight (1953). Value in parenthesis is mass number of the most stable known isotope.
2. See Niobium.
3. See Wolfram.

COMMON AND SCIENTIFIC NAMES FOR CHEMICALS

Popular Name	Chemical Name	Formula
Alcohol, grain	Ethyl alcohol	C_2H_5OH
Alcohol, wood	Methyl alcohol	CH_3OH
Alum, common	Aluminum potassium sulfate	$AlK(SO_4)_2 \cdot 12H_2O$
Alumina	Aluminum oxide	Al_2O_3
Alundum	Fused aluminum oxide	Al_2O_3
Antichlor	Sodium thiosulfate	$Na_2S_2O_3 \cdot 5H_2O$
Aqua ammonia	Ammonium hydroxide solution	$NH_4OH + H_2O$
Aqua fortis	Nitric acid	HNO_3
Aqua regia	Nitric and hydrochloric acids	$HNO_3 + HCl$
Aromatic spirits of ammonia	Ammonia gas in alcohol	
Asbestos	Magnesium silicate	$Mg_3Si_2O_7 \cdot 2H_2O$
Aspirin	Acetylsalicylic acid	$C_2H_3O_2C_6H_4CO_2H$
Baking soda	Sodium bicarbonate	$NaHCO_3$
Banana oil	Amyl acetate	$CH_3CO_2C_5H_{11}$
Baryta	Barium oxide	BaO
Bauxite	Impure aluminum oxide	Al_2O_3
Benzol	Benzene	C_6H_6
Bichloride of mercury	Mercuric chloride	$HgCl_2$
Black lead	Graphite	C
Black oxide of copper	Cupric oxide	CuO
Black oxide of mercury	Mercurous oxide	Hg_2O
Bleaching powder	Calcium hypochlorite	$CaOCl_2$
Bluestone	Copper sulfate	$CuSO_4 \cdot 5H_2O$
Blue vitriol	Copper sulfate	$CuSO_4 \cdot 5H_2O$
Boracic acid	Boric acid	H_3BO_3
Borax	Sodium borate	$Na_2B_4O_7 \cdot 10H_2O$
Brimstone	Sulfur	S
Brine	Strong sodium chloride solution	$NaCl\ H_2O$
"Butter of"	Chloride or trichloride of	
Caliche	Impure sodium nitrate	$NaNO_3$
Calomel	Mercurous chloride	Hg_2Cl_2
Carbolic acid	Phenol	C_6H_5OH
Carbonic acid gas	Carbon dioxide	CO_2
Caustic potash	Potassium hydroxide	KOH
Caustic soda	Sodium hydroxide	$NaOH$
Chalk	Calcium carbonate	$CaCO_3$
Chile saltpeter	Sodium nitrate	$NaNO_3$
Chloroform	Trichloromethane	$CHCl_3$
Chrome alum	Chromium potassium sulfate	$CrK(SO_4)_2 \cdot 12H_2O$
Chrome yellow	Lead chromate	$PbCrO_4$
Copperas	Ferrous sulfate	$FeSO_4 \cdot 7H_2O$
Corrosive sublimate	Mercuric chloride	$HgCl_2$
Cream of tartar	Potassium bitartrate	$KHC_4H_4O_6$
Crocus powder	Ferric oxide	Fe_2O_3
DDT	Dichlorodiphenyl-trichloroethane	$(C_6H) \cdot Cl_2 \cdot CH \cdot CCl_3$

Popular Name	Chemical Name	Formula
Dry ice	Solid carbon dioxide	CO_2
Dutch liquid	Ethylene dichloride	$CH_2Cl \cdot CH_2Cl$
Emery powder	Impure aluminum oxide	Al_2O_3
Epsom salts	Magnesium sulfate	$MgSO_4 \cdot 7H_2O$
Ethanol	Ethyl alcohol	C_2H_5OH
Ether	Ethyl ether	$(C_2H_5)_2O$
Fluorspar	Natural calcium fluoride	CaF_2
Formalin	Formaldehyde	$HCOH$
French chalk	Natural magnesium silicate	$H_2Mg_3(SiO_3)_4$
Galena	Natural lead sulfide	PbS
Glauber's salt	Sodium sulfate	$Na_2SO_4 \cdot 10H_2O$
Green vitriol	Ferrous sulfate	$FeSO_4 \cdot 7H_2O$
Gypsum	Natural calcium sulfate	$CaSO_4 \cdot 2H_2O$
Hypo	Sodium thiosulfate	$Na_2S_2O_3 \cdot 5H_2O$
Labarraque's solution	Sodium hypochlorite solution	$NaOCl + H_2O$
Lime, unslaked	Calcium oxide	CaO
Limewater	Calcium hydroxide solution	$Ca(OH)_2 + H_2O$
Litharge	Lead oxide	PbO
Lithopone	Zinc sulfide plus barium sulfate	$ZnS + BaSO_4$
Magnesia	Magnesium oxide	MgO
Magnesite	Magnesium carbonate	$MgCO_3$
Marble	Calcium carbonate	$CaCO_3$
Marsh gas	Methane	CH_4
Methanol	Methyl alcohol	CH_3OH
Methylated spirits	Methyl alcohol	CH_3OH
Milk of magnesia	Magnesium hydroxide in water	$Mg(OH)_2$
Minium	Lead tetroxide	Pb_3O_4
"Muriate of"	Chloride of	
Muriatic acid	Hydrochloric acid	HCl
Natural gas	Mostly methane	CH_4
Niter	Potassium nitrate	KNO_3
Oil of bitter almonds (artificial)	Benzaldehyde	C_6H_5CHO
Oil of mirbane	Nitrobenzene	$C_6H_5NO_3$
Oil of vitriol	Sulfuric acid	H_2SO_4
Oil of wintergreen (artificial)	Methyl salicylate	$C_6H_4OHCOOCH_3$
Oleum	Fuming sulfuric acid	$H_2SO_4SO_3$
Orpiment	Arsenic trisulfide	As_2S_3
Paris green	Copper aceto-arsenite	$3Cu(AsO_2)_2 \cdot Cu(C_2H_3O_2)_2$
Pearl ash	Potassium carbonate	K_2CO_3
Peroxide	Peroxide of hydrogen solution	$H_2O_2 + H_2O$
Phosgene	Carbonyl chloride	$COCl_2$
Plaster of Paris	Calcium sulfate	$(CaSO_4)_2 \cdot H_2O$
Plumbago	Graphite	C
Potash	Potassium carbonate	K_2CO_3
Prussic acid	Hydrocyanic acid	HCN
Pyro	Pyrogallic acid	$C_6H_3(OH)_3$
Quicklime	Calcium oxide	CaO
Quicksilver	Mercury	Hg
Red lead	Lead tetroxide	Pb_3O_4
Red oxide of copper	Cuprous oxide	Cu_2O

Popular Name	Chemical Name	Formula
Red oxide of mercury	Mercuric oxide	HgO
Red prussiate of potash	Potassium ferricyanide	$K_3Fe(CN)_6$
Rochelle salt	Potassium sodium tartrate	$KNaC_4H_4O_6 \cdot 4H_2O$
Rouge	Ferric oxide	Fe_2O_3
Sal ammoniac	Ammonium chloride	NH_4Cl
Saleratus	Sodium bicarbonate	$NaHCO_3$
Sal soda	Crystalline sodium carbonate	$Na_2CO_3 \cdot 10H_2O$
Salt	Sodium chloride	$NaCl$
Salt cake	Impure sodium sulfate	Na_2SO_4
Saltpeter	Potassium nitrate	KNO_3
Saltpeter (Chile)	Impure sodium nitrate	$NaNO_3$
Salt of lemon	Potassium binoxalate	$KHC_2O_4 \cdot H_2O$
Salts of tartar	Potassium carbonate	K_2CO_3
Silica	Silicon dioxide	SiO_2
Slaked lime	Calcium hydroxide	$Ca(OH)_2$
Soapstone	Impure magnesium silicate	$H_2Mg_3(SiO_3)_4$
Soda ash	Dry sodium carbonate	Na_2CO_3
Spirit of hartshorn	Ammonia gas in alcohol	
Spirits of salt	Hydrochloric acid	HCl
Spirits of wine	Ethyl alcohol	C_2H_5OH
Sugar of lead	Lead acetate	$Pb(C_2H_3O_2)_2 \cdot 3H_2O$
Sulfuric ether	Ethyl ether	$(C_2H_5)_2O$
Talc	Magnesium silicate	$H_2Mg_3(SiO_3)_4$
TNT	Trinitrotoluene	$C_6H_2CH_3(NO_3)_3$
Toluol	Toluene	$C_6H_5CH_3$
Vinegar	Dilute and impure acetic acid	CH_3COOH
Washing soda	Crystalline sodium carbonate	$Na_2CO_3 \cdot 10H_2O$
Water glass	Sodium silicate	Na_2SiO_3
White arsenic	Arsenic trioxide	As_2O_3
White lead	Basic lead carbonate	$(PbCO_3)_2 \cdot Pb(OH)_2$
White vitriol	Zinc sulfate	$ZnSO_4 \cdot 7H_2O$
Whiting	Powdered calcium carbonate	$CaCO_3$
Wood alcohol	Methyl alcohol	CH_3OH
Xylol	Xylene	$C_6H_4(CH_3)_2$
Zinc white	Zinc oxide	ZnO

PROPERTIES OF METALS

Metal or Composition	Symbol	Specific Gravity	Weight per Cubic Ft., (Lbs.)	Melting Point, (°F.)	Electric Conductivity (Silver=100)
Aluminum	Al	2.70	168.5	1220	63.0
Antimony	Sb	6.618	413.0	1167	3.59
Barium	Ba	3.78	235.9	1562	30.61
Bismuth	Bi	9.781	610.3	520	1.40
Boron	B	2.535	158.2	4172	---
Cadmium	Cd	8.648	539.6	610	24.38
Calcium	Ca	1.54	96.1	1490	21.77
Chromium	Cr	6.93	432.4	2939	16.00
Cobalt	Co	8.71	543.5	2696	16.93
Copper	Cu	8.89	554.7	1981	97.61
Gold	Au	19.3	1204.3	1945	76.61
Iridium	Ir	22.42	1399.0	4262	13.52
Iron, wrought	Fe	7.80 - 7.90	486.7 - 493.0	2750	14.57
Lead	Pb	11.342	707.7	621	8.42
Magnesium	Mg	1.741	108.6	1204	39.44
Manganese	Mn	7.3	455.5	2300	15.75
Mercury (68°F)	Hg	13.546	845.3	-38	1.75
Molybdenum	Mo	10.2	636.5	4748	17.60
Nickel	Ni	8.8	549.1	2651	12.89
Platinum	Pt	21.37	1333.5	3224	14.43
Potassium	K	0.870	54.3	144	19.62
Silver	Ag	10.42 - 10.53	650.2 - 657.1	1761	100.00
Sodium	Na	0.9712	60.6	207	31.98
Tantalum	Ta	16.6	1035.8	5162	54.63
Tellurium	Te	6.25	390.0	846	0.001
Tin	Sn	7.29	454.9	449	14.39
Titanium	Ti	4.5	280.1	3272	13.73
Tungsten	W	18.6 - 19.1	1161 - 1192	6098	14.00
Uranium	U	18.7	1166.9	<3362	16.47
Vanadium	V	5.6	349.4	3110	4.95
Zinc	Zn	7.04 - 7.16	439.3 - 446.8	788	29.57

pH OF COMMON MATERIALS

	pH*		pH*
Hydrochloric acid, normal	0.1	Average garden soils	4.5 - 7.0
Sulfuric acid, normal	0.3	Boric acid, 0.1 normal	5.2
Oxalic acid, 0.1 normal	1.6	Best pH for most plants	6.0 - 7.0
Limes	1.8 - 2.0	Cow's milk	6.3 - 6.6
Ginger Ale	2.0 - 4.0	Drinking water	6.5 - 6.8
Lemons	2.2 - 2.4	Pure water	7.0
Swamp peats	2.7 - 3.4	Human blood plasma	7.3 - 7.5
Apples	2.9 - 3.3	Sodium bicarbonate, 0.1 normal	8.4
Grapefruit	3.0 - 3.3		
Bananas	4.5 - 4.7		

* A measure of the acidity of an aqueous solution.

COMMON ALLOYS

Name	Composition (typical)	Uses or Properties
Alnico-4	55%Fe, 28%Ni, 12%Al, 5%Co	Magnets
Babbitt metal	91%Sn, 4.5%Sb, 4.5%Cu	Bearings
Brass	60%Cu, 40%Zn	Wide general use
Bronze	92%Cu, 8%Sn	Wide general use
Coinage metal	95%Cu, 4%Sn, 1%Zn	"Copper" coins
Coinage metal	75%Cu, 25%Ni	"Silver" coins
Constantan	55%Cu, 45%Ni	Thermocouples
Dental amalgam	52%Hg, 33%Ag, 12.5%Sn, 2%Cu, 0.5%Zn	Dental fillings
Elektron	86.5%Mg, 11%Al, 1.5%Zn, 1%Mn	Very light aircraft parts
German silver	56%Cu, 24%Zn, 20%Ni	Base for electroplating
Gun metal	88%Cu, 10%Sn, 2%Zn	Strong and tough
Invar	64%Fe, 36%Ni	Zero temperature coefficient of expansion
Monel metal	67%Ni, 33%Cu	Corrosion resistant
Nichrome	60%Ni, 25%Fe, 15%Cr	Electrical heating elements
Pewter	65%Sn, 30%Pb, 5%Sb	Drinking vessels
Solder	60%Pb, 35%Sn, 5%Bi	Electrical connections
Stainless steel	73%Fe, 18%Cr, 8%Ni, 1%C	Corrosion-resistant
Wood's metal	50%Bi, 25%Pb, 12.5%Sn, 12.5%Cd	Low melting point

TEMPERATURE STANDARDS

Degrees Celsius (Centigrade)		Degrees Fahrenheit
-273	Absolute zero	-459.4
-130	Alcohol freezes	-202
-78.5	Dry ice sublimes	-109.3
-38.9	Mercury freezes	-38
0	Ice melts	32
34.5	Ether boils	94.1
37	Temperature of human body	98.6
78.5	Alcohol boils	173.3
100	Water boils	212
232	Tin melts	450
327	Lead melts	621
658	Aluminum melts	1,216
700	Dull red heat	1,292
1,000	Bright red heat	1,832
1,400	White heat	2,552
1,500	Temperature of Bunsen flame	2,732
1,530	Iron melts	2,786
6,000	Temperature of sun's surface	10,800

Note: Use the following formulas to convert from one standard to the other.

Degrees Fahrenheit $= \dfrac{9 \times \text{degrees C}}{5} + 32$ or $(1.8 \times \text{degrees C}) + 32$

Degrees Celsius $= \dfrac{5 \times (\text{degrees F} - 32)}{9}$ or $.55556 \times (\text{degrees F} - 32)$

EARTHQUAKE INTENSITIES

Intensity	Characteristic Effects	Magnitude on the Richter Scale [1]
Instrumental	Detected only by seismographs.	<3
Feeble	Noticed only by sensitive people.	3 - 3.4
Slight	Similar to vibrations caused by heavy trucks.	3.5 - 4
Moderate	Loose objects disturbed.	4 - 4.4
Rather strong	Can wake sleeping people.	4.5 - 4.8
Strong	Trees sway, loose objects fall.	4.9 - 5.4
Very strong	Walls crack.	5.5 - 6
Destructive	Chimneys fall; some buildings collapse.	6.1 - 6.5
Ruinous	Most houses collapse.	6.6 - 7
Disastrous	Ground badly cracked; landslides.	7.1 - 7.3
Very disastrous	Most buildings, railroads and pipelines destroyed.	7.4 - 8.1
Catastrophic[2]	Total destruction.	>8.1

1. Measured at earthquake's epicenter.
2. Greatest recorded intensity is in Iran, 1972; measured 9.5 on Richter scale.

BEAUFORT WIND STRENGTH SCALE

Beuafort Number	Wind Speed (miles/hour)	
0	< 1	**Calm:** Smoke rises vertically.
1	1-5	**Light Air:** Rising smoke drifts.
2	6-11	**Light Breeze:** Leaves rustle, you can feel breeze on your face.
3	12-19	**Gentle Breeze:** Light weight flags extend.
4	20-28	**Moderate Breeze:** Dust and paper blown around.
5	29-38	**Fresh Breeze:** Small trees sway.
6	39-49	**Strong Breeze:** Umbrellas are difficult to control.
7	50-61	**Moderate Gale:** Noticeably difficult to walk, large trees sway.
8	62-74	**Fresh Gale:** Walking into wind very difficult, small branches break.
9	75-88	**Strong Gale:** Slight building damage, shingles blown off roofs.
10	89-102	**Whole Gale:** Large trees uprooted, considerable building damage.
11	103-117	**Storm:** Widespread damage. (*Storm* winds occur mainly at sea.)
12	> 117	**Hurricane:** Extreme destruction.

ELECTRICS

ELECTRICAL TERMS AND DEFINITIONS

Unit	Symbol	Definition
Volt	V	The pressure required to force one ampere through a resistance of one ohm.
Ampere (Amp)	A	The electric current that will flow through one ohm under a pressure of one volt.
Ohm	Ω	The resistance through which one volt will force one ampere.
Hertz	Hz	Frequency in cycles / second.
Coulomb	C	The quantity of electricity transported in one second by a current of one ampere.
Watt	W	One joule* per second.
Horsepower	hp	745.6999 watts.
Farad	F	The capacitance of a capacitor between the plates of which there appears a difference of potential of one volt when it is charged by a quantity of electricity equal to one coulomb.

* See page 213 for definition of a joule.

ELECTRICAL ANALOGIES AND EXPLANATIONS

Electro motive force (voltage) is analogous to the pressure of water flowing in a pipe. The quantity of water flowing is comparable to the **current** (amperes); the friction between water and the pipe is similar to electrical **resistance** (ohms).

Resistance, inductance and capacitance: Resistance is the property of limiting the passage of electric current to a predictable level. Value of the resistor is expressed in ohms. Capacitance is the property of an electric non-conductor to store energy as a result of electric displacement, where opposite plates are held at different potentials. Inductance is the property of an electric component where electromotive force is induced into it by the circuit, or by a neighboring circuit.

Conductors and insulators: If a material will conduct an electric current, it is called a "conductor." If a material will not conduct an electric current, it is called an "insulator." Insulating materials are therefore used as insulation for conductors by enclosing conductors, such as wires, in a layer of the insulation.

ELECTRIC FORMULAS WHEEL

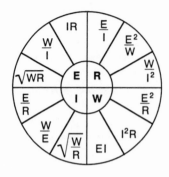

E = Electro Magnetic Force (Volts)
R = Resistance (Ohms)
I = Intensity (Amps)
W = Watts (or power)

The formulas associated with this wheel apply to DC circuits, and common AC circuits (like normal household 110VAC) in which the phase angle is 0° and impedance is equal to resistance.

VOLTAGE DROP FORMULAS

Three-Phase Circuits   (18.7 is 21.6 times 0.866, which is the square root of 3, divided by 2)

$$\frac{\text{amperes x one-way distance x 18.7}}{\text{cmils}} = \text{voltage drop}$$

Three-Wire 120/208 Derived from Four-Wire, Three-Phase System   (used when a three-wire 120/208-V feeder cable is created from four-wire, three-phase system)

$$\frac{\text{amperes x one-way distance x 18.7 x 1.5}}{\text{cmils}} = \text{voltage drop}$$

Wire Size   (used to calculate the wire size needed to limit the line loss to a particular number of volts)

$$\frac{\text{amperes x one-way distance x 21.6}}{\text{voltage drop desired}} = \text{cmils} \qquad \text{(single-phase circuits)}$$

$$\frac{\text{amperes x one-way distance x 21.6 x 0.866}}{\text{voltage drop desired}} = \text{cmils} \quad \text{(three-phase circuits)}$$

Distance   (used to calculate the maximum lentgh of a particular cable for a given line loss)

$$\frac{\text{voltage drop x cmils}}{\text{amperes x 21.6}} = \text{one-way distance in feet} \qquad \text{(single-phase circuits)}$$

$$\frac{\text{voltage drop x cmils}}{\text{amperes x 18.7}} = \text{one-way distance in feet} \qquad \text{(three-phase circuits)}$$

Resistance Of Copper Wire at 25° C

Size:	4/0	2/0	2AWG	4AWG	6AWG	8AWG	10AWG	12AWG
cmils*:	211,600	133,100	66,360	41,740	26,240	16,510	10,380	6,530

* Cross-sectional area of cable measured in circular mils.
Formulas courtesy Harry Box, *Set Lighting Technician's Handbook: Film Lighting Equipment, Practice, and Electrical Distribution.*

TERMINAL COLOR CODES

Color	Function
Copper or Brass	Hot wires (live)
Nickle, Tin or Zinc (whitish)	Neutral wires (grounded)
Green	Grounding wires

Source: NEC

WIRE COLOR CODES

Color	Function
White	Neutral wire (grounded)
Black	Hot wire
Red	Hot wire*
Blue	Hot wire
White coded black*	Hot wire
Green	Grounding wire
Bare copper	Grounding wire

*Red in 3-way household circuits is normally the "traveler" wire. White is always a neutral wire, with the exception of a switch loop where it must be identified as hot with a dab of black paint or wrapping at the end with black electrician's tape.

Source: NEC

SERIES AND PARALLEL CIRCUITS

Series Circuit

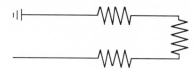

$R_{(total)} = R_1 + R_2 + R_3 +$ etc.

$E_{(total)} = E_1 + E_2 + E_3 +$ etc.

$I_{(total)} = I_1 = I_2 = I_3 =$ etc.

Parallel Circuit

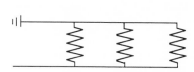

$$\frac{1}{R_{(total)}} = \frac{1}{R_1} + \frac{1}{R_2} + \frac{1}{R_3} + \text{ etc.}$$

$E_{(total)} = E_1 = E_2 = E_3 =$ etc.

$I_{(total)} = I_1 + I_2 + I_3 +$ etc.

R = Resistance (Ohms)
E = Electro Magnetic Force (Volts)
I = Intensity (Amps)

WIRE, CORD, AND CABLE TYPES

Wire	An individual strand (solid or stranded).

Wire

Cord*	Two or more stranded wires with flexible insulation intended for temporary use.
Cable*	Two or more wires combined in the same sheathing and intended for permanent installation.
T Wire	Wire wrapped in thermoplastic insulation for protection from below 32° to 150°.
TW Wire	T wire with water-resistant insulation. Should not be buried directly in ground.
THW Wire	TW wire with heavier heat-resistant insulation.
THHN Wire	Thermoplastic insulation with outer nylon (or equivalent) jacket; heat-resistant.
THWN Wire	Thermoplastic insulation with outer nylon (or equivalent) jacket; water-resistant.
SPT Cord	Fixture or "zip" cord, 2 or 3 wire stranded. Designated by gauge and number of wires. e.g. "18-3" is 18 gauge, 3 wire.

SPT or "Zip" Cord

S Cord	Two or more stranded conductors with a serving of cotton between the copper and the insulation. Jute or other "fillers" are twisted together with the conductors to make a round assembly. Outer jacket of high-quality rubber.
SJ Cord	Same as S Cord, with lighter jacket.
SV Cord	Same as SJ Cord, with even lighter jacket.
ST, SJT & SVT Cord	Same as S, SJ, and SV except with outer jacket of (thermo) plastic materials.
SO & SJO Cord	Same as S and SJ except with oil resistant jacket of neoprene or similar material.

SO Cord

SC Cord	NEC (National Electrical Code) designation for Entertainment Industry and Stage Lighting Cable; rated 600 volts Extra Hard Usage.
SCE Cord	Same as SC, with PVC jacket.
SCT Cord	Same as SC, with TPE based jacket.
W Cord	Rated 2000 volts Extra Hard Usage; replaced welding cable as an acceptatble stage cable until type SC was developed.

* In common stage use "Cord" refers to "Zip Cord" and "Cable" refers to SO Cord.

WIRE, CORD, AND CABLE TYPES (continued)

NM Cable	Non-metallic cable with paper wrapping between conductors and plastic sheathing. Known by the trade name *Romex*.

NM Cable

NMC Cable	Non-metallic cable with solid plastic sheathing. Also known by the trade name *Romex*.

NMC Cable

UF Cable	Underground feeder. A water-proof version of NMC, rated for burial in the ground.
Armored Cable	Has a flexible steel or aluminum spiral armor (known by the trade name *BX*).

Armored Cable or "BX"

Source: NEC

RECOMMENDED EXTENSION CORD WIRE GAUGES

Excessive voltage drop occurs in extension cords which do not have large enough conductors to carry the load. The following table gives adequate wire gauges for extension cords of given lengths under certain rated loads. The recommendations ensure that the line voltage drop does not exceed 5 volts under a load of 150% of the rated amps.

Length	2	3	4	5	6	8	10	12	14	16	18	20
				Rated Load (in amps)								
25'	18	18	18	18	18	18	18	16	16	16	14	14
50'	18	18	18	18	16	16	14	14	12	12	12	12
100'	18	16	16	14	14	12	12	10	10	10	8	8
150'	16	14	14	12	12	10	10	8	8	8	6	6
200'	16	14	12	12	10	10	8	8	6	6	6	6
250'	14	12	12	10	10	8	8	6	6	6	4	4
300'	14	12	10	10	8	6	6	6	6	4	4	4
400'	12	10	10	8	8	6	6	4	4	4	2	2
500'	12	10	8	8	6	6	4	4	2	2	2	2

UNDERWRITERS KNOT

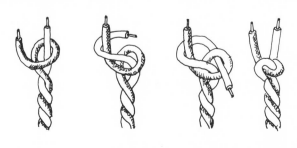

INTERNATIONAL POWER REQUIREMENTS

Country	City	Frequency (Hz)	Voltage (V)
Australia	Melbourne	50	240
	Sydney	50	240
Austria	Vienna	50	220
Belgium	Brussels	50	220
Canada	Montreal	60	120
	Toronto	60	120
	Vancouver	50	220
Denmark	Copenhagen	50	220
Egypt	Cairo	50	220
Finland	Helsinki	50	220
France	Nice	50	220/127
	Paris	50	220/127
Germany	Former E. Berlin	50	220/127
	Former W. Berlin	50	220
	Hamburg	50	220
	Munich	50	220
Great Britain	London	50	240
Greece	Athens	50	220
Hong Kong	Victoria	50	200
India	Bombay	50	230
Ireland (Rep.)	Dublin	50	220
Israel	Tel Aviv	50	220
Italy	Rome	50	220/127
Japan	Tokyo	50/60	100
Malaysia	Kuala Lumpur	50	240
Mexico	Mexico City	60	220/120
Netherlands	Amsterdam	50	220
Norway	Oslo	50	220
Pakistan	Karachi	50	230
Philippines	Manila	60	110
Portugal	Lisbon	50	220
Russia	Moscow	50	127
Singapore	Singapore	50	230
South Africa	Johannesburg	50	220
Spain	Madrid	50	220/127
Sweden	Stockholm	50	220
Switzerland	Geneva	50	220
	Zurich	50	220
United States	(all)	60	120
Yugoslavia	Belgrade	50	220

Table courtesy Harry Box, *Set Lighting Technician's Handbook: Film Lighting Equipment, Practice, and Electrical Distribution.*

LIGHTING TERMS

Physical Quantity	Name	Symbol	Definition
Luminous Intensity	candela	cd	The luminous intensity, in the perpendicular direction, of a surface of 1/600,000 square meter of a black body at the temperature of freezing platinum under a pressure of 101.325 newtons per square meter.
Luminous Flux*	lumen	lm	The flux emitted within a unit solid angle of one steradian by a point source having a uniform intensity of one candela.
Illumination	lux	lx	An illumination of one lumen per square meter.
	Transparent		Capable of transmitting light so that objects or images can be seen as if there were no intervening material.
	Translucent		Transmitting light but causing sufficient diffusion to eliminate perception of distinct images.
	Opaque		Impenetrable by light.

* Flux or Luminous Flux is the out-put of light from a source (such as a candle or light bulb). This flux is measured in lumens (lm), or most commonly lumens per square foot (lm/ft^2). One lumen per square foot equals 1 foot candle (fc). Light bulbs are commonly rated in watts but this can be deceiving, because the relationship between watts and lumens varies depending on the efficiency of the light source.

Source: MH

LAW OF SQUARES

Light intensity decreases in inverse proportion to the square of the distance.

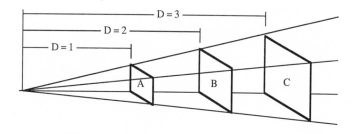

Source = 1 candela

A = 1 square foot   Illumination = 1 footcandle
B = 4 square feet   Illumination = $^1/_4$ footcandle
C = 9 square feet   Illumination = $^1/_9$ footcandle

ELECTROMAGNETIC AND COLOR SPECTRUM

.00001 nm	.001 nm	.1 nm	10 nm		.0001 ft	.01 ft	1 ft	100 ft	1-3100 mi
Cosmic Rays	Gamma Rays	X-Rays	Ultra-Violet		Infra-Red	Micro Waves	TV	Radio	Electric Power

Visible Spectrum

Violet	Blue	Green	Yellow	Orange	Red

450 nm*	500 nm	550 nm	600 nm	650 nm

* Nanometer

COLOR WHEELS

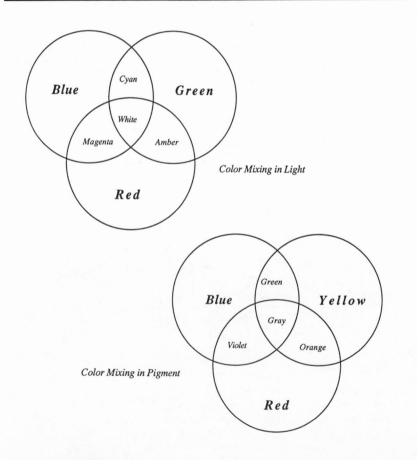

Color Mixing in Light

Color Mixing in Pigment

COLOR TEMPERATURES

Source	Color Temp. (K)	MIREDs
Match or candle flame	1900	526
Sunlight, dawn or dusk	2000-2500	500-400
Household bulb	2800-2900	357-345
Tungsten halogen bulb	3200	312
Photoflood bulb	3400	294
Sunlight, one hour after sunrise	3500	286
Sunlight, late afternoon	4500	233
Blue glass photoflood bulb	4800	208
3200 lamp with dichroic filter	4800-5000	208-200
FAY lamp	5000	200
Sunlight, summer	5500-5700	182
White-flame carbon arc light with Y-1 filter	5700	175
HMI light	5600 or 6000	179 or 167
Sunlight with blue or white sky	6500	154
Summer, shade	7000	141
Overcast sky	7000	141
Color television	9300	108
Skylight	10,000-20,000	100-50

Table courtesy Harry Box, *Set Lighting Technician's Handbook: Film Lighting Equipment, Practice, and Electrical Distribution.*

KELVIN / MIRED CONVERSION

Color Temp. (K)	MIRED Value									
	+0	100	200	300	400	500	600	700	800	900
2000	500	476	455	534	417	400	385	370	357	345
3000	333	323	312	303	294	286	278	270	263	256
4000	250	244	238	233	227	222	217	213	208	204
5000	200	196	192	189	185	182	179	175	172	169
6000	167	164	161	159	156	154	152	149	147	145

The MIRED (microreciprocal degrees) scale is used to quantify the effect of color correction gels. The MIRED value of a light source is equal to 1,000,000 divided by the Kelvin color temperature. To use the above table to find the MIRED value of 5600K, for example, read across on the 5000 row and down the 600 column.

Table courtesy Harry Box, *Set Lighting Technician's Handbook: Film Lighting Equipment, Practice, and Electrical Distribution.*

COLOR CORRECTION GEL

Type	Rosco Cinegel No.	Lee No.	GAM No.	Color Temp. Shift (Degrees K)	Exposure Change (Stops)
Daylight (Correct To Orange)					
Extra CTO	n/a*	n/a	1540	20,000 to 3200 5500 to 2200	1
CTO	3407	204	1543	6500 to 3200 5500 to 2900	$2/3$
Sun 85	3401	204	n/a	5500 to 3200	$2/3$
$3/4$ CTO	3411	285	1546	5500 to 3200	$2/3$
$1/2$ CTO	3408	205	1549	5500 to 3800	$1/2$
$1/4$ CTO	3409	206	1552	5500 to 4500	$1/3$
$1/8$ CTO	3410	223	1555	5500 to 4900	$1/4$
Neutral-Density and Neutral-Density/Daylight					
.15 ND	3415	298	1514	0	$1/2$
.3 ND	3402	209	1515	0	1
.6 ND	3403	210	1516	0	2
.9 ND	3404	211	1517	0	3
1.2 ND	n/a	299	1518	0	4
CTO .3 ND	3405	207	1556	5500 to 3200	1
CTO .6 ND	3406	208	1557	5500 to 3200	2
CTO .9 ND	n/a	n/a	1558	5500 to 3200	3
Tungsten (Correct To Blue)					
Extra CTB	n/a	n/a	1520	3200 to 6000	$1 3/4$
Full CTB	3202	201	1523	3200 to 5500	$1 1/2$
$3/4$ CTB	n/a	281	1526	3200 to 5000	$1 1/4$
$1/2$ CTB	3204	202	1529	3200 to 4100	1
$1/3$ CTB	3206	n/a	n/a	3200 to 3800	$2/3$
$1/4$ CTB	3208	203	1532	3200 to 3500	$1/2$
$1/8$ CTB	3216	218	1535	3200 to 3300	$1/3$

* Not applicable.

Table courtesy Harry Box, *Set Lighting Technician's Handbook: Film Lighting Equipment, Practice, and Electrical Distribution.*

Editor's note: The information in this table is based on data published by each manufacturer. However, the color temperature shift values and the exposure change figures (ƒ-stops) are generalizations made by Mr. Box and do not represent manufacturer's specifications.

DIFFUSION MATERIALS

Types of Diffusion	Product No.	Exposure Change (Stops)	Notes
Lee			
Full Tough Spun	214	2^1/$_2$	Slight softening of field and beam edge.
Half Tough Spun	215	1^1/$_2$	Slight softening of field and beam edge.
Quarter Tough Spun	229	^{3}/$_4$	Slight softening of field and beam edge.
Full Tough Spun-FR	261	2	Flame retardant. Slight softening of field and beam edge.
^{3}/$_4$ Tough Spun-FR	262	1^2/$_3$	Flame retardant.
^{1}/$_2$ Tough Spun-FR	263	1^1/$_3$	Flame retardant.
^{3}/$_8$ Tough Spun-FR	264	1	Flame retardant.
^{1}/$_4$ Tough Spun-FR	265	^{3}/$_4$	Flame retardant.
216 White Diffusion	216	1^1/$_2$	Moderate/heavy diffusion; available in 60" width.
^{1}/$_2$ 216	250	^{3}/$_4$	Moderate beam spread and softening.
^{1}/$_4$ 216	251	^{1}/$_3$	Moderate beam spread and softening.
^{1}/$_8$ 216	252	^{1}/$_8$	Moderate beam spread and softening.
Blue Diffusion	217	1^1/$_2$	Increases color temperature very slightly.
Daylight Blue Frost	224	2^1/$_4$	CTB frost.
Neutral Density Frost	225	2	ND.6 frost.
Brushed Silk	228	^{3}/$_4$	Diffuses light in one direction only.
Hampshire Frost	253	^{1}/$_4$	Very light frost.
Heavy Frost	129	1^1/$_3$	Flame retardant.
White Frost	220	1^1/$_3$	Flame retardant.
Blue Frost	221	1^1/$_3$	Flame retardant. Increases color temp. very slightly.
Rosco			
Tough Spun	3006	2^1/$_2$	Slight softening of field and beam edge.
Light Tough Spun	3007	1^2/$_3$	Slight softening of field and beam edge.
^{1}/$_4$ Tough Spun	3022	1	Slight softening of field and beam edge.
Tough Frost	3008	2	Slight to moderate softening, moderate beam spread, but with discernible beam center.
Light Tough Frost	3009	1^1/$_2$	Slight to moderate softening, moderate beam spread, but with discernible beam center.
Opal Tough Frost	3010	1	Slight to moderate softening, moderate beam spread, but with discernible beam center.
Light Opal	3020	^{1}/$_2$	Slight to moderate softening, moderate beam spread, but with discernible beam center.
Tough White Diffusion	3026	3^1/$_2$	Dense diffusion with wide beam spread creating even field of shadowless light.
^{1}/$_2$ White Diffusion	3027	2^1/$_2$	Moderately dense diffusion with wide beam spread.

DIFFUSION MATERIALS (continued)

1/4 White Diffusion	3028	1½	Moderate diffusion with wide beam spread.
Tough Rolux	3000	2½	Moderately dense diffusion with wide beam spread.
Light Tough Rolux	3001	*	Moderate diffusion with wide beam spread.
Grid Cloth	3030	5	Comes in 54" width rolls. Very dense diffusion with very wide beam spread which creates soft shadowlesslight. Ideal for large area diffusion. Not tolerant of high heat.
Light Grid Cloth	3032	3½	Smaller weave than grid cloth. Considerable softening. Comes in 54" width rolls.
1/4 Grid Cloth	3034	2½	Considerable softening. Comes in 54" width rolls.
Silent Frost	3029	3	Diffusion made of a rubbery plastic that does not crinkle and rattle in the wind.
Hilite	3014	1	Quiet like Silent Frost. Comes in 54" rolls.
Soft Frost	3002	2	Quiet like Silent Frost. Denser than Hilite.
Wide Soft Frost	3023	2	72" width.
1/2 Soft Frost	3004	½	Quiet, light diffuser.
Tough Silk	3011	1½	Considerable softening in one direction only.
Light Tough Silk	3015	1	Considerable softening in one direction only.
Tough Booster Silk	3012	*	Raises color temperature from 3200K to 3500K with silk softening characteristics.
Tough Booster Frost	3013	*	Raises color temperature from 3200K to 3800K with frost softening characteristics.
Full Blue Frost	3017	*	Raises color temperature from 3200K to daylight (5600K) with frost softening characteristics.

GAM–Great American Market

Medium GAM Frost	10	*	Soft light, warm center, diffuse edge.
Light GAM Frost	15	*	Soft light, warm center, diffuse edge.
Full GAM Spun	32	2½	Textural, warm center, defined edge.
Medium GAM Spun	35	1⅔	Textural, warm center, defined edge.
Light GAM Spun	38	1	Textural, warm center, defined edge.
Gamvel	45	3	Soft light with diffuse shadow line.
216 GAM White	55	*	Shadowless, white light. Heavy diffusion with no center or edge visible.
Medium GAM Silk	65	*	Spreads light predominantly in one direction.
Light GAM Silk	68	*	Spreads light predominantly in one direction.

* Information on f-stop change not published by manufacturer.

Table courtesy Harry Box, *Set Lighting Technician's Handbook: Film Lighting Equipment, Practice, and Electrical Distribution.*

Editor's note: The information in this table is based on data published by each manufacturer. However, in some cases, the exposure change figures (f-stops) are generalizations made by Mr. Box and do not represent manufacturer's specifications.

BEAM AND FIELD AREAS

Lighting instruments with reflectors give off a cone-shaped beam of light which is most intense at the center. The **beam area** is the center portion of the cone where the intensity is at least 50% of maximum. The **field area** is roughly the "whole beam of light" or more precisely that portion of the cone where the intensity is greater than 10% of maximum.

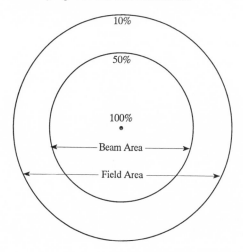

TYPICAL FIELD ANGLES

The field angle is derived from the field area. The following table gives averages of some standard equipment. Beam angles are not included since they vary enormously depending on instrument brand, lamp alignment and lamp type. Roughly, however the beam area is $2/3$ of the field area.

Ellipsoidal Reflector Spotlight (ERS)	Field Angle	Field Diameter* (per 1' of throw)
$4^1/_2$ x $6^1/_2$	50°	.9326 ft.
6 x 9	37°	.6692 ft.
6 x 12	27°	.4802 ft.
6 x 16	17°	.2989 ft.
6 x 22	10°	.1750 ft.
8 x 8	20°	.3527 ft.
8 x 11	16°	.2811 ft.
8 x 14	10°	.1750 ft.
6" and 8" Fresnels		
spot focus:	20°	.3527 ft.
flood focus:	50°	.9326 ft.

* When the field angle and throw distence are known, the field diameter can be calculated using the following foumula: diameter = 2 x (distance x tangent of half of the field angle).

Fresnel

Available Sizes*:

3¹/₂"	(75w, 150w)
6"	(500w, 750w, 1000w)
8"	(1000w, 1500w, 2000w)
10"	(1000w, 5000w)
12"	(5000w - 10,000w)

* Lens diameter (typical wattage)

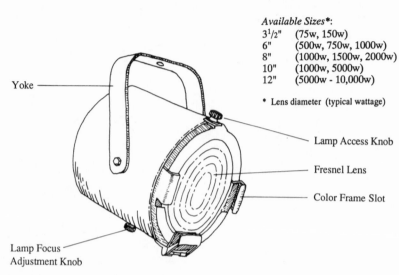

Yoke

Lamp Access Knob

Fresnel Lens

Color Frame Slot

Lamp Focus
Adjustment Knob

Elipsoidal Reflector Spotlight (ERS)

("Leko")

Available Sizes*:

3" x 10"	(250w, 400w, 500w)
3" x 12"	(250w, 400w, 500w)
4¹/₂" x 6¹/₂"	(500w, 750w)
6" x 9"	(750w, 1000w)
6" x 12"	(750w, 1000w)
6" x 16"	(750w, 1000w)
6" x 22"	(750w, 1000w)
8" x 8"	(1000w)
8" x 10"	(1000w)
8" x 16"	(1000w)

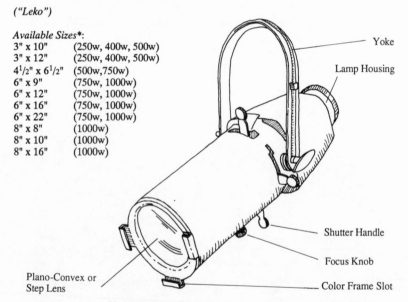

Yoke

Lamp Housing

Shutter Handle

Focus Knob

Color Frame Slot

Plano-Convex or
Step Lens

* Lens diameter x focal length of lens (typical wattage)

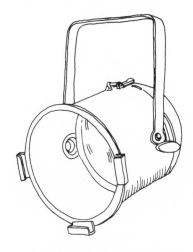

Beam Projector

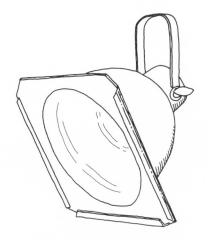

Scoop

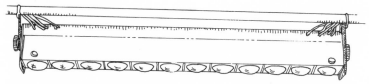

Strip Light, Border Light or X-Ray

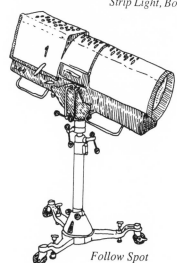

Follow Spot

PAR Head or PAR Can

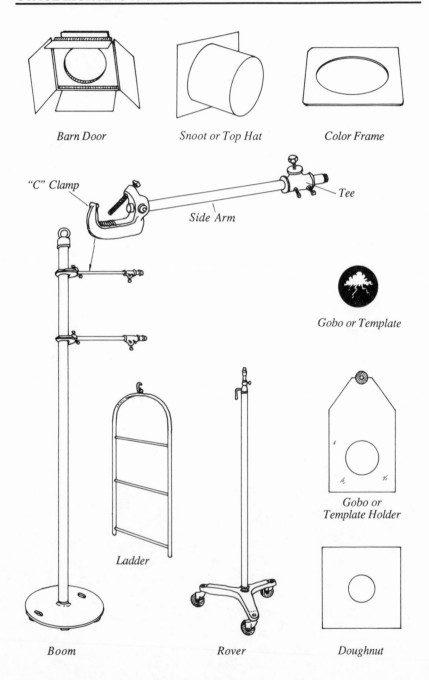

Barn Door

Snoot or Top Hat

Color Frame

"C" Clamp

Tee

Side Arm

Gobo or Template

Gobo or
Template Holder

Ladder

Boom

Rover

Doughnut

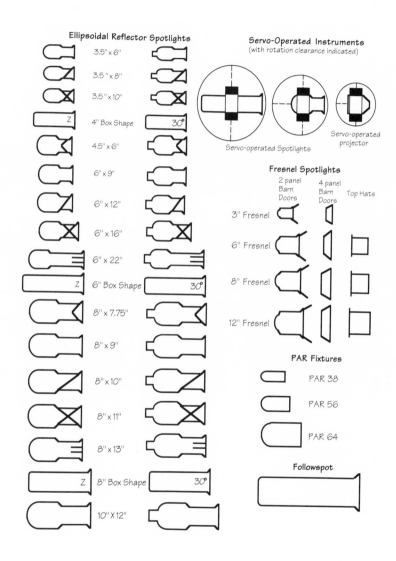

Ellipsoidal Reflector Spotlights

- 3.5" x 6"
- 3.5" x 8"
- 3.5" x 10"
- 4" Box Shape
- 4.5" x 6"
- 6" x 9"
- 6" x 12"
- 6" x 16"
- 6" x 22"
- 6" Box Shape
- 8" x 7.75"
- 8" x 9"
- 8" x 10"
- 8" x 11"
- 8" x 13"
- 8" Box Shape
- 10" X 12"

Servo-Operated Instruments
(with rotation clearance indicated)

Servo-operated Spotlights

Servo-operated projector

Fresnel Spotlights

2 panel Barn Doors   4 panel Barn Doors   Top Hats

- 3" Fresnel
- 6" Fresnel
- 8" Fresnel
- 12" Fresnel

PAR Fixtures

- PAR 38
- PAR 56
- PAR 64

Followspot

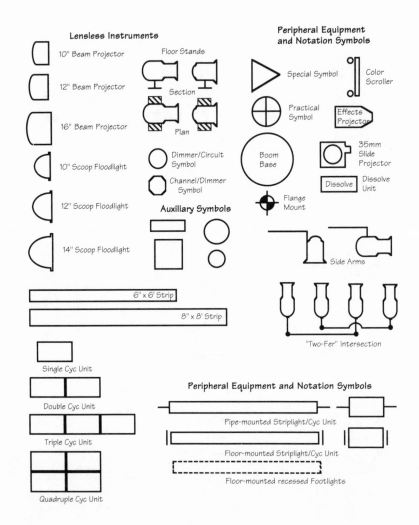

Lensless Instruments

10" Beam Projector

12" Beam Projector

16" Beam Projector

10" Scoop Floodlight

12" Scoop Floodlight

14" Scoop Floodlight

Floor Stands

Section

Plan

Dimmer/Circuit Symbol

Channel/Dimmer Symbol

Auxiliary Symbols

6" x 6' Strip

8" x 8' Strip

Single Cyc Unit

Double Cyc Unit

Triple Cyc Unit

Quadruple Cyc Unit

Peripheral Equipment and Notation Symbols

Special Symbol

Practical Symbol

Boom Base

Flange Mount

Color Scroller

Effects Projector

35mm Slide Projector

Dissolve

Dissolve Unit

Side Arms

"Two-Fer" Intersection

Peripheral Equipment and Notation Symbols

Pipe-mounted Striplight/Cyc Unit

Floor-mounted Striplight/Cyc Unit

Floor-mounted recessed Footlights

Instrument Notation

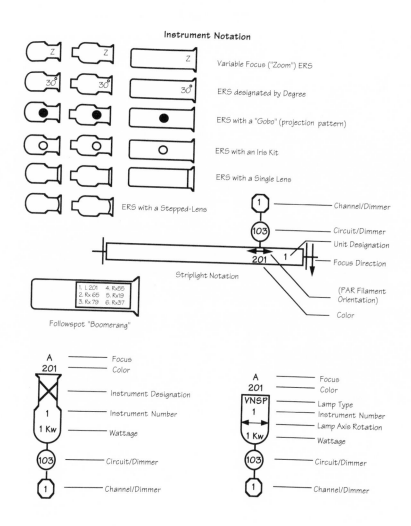

Variable Focus ("Zoom") ERS

ERS designated by Degree

ERS with a "Gobo" (projection pattern)

ERS with an Iris Kit

ERS with a Single Lens

ERS with a Stepped-Lens

Channel/Dimmer

Circuit/Dimmer

Unit Designation

Focus Direction

(PAR Filament Orientation)

Color

Striplight Notation

Followspot "Boomerang"

1. L 201   4. Rx55
2. Rx 65   5. Rx19
3. Rx 79   6. Rx37

Focus
Color
Instrument Designation
Instrument Number
Wattage
Circuit/Dimmer
Channel/Dimmer

Focus
Color
Lamp Type
Instrument Number
Lamp Axis Rotation
Wattage
Circuit/Dimmer
Channel/Dimmer

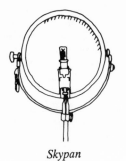

Skypan

Non-Focusable Open-Face Fixtures

Name	Available Sizes
Skypan	2K, 5K
Conelight	1K, 2K
Barebulb	1K, 2K
Broadlight	1K, 2K, 2K double (2 x 1K)
Nook Light	650W, 1950W (3 x 650W), 1K, 2K
Space Light	6 1K Nook Lights in silk cylinder

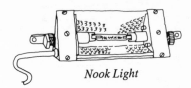

Nook Light

1K Mickey

Focusable Open-Face Fixtures

Name	Available Sizes
Mighty or Blonde	2K
Mickey or Redhead	1K
Teenie	650W
Teenie Weenie	600W

1K Redhead

Soft Light

Soft Lights

Name	Available Sizes
Studio Soft Lights	8K, 4K, 2K, 750W
Zip Lights	4K, 2K, 1K
Pepper	400W
Coop Light	(a.k.a. Chicken Coop or Bay Light)

Egg Crate

Coop Light

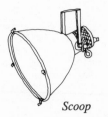

Scoop

Sun Gun
(Portable battery powered;
HMI or tunsgten)

HMI Gas Arc Fresnel*

Available Sizes

24K, 220 volt
18K, 220 volt
12K, 220 volt
8K, 220 volt
6K, 220 or 110 volt
4K, 220 or 110 volt
2.5K, 220 or 110 volt
1.2K, 110 volt
575w, 110 volt
200w, 110 volt

HMI PAR Lights

Available Sizes

6K
4K
2.5K
1.2K
575w
200w

* HMI is an acronym for "Hydrargyrum Medium
Arc Length Iodide." (Hydrargyrum is the
chemical name for mercury (Hg).)
HMI's are available with electronic "flicker-free"
ballasts for off-speed filming.

PAR

PAR Lamp Types

Name

VNSP (Very Narrow Spot)
NSP (Narrow Spot)
MFL (Medium Flood)
WFL (Wide Flood)

Xenon

Available Sizes

7K
4K
2K, 110 or 220v
1K, 110 or 220v

PARs   *Fay Light*

Name	Available Sizes
Dino Light	24 x PAR 64s
Maxi Brute	6 x PAR 64s or - 9 x PAR 64s
Fay Lights	single or multiple PAR 36, 650W lamps with dichroic daylight filters

Tungsten Fresnels

Nickname	Available Sizes
20K	20K, 220 volt
Tenner, Studio 10K	10K
Big Eye Tenner	10K with 24" lens
Baby 10K*	10K
Senior	5K
Baby 5K*	5K
Deuce, Junior	2K
Baby Deuce*, Baby Junior, BJ	2K
Baby, Ace, Pup, 407	1K or 750W
Baby Baby*	1K
Teenie Weenie	650W
Tweenie	600W or 500W
Inkie, Midget	200W
Pepper	100W

*"Baby" indicates a smaller, lighter weight unit.

Focal Spot

Carbon Arc Fresnels

Name	Available Sizes
Titan	350A
Litewate Brute	225A
Heavyhead or English Brute	225A
Baby Brute	225A

Arc Fresnel

Far Cyc Fixture

Fluorescents*

* Color corrected lamps are generally used, either 5000K or 3200K. Kino Flo, Inc. makes a line of fluorescent fixtures with high output, flicker-free ballasts; 9", 15", 24", 48" lamps in various configurations.

"Kino Flo"

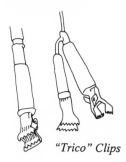

"Trico" Clips

Bus Bar Lug

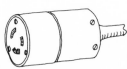

"Anderson" Clamp & Wrench

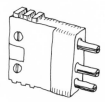

*Bates, Stage Pin or
Union Connector*

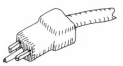

Twist-lock

"Cam-lok®" Connectors

Edison Connector

*Two-fer Pin Plug Adapter or
Paralleling "T", (female-female-male)*

*Three-fer Pin Plug Adapter
(female-female-female-male)*

Pin Plug, "Mole Pin" or "Slip Pin"

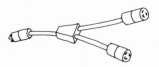

*Two-fer Adapter or
Y Splice (twist-lock)*

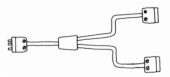

*Two-fer Adapter or
Y Splice (pin connectors)*

Stage Plug

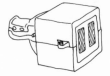

*Two Hole Plugging Box
or Stage Box*

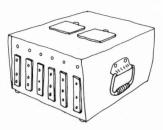

Temporary Distribution Box

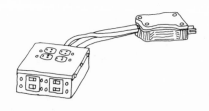

Receptacle Box to Pin Plug

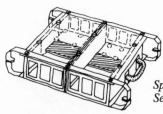

*Spider Box (cable splicing block)
See-thru, 2 bar, 12 lug*

SPIDER BOX CAPACITIES

Input Feeder Cables per Bar	Continuous Use per cable	per bar	Intermittent Use per cable	per bar	(minutes on/off)
2	300 amps	600 amps	325 amps	650 amps	(20/6)
3	280 amps	840 amps	325 amps	975 amps	(20/10)
4	270 amps	1080 amps	325 amps	1300 amps	(20/14)

Mole-Richardson specifications using 4/0 AWG Copper Feeder Cables

STAGE PLUG

(Amperages vary)
2 Pole 2 Wire
Stage Use: generally have been
replaced by Pin Connectors
(No NEMA* code)

* National Electrical Manufacturers Association.

STAGE OR "PIN" TYPE RECEPTACLES

H   G   N

20 Amp 125 Volt
Grounding
2 Pole 3 Wire
Standard for stage use.
(No NEMA code)

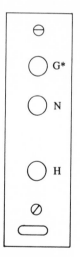

30 Amp 250 Volt
Grounding
2 Pole 3 Wire
(No NEMA code)

60 Amp 250 Volt
Grounding
2 Pole 3 Wire
(No NEMA code)

100 Amp 250 Volt
Grounding
2 Pole 3 Wire
(No NEMA code)

* Note that ground and neutral positions are reversed.

Source: UC

NON-GROUNDING RECEPTACLES

Non-grounded plugs and receptacles like those shown here should only be used in replacement situations where a ground wire is not available.

15 Amp 125 Volt
2 Pole 2 Wire
1-15 R (receptacle); 1-15 P (plug)

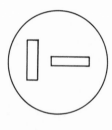

20 Amp 250 Volt
2 Pole 2 Wire
2-20 R (receptacle); 2-20 P (plug)

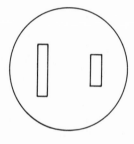

30 Amp 250 Volt
2 Pole 2 Wire
2-30 R (receptacle); 2-30 P (plug)

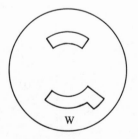

15 Amp 125 Volt
2 Pole 2 Wire
L1-15 R (receptacle); L1-15 P (plug)

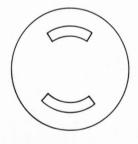

20 Amp 250 Volt
2 Pole 2 Wire
L2-20 R (receptacle); L2-20 P (plug)

Source: H

GROUNDING RECEPTACLES

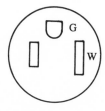

15 Amp 125 Volt Grounding
2 Pole 3 Wire
Standard for residential / commercial.
5-15 R (receptacle); 5-15 P (plug)

20 Amp 125 Volt Grounding
2 Pole 3 Wire
Room air-conditioners, heavy-duty tools.
5-20 R (receptacle); 5-20 P (plug)

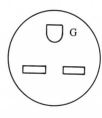

15 Amp 250 Volt Grounding
2 Pole 3 Wire
Room air-conditioners, heavy-duty tools.
6-15 R (receptacle); 6-15 P (plug)

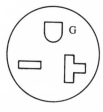

20 Amp 250 Volt Grounding
2 Pole 3 Wire
Room air-conditioners, heavy-duty tools.
6-20 R (receptacle); 6-20 P (plug)

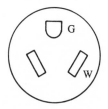

15 Amp 277 Volt Grounding
2 Pole 3 Wire
7-15 R (receptacle); 7-15 P (plug)

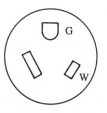

20 Amp 277 Volt Grounding
2 Pole 3 Wire
7-20 R (receptacle); 7-20 P (plug)

LOCKING TYPE (TWISTLOCK) RECEPTACLES

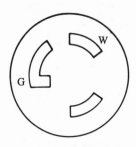

15 Amp 125 Volt Grounding
2 Pole 3 Wire
Common in older stages.
L5-15 R (receptacle); L5-15 P (plug)

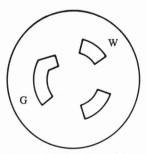

20 Amp 125 Volt Grounding
2 Pole 3 Wire
Standard for stage use.
L5-20 R (receptacle); L5-20 P (plug)

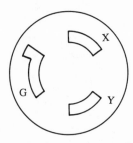

15 Amp 250 Volt Grounding
2 Pole 3 Wire
For special stage applications.
L6-15 R (receptacle); L6-15 P (plug)

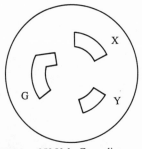

20 Amp 250 Volt Grounding
2 Pole 3 Wire
For high voltage stage use:
heaters, fog barrels, etc.
L6-20 R (receptacle); L6-20 P (plug)

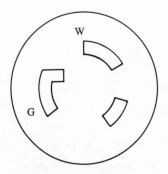

30 Amp 125 Volt Grounding
2 Pole 3 Wire
Not standard for stage use.
L5-30 R (receptacle); L5-30 P (plug)

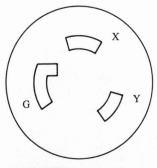

30 Amp 250 Volt Grounding
2 Pole 3 Wire
Not standard for stage use.
L6-30 R (receptacle); L6-30 P (plug)

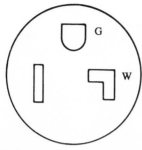

30 Amp 125 Volt Grounding
2 Pole 3 Wire
5-30 R (receptacle); 5-30 P (plug)

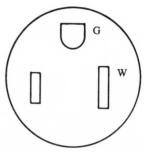

50 Amp 125 Volt Grounding
2 Pole 3 Wire
5-50 R (receptacle); 5-50 P (plug)

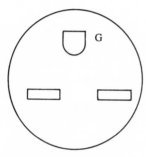

30 Amp 250 Volt Grounding
2 Pole 3 Wire
6-30 R (receptacle); 6-30 P (plug)

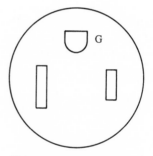

50 Amp 250 Volt Grounding
2 Pole 3 Wire
6-50 R (receptacle); 6-50 P (plug)

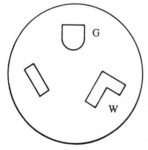

30 Amp 277 Volt Grounding
2 Pole 3 Wire
7-30 R (receptacle); 7-30 P (plug)

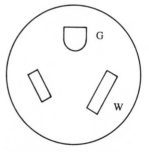

50 Amp 277 Volt Grounding
2 Pole 3 Wire
7-50 R (receptacle); 7-50 P (plug)

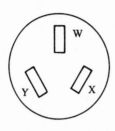

20 Amp 125/250 Volt
3 Pole 3 Wire
10-20 R (receptacle); 10-20 P (plug)

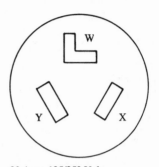

30 Amp 125/250 Volt
3 Pole 3 Wire
10-30 R (receptacle); 10-30 P (plug)

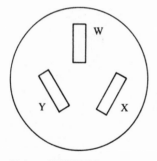

50 Amp 125/250 Volt
3 Pole 3 Wire
10-50 R (receptacle); 10-50 P (plug)

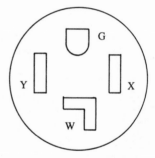

30 Amp 125/250 Volt Grounding
3 Pole 4 Wire
14-30 R (receptacle); 14-30 P (plug)

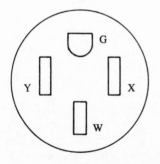

50 Amp 125/250 Volt Grounding
3 Pole 4 Wire
14-50 R (receptacle); 14-50 P (plug)

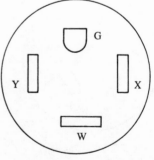

60 Amp 125/250 Volt Grounding
3 Pole 4 Wire
14-60 R (receptacle); 14-60 P (plug)

MIDGET LOCKING TYPE (TWISTLOCK) RECEPTACLES

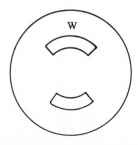

15 Amp 125 Volt
A.C. or D.C.
Often used for speaker connections.
ML-1R (receptacle); ML-1P (plug)

15 Amp 125 Volt Grounding
A.C. or D.C.
Often used for speaker connections.
ML-2R (receptacle); ML-2P (plug)

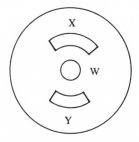

15 Amp 125/250 Volt A.C.
Misc. stage uses.
ML-3R (receptacle); ML-3P (plug)

OBSOLETE LOCKING TYPE (TWISTLOCK) RECEPTACLES

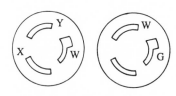

20 Amp 125/250 Volt A.C. or D.C.
or
20 Amp 250 Volt A.C. or D.C.
or
10 Amp 600 Volt A.C.

This type of locking receptacle was in use before NEMA standards were adopted.

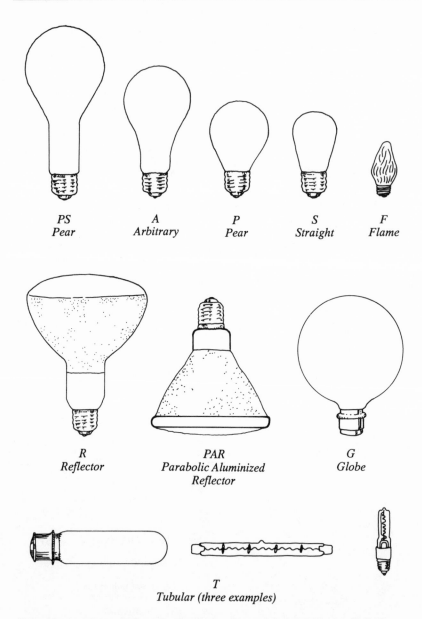

PS
Pear

A
Arbitrary

P
Pear

S
Straight

F
Flame

R
Reflector

PAR
Parabolic Aluminized
Reflector

G
Globe

T
Tubular (three examples)

The mechanical size and shape of an incandescent lamp are designated by standardized abbreviations such as A-19, PS-35, F-15. The letter designates the shape in accordance with the outlines shown. The numeral designates the diameter in eighths of an inch. Thus a T-12 lamp has the T shape and is $^{12}/_8$ ($1^1/_2$) inches in diameter.

Source: LH

EFFECT OF VOLTAGE ON LAMPS

Actual Voltage*	Average Life	Total Output	Actual Watts
85%	825%	58%	78%
90%	400%	70%	85%
95%	200%	84%	93%
100%	100%	100%	100%
105%	54%	119%	108%
110%	29%	138%	116%
115%	16%	160%	124%

* As percentage of the rated voltage of lamp. For instance, if the rated voltage of a lamp is 115v and the measured circuit voltage is 103v the actual voltage would be 90%.

SCREW BASES (actual size)

0.465"

Candelabra

0.651"

Intermediate

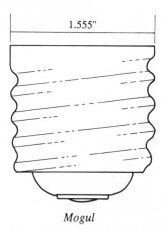

1.555"

Mogul

1.037"

Medium

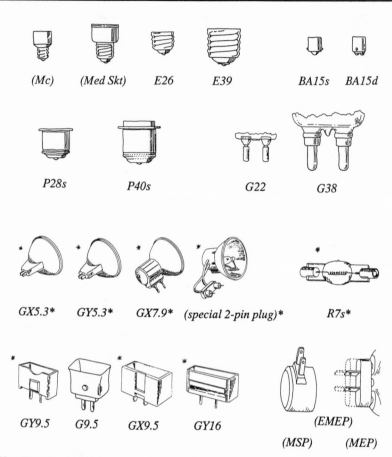

(Mc)   (Med Skt)   E26   E39   BA15s   BA15d

P28s   P40s   G22   G38

GX5.3*   GY5.3*   GX7.9*   (special 2-pin plug)*   R7s*

GY9.5   G9.5   GX9.5   GY16   (EMEP)   (MSP)   (MEP)

Note: illustrations not to scale.

(Mc)	Mini-Can Screw (Mc)	GX5.3	2-pin (MR-16 lamp)
(Med Skt)	Medium skirted	GY5.3	Oval 2-pin (MR-16 120 V. lamp)
E26	Medium screw (Med)	GX7.9	(MARC 300 lamp)
E39	Mogul screw (Mog)	——	special 2-pin plug (MARC 350 lamp)
BA15s	Single contact bayonet candelabra (SC Bay)	R7s	Recessed Single-Contact (RSC)
		GY9.5	(no common name)
BA15d	Double contact bayonet candelabra (DC Bay)	G9.5	Medium 2-pin (Med 2P)
		GX9.5	(no common name)
P28s	Medium prefocus (Med Pf)	GY16	(no common name)
P40s	Mogul prefocus (Mog Pf)	(MSP)	Medium side prong (MSP)
G22	Medium bipost (Med Bp)	(EMEP)	Extended mogul end prong (EMEP)
G38	Mogul bipost (Mog Bp)	(MEP)	Mogul end prong (MEP)

* Illustrations by Robert Mumm.

PROJECTION DISTANCES FOR SLIDE PROJECTORS

Nominal Aperature Dimensions of 2 x 2 inch Slide Mounts *(shown approx. half size)*	Screen-Image Width	1.4	2	3	4	5	7	9	11	4 to 6 Zoom
		Projection Distances (in feet)								

Lens Focal Length (in inches)

22.9 mm — 34.2 mm
135-35 mm

		1.4	2	3	4	5	7	9	11	4 to 6 Zoom
	20 in.	2	2½	4	5	7	9	12	15	5 to 8
	30 in.	3	4	6	8	10	14	18	22	8 to 12
	40 in.	4	5	8	10	13	18	23	29	10 to 16
	50 in.	4½	6	10	13	16	23	29	35	13 to 19
	5 ft.	6	8	11	15	19	27	34	42	15 to 23
	6 ft.	7	9	14	18	23	32	41	50	18 to 27
	8 ft.	9	12	18	24	30	42	54	66	24 to 36
	10 ft.	11	15	23	30	38	53	68	83	30 to 45
	12 ft.	13	18	27	36	45	63	81	99	36 to 54

26.5 mm — 26.5 mm
126

	20 in.	2½	3	5	7	8	12	15	18	7 to 10
	30 in.	3½	5	7	10	12	17	22	27	10 to 15
	40 in.	5	6	10	13	16	23	30	36	13 to 20
	50 in.	6	8	12	16	20	29	37	45	16 to 25
	5 ft.	8	10	15	20	24	34	44	54	20 to 30
	6 ft.	9	12	18	23	29	41	52	64	23 to 35
	8 ft.	12	16	23	31	39	54	70	85	31 to 46
	10 ft.	14	19	29	39	48	68	87	106	39 to 58
	12 ft.	16	23	35	46	58	81	104	128	46 to 69

38 mm — 26.2 mm — 38 mm
127 Super-Slide (38x38 mm)
828 (26.2 x 38 mm)

	20 in.	1½	2	3½	5	6	8	11	13	5 to 7
	30 in.	2½	3	5	7	9	12	16	19	7 to 11
	40 in.	3½	4½	7	9	12	16	21	26	9 to 14
	50 in.	4	6	8	12	14	20	26	32	12 to 17
	5 ft.	5	7	10	14	17	24	31	38	14 to 21
	6 ft.	6	8	12	16	20	29	37	45	16 to 25
	8 ft.	8	11	16	22	27	38	49	60	22 to 33
	10 ft.	10	13	20	27	34	48	61	74	27 to 41
	12 ft.	11	16	24	32	41	57	73	89	32 to 49

30.7 mm — 30.7 mm
"Kodachrome" Duplicate or
"Kodacolor" Transparency

	20 in.	2	3	4½	6	8	10	13	16	6 to 9
	30 in.	3	4	6	8	11	16	19	24	8 to 13
	40 in.	4	6	8	11	14	20	26	31	11 to 17
	50 in.	5	7	11	14	18	25	32	39	14 to 21
	5 ft.	6	8	13	17	22	30	38	46	17 to 25
	6 ft.	8	10	15	20	26	36	45	56	20 to 30
	8 ft.	10	13	20	27	34	48	60	74	27 to 40
	10 ft.	12	17	25	34	42	60	75	92	34 to 50
	12 ft.	14	20	30	40	50	70	90	110	40 to 60

(from 1⅝ x 1⅝ inch or 2¼ x 2¼ inch transparency or negative, respectively.)

SOUND TERMS AND DEFINITIONS

Vibrate: To move regularly, backwards and forwards. The ends of a tuning fork vibrate back and forth. Vibration in a fluid takes place at the molecular level, with each molecule moving backwards and forwards about a fixed point.

Frequency: The rate at which an event is regularly repeated. Also the number of cycles per second of a wave.

Hertz: The Standard International Unit of frequency. One hertz is equal to one cycle per second. The standard symbol is *Hz*.

Amplitude: The distance between the extreme and middle positions of a vibrating object. Also the distance between the middle and the top (or bottom) of a wave.

Octave: The interval between any two frequencies having a ratio of 2:1, e.g. notes with pitches of 440 Hz and 880 Hz are an octave apart. Also in any wave motion, the band of frequencies between any two frequencies which are in the ratio of 2:1.

Pitch: The highness or lowness of a musical note. Also a measure of the frequency of vibration of the source of the note, e.g. a high frequency vibration produces a note of high pitch.

Quality: If two notes have the same pitch and loudness, the difference between them (caused by overtones) is called the note's quality. The quality of notes enables us to recognize the same notes produced by different instruments.

Wave motion: Energy from a periodic movement (vibration) is transmitted in a medium (air, water, etc.) in the form of a wave (see diagram). The wave motion is actually produced by the vibration of the particles in the medium about a fixed point.

Sound wave: A longitudinal wave produced by a vibrating object. As the object vibrates, it sends out (1) a wave of high pressure, known as a *compression,* and (2) a wave of low pressure, a *rarefaction.* In between, in air, the pressure returns to atmospheric pressure. The wavelength of a sound wave is the distance between one compression and the next. A sound wave has a speed of about 330 m/s in air.

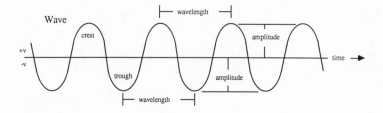

SOUND INTENSITIES

Decibels	Description
140	Jet aircraft
130	Threshold of pain; causes immediate hearing damage.
120	Thunder
100	Lawn mower, table saw
90	Symphony orchestra; extended exposure to levels above 90 dB can cause damage.
80	Alarm clock
70	Street noise
60	Conversation
50	Office background noise
20	Empty theatre
10	Empty recording studio

Note: The sound intensity scale is a logarithmic scale rather than a linear one. Thus the increase in sound intensity between 90 dB and 100 dB is much greater than it is between 10 dB and 20 dB.

HEARING PROTECTION STANDARDS

Sound Intensity	Permissible Duration of Exposure*	
115 dB	15 minutes	Properly fitted ear muffs or foam ear plugs
110	30	reduce noise levels approximately
105	60	25 to 29 dB.
102	90	
100	120	
97	3 hours	
95	4	
92	6	
90	8	

*Good health and safety practices require hearing protection when exposure exceeds the above durations.

ANALOG RECORDING TAPE:
LENGTH, TIME, SPEED AND FREQUENCY

| Reel Size | Amount of Tape | -------------Time---------- | | | Tape Speed (ips) | Highest Frequency** |
		$3^3/_4$ ips*	$7^1/_2$ ips	15 ips		
5"(1.5 mil)	600'	32 min.	16 min.	8 min.	15	25,000 Hz
5"(1.0 mil)	900'	48 min.	24 min.	12 min.	$7^1/_2$	20,000 Hz
7"(1.5 mil)	1200'	64 min.	32 min.	16 min.	$3^3/_4$	12,000 Hz
7"(1.0 mil)	1800'	96 min.	48 min.	24 min.	$1^7/_8$	8,000 Hz
10.5"(1.5 mil)	2400'	128 min.	64 min.	32 min.	$^{15}/_{16}$	4,000 Hz
10.5"(1.0 mil)	3600'	192 min.	96 min.	48 min.		

* Inches per second.
** Tape speed governs frequency range and although there are constant technical developments in both tape and electronics the average highest frequencies reproduced by most non-studio quality recorders are given.

WIRING MIC AND LINE LEVEL XLR-3 PLUGS

The standard pin configuration for XLR-3 connectors when used with microphone and line level signals is as follows:

Pin 1   Cable screen and circuit ground, if connected.
Pin 2   Positive signal (+), high (red)
Pin 3   Negative signal (-), low (black)

Note: the signal carrying connector should always be *male*. The case of the mic is connected to pin 1: do not connect pin 1 to the connector case.

SOUND CONNECTORS

3-Pin XLR Plug

¹/₄" Phone Plug (Mono)

RCA or Phone Plug

¹/₈" or Mini Phone Plug (Stereo)

WIRING ¹/₄" PHONE PLUGS

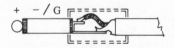

Unbalanced Plug

1-conductor
with shield

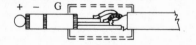

Balanced Plug ("TRS")

2-conductor
with shield

SHOP MATH

DECIMAL EQUIVALENTS OF FRACTIONS

$1/64$ = 0.015 625	$33/64$ = 0.515 625
$1/32$ = 0.031 25	$17/32$ = 0.531 25
$3/64$ = 0.046 875	$35/64$ = 0.546 875
$1/16$ = 0.062 5	$9/16$ = 0.562 5
$5/64$ = 0.078 125	$37/64$ = 0.578 125
$3/32$ = 0.093 75	$19/32$ = 0.593 75
$7/64$ = 0.109 375	$39/64$ = 0.609 375
$1/8$ = 0.125	$5/8$ = 0.625
$9/64$ = 0.140 625	$41/64$ = 0.640 625
$5/32$ = 0.156 25	$21/32$ = 0.656 25
$11/64$ = 0.171 875	$43/64$ = 0.671 875
$3/16$ = 0.187 5	$11/16$ = 0.687 5
$13/64$ = 0.203 125	$45/64$ = 0.703 125
$7/32$ = 0.218 75	$23/32$ = 0.718 75
$15/64$ = 0.234 375	$47/64$ = 0.734 375
$1/4$ = 0.25	$3/4$ = 0.75
$17/64$ = 0.265 625	$49/64$ = 0.765 625
$9/32$ = 0.281 25	$25/32$ = 0.781 25
$19/64$ = 0.296 875	$51/64$ = 0.796 875
$5/16$ = 0.312 5	$13/16$ = 0.812 5
$21/64$ = 0.328 125	$53/64$ = 0.828 125
$11/32$ = 0.343 75	$27/32$ = 0.843 75
$23/64$ = 0.359 375	$55/64$ = 0.859 375
$3/8$ = 0.375	$7/8$ = 0.875
$25/64$ = 0.390 625	$57/64$ = 0.890 625
$13/32$ = 0.406 25	$29/32$ = 0.906 25
$27/64$ = 0.421 875	$59/64$ = 0.921 875
$7/16$ = 0.437 5	$15/16$ = 0.937 5
$29/64$ = 0.453 125	$61/64$ = 0.953 125
$15/32$ = 0.468 75	$31/32$ = 0.968 75
$31/64$ = 0.484 375	$63/64$ = 0.984 375
$1/2$ = 0.5	1 = 1.00

METRIC UNITS

Basic units of measurement:

Unit	Symbol	Measures
meter	m	distance
liter	l	volume (dry and liquid)
gram	g	weight (mass)

Common divisions of the above units:

Prefix	Abbreviation	Multiplier		
tera	T	10^{12}	or	1,000,000,000,000
giga	G	10^9	or	1,000,000,000
mega	M	10^6	or	1,000,000
kilo	k	10^3	or	1,000
hecto	h	10^2	or	100
deka	da	10	or	10
deci	d	10^{-1}	or	.1
centi	c	10^{-2}	or	.01
milli	m	10^{-3}	or	.001
micro	u	10^{-6}	or	.000001
nano	n	10^{-9}	or	.000000001
pico	p	10^{-12}	or	.000000000001
femto	f	10^{-15}	or	.000000000000001
atto	a	10^{-18}	or	.000000000000000001

SQUARE ROOTS OF NUMBERS

	.0	.1	.2	.3	.4	.5	.6	.7	.8	.9
1	1.000	1.049	1.095	1.140	1.183	1.225	1.265	1.304	1.342	1.378
2	1.414	1.449	1.483	1.517	1.549	1.581	1.612	1.643	1.673	1.703
3	1.732	1.761	1.789	1.817	1.844	1.871	1.897	1.924	1.949	1.975
4	2.000	2.025	2.049	2.074	2.098	2.121	2.145	2.168	2.191	2.214
5	2.236	2.258	2.280	2.302	2.324	2.345	2.366	2.387	2.408	2.429
6	2.449	2.470	2.490	2.510	2.530	2.550	2.569	2.588	2.608	2.627
7	2.646	2.665	2.683	2.702	2.720	2.739	2.757	2.775	2.793	2.811
8	2.828	2.846	2.864	2.881	2.898	2.915	2.933	2.950	2.966	2.983
9	3.000	3.017	3.033	3.050	3.066	3.082	3.098	3.114	3.130	3.146

	0	1	2	3	4	5	6	7	8	9
10	3.162	3.317	3.464	3.606	3.742	3.873	4.000	4.123	4.243	4.359
20	4.472	4.583	4.690	4.796	4.899	5.000	5.099	5.196	5.292	5.385
30	5.477	5.568	5.657	5.745	5.831	5.916	6.000	6.083	6.164	6.245
40	6.325	6.403	6.481	6.557	6.633	6.708	6.782	6.856	6.928	7.000
50	7.071	7.141	7.211	7.280	7.348	7.416	7.483	7.550	7.616	7.681
60	7.746	7.810	7.874	7.937	8.000	8.062	8.124	8.185	8.246	8.307
70	8.367	8.426	8.485	8.544	8.602	8.660	8.718	8.775	8.832	8.888
80	8.944	9.000	9.055	9.110	9.165	9.220	9.274	9.327	9.381	9.434
90	9.487	9.539	9.592	9.644	9.695	9.747	9.798	9.849	9.899	9.950

Note: To use this table, find the integer (or tens) portion of a number in the left column and the decimal (or ones) portion along the top. For instance the square root of 4.0 (2.000) is found in the first column and fourth row of the upper part of the table; the square root of 55 (7.416) is found in the sixth column and fifth row of the lower part of the table.

ROMAN NUMERALS

Arabic	Roman	Arabic	Roman	Arabic	Roman
1	I	17	XVII	600	DC
2	II	18	XVIII	700	DCC
3	III	19	XIX	800	DCCC
4	IV	20	XX	900	DCCCC or CM
5	V	30	XXX	1,000	M
6	VI	40	XL	2,000	MM
7	VII	50	L	3,000	MMM
8	VIII	60	LX	4,000	MMMM
9	IX	70	LXX	5,000	$\overline{\text{V}}$
10	X	80	LXXX	10,000	$\overline{\text{X}}$
11	XI	90	XC	50,000	$\overline{\text{L}}$
12	XII	100	C	100,000	$\overline{\text{C}}$
13	XIII	200	CC	500,000	$\overline{\text{D}}$
14	XIV	300	CCC	1,000,000	$\overline{\text{M}}$
15	XV	400	CCCC or CD		
16	XVI	500	D		

If the lesser number is placed before the greater, the lesser is deducted from the greater; for example IV=4, IX=9, XC=90. If the lesser number is placed after the greater, the lesser is added to the greater; for example VI=6, XI=11, CX=110. A horizontal stroke over a numeral denotes 1,000; thus $\overline{\text{V}}$ = 5,000, $\overline{\text{L}}$ = 50,000 and $\overline{\text{M}}$ = 1,000,000 (1,000 x 1,000)

HEXADECIMAL AND BINARY EQUIVALENTS

Hexadecimal	Decimal	Binary	Hexadecimal	Decimal	Hexadecimal	Decimal
0	0	0	1A	26	700	1792
1	1	1	1B	27	800	2048
2	2	10	1C	28	900	2304
3	3	11	1D	29	A00	2560
4	4	100	1E	30	B00	2816
5	5	101	1F	31	C00	3072
6	6	110	20	32	D00	3328
7	7	111	30	48	E00	3584
8	8	1000	40	64	F00	3840
9	9	1001	50	80	1000	4096
A	10	1010	60	96	2000	8192
B	11	1011	70	112	3000	12288
C	12	1100	80	128	4000	16384
D	13	1101	90	144	5000	20480
E	14	1110	A0	160	6000	24576
F	15	1111	B0	176	7000	28672
10	16	etc.	C0	192	8000	32768
11	17		D0	208	9000	36864
12	18		E0	224	A000	40960
13	19		F0	240	B000	45056
14	20		100	256	C000	49152
15	21		200	512	D000	53248
16	22		300	768	E000	57344
17	23		400	1024	F000	61440
18	24		500	1280		
19	25		600	1536		

ASCII CODES FOR COMPUTERS

D	Character	H	D	Character	H	D	Character	H
0	nul	00	45	-	2D	90	Z	5A
1	soh	01	46	.	2E	91	[	5B
2	stx	02	47	/	2F	92	\	5C
3	etx	03	48	0	30	93	]	5D
4	eot	04	49	1	31	94	^	5E
5	enq	05	50	2	32	95	_	5F
6	ack	06	51	3	33	96	`	60
7	bel	07	52	4	34	97	a	61
8	bs	08	53	5	35	98	b	62
9	ht	09	54	6	36	99	c	63
10	lf	0A	55	7	37	100	d	64
11	vt	0B	56	8	38	101	e	65
12	ff	0C	57	9	39	102	f	66
13	cr	0D	58	:	3A	103	g	67
14	so	0E	59	;	3B	104	h	68
15	si	0F	60	<	3C	105	i	69
16	dle	10	61	=	3D	106	j	6A
17	dc1(xon)	11	62	>	3E	107	k	6B
18	dc2	12	63	?	3F	108	l	6C
19	dc3(xoff)	13	64	@	40	109	m	6D
20	dc4	14	65	A	41	110	n	6E
21	nak	15	66	B	42	111	o	6F
22	syn	16	67	C	43	112	p	70
23	etb	17	68	D	44	113	q	71
24	can	18	69	E	45	114	r	72
25	em	19	70	F	46	115	s	73
26	sub	1A	71	G	47	116	t	74
27	esc	1B	72	H	48	117	u	75
28	fs	1C	73	I	49	118	v	76
29	gs	1D	74	J	4A	119	w	77
30	rs	1E	75	K	4B	120	x	78
31	us	1F	76	L	4C	121	y	79
32	sp	20	77	M	4D	122	z	7A
33	!	21	78	N	4E	123	{	7B
34	"	22	79	O	4F	124			7C
35	#	23	80	P	50	125	}	7D
36	$	24	81	Q	51	126	~	7E
37	%	25	82	R	52	127	del	7F
38	&	26	83	S	53			
39	'	27	84	T	54			
40	(	28	85	U	55			
41	)	29	86	V	56			
42	*	2A	87	W	57			
43	+	2B	88	X	58			
44	,	2C	89	Y	59			

MATH SIGNS AND SYMBOLS

+	Plus (addition) or positive	sin	Sine
-	Minus (subtraction) or negative	cos	Cosine
±	Plus or minus	tan	Tangent (also tg, tang)
x	Multiplied by	cot	Cotangent (also ctg)
*	Multiplied by	sec	Secant
•	Multiplied by	cosec	Cosecant
÷	Divided by	versin	Versed sine
/	Divided by	covers	Coversed sine
=	Equals	$\sin^{-1} a$	Arc the sine of which is a (also arcsin a)
≠	Is not equal to		
:	Is to (in proportion)	$(\sin a)^{-1}$	Reciprocal of sin a (1÷sin a)
::	Equals (in proportion)	$\sinh x$	Hyperbolic sine of x
≡	Is identical to	$\cosh x$	Hyperbolic cosine of x
≈	Approximately equals (also ≅)	∠	Angle
>	Greater than	∟	Right angle
<	Less than	⊥	Perpendicular to
≥	Greater than or equal to	△	Triangle
≤	Less than or equal to	⊙	Circle
∴	Therefore	▱	Parallelogram
d	Differential (in calculus)	°	Degree (circular arc or temperature)
∫	Integral (in calculus)		
$\int_b^a$	Integral between limits a and b	'	Minutes or feet
!	Factorial (5! = 1 x 2 x 3 x 4 x 5)	"	Seconds or inches
√	Square root	log	Logarithm
a^2	a squared	hyp. log	Hyperbolic logarithm
a^3	a cubed	nat. log	Natural logarithm
a^n	nth power of a	a'	a prime
a^{-n}	$\frac{1}{a^n}$	a''	a double prime
$\frac{1}{n}$	Reciprocal value of n	a_1	a sub one
∞	Infinity	a_2	a sub two
π	Pi (3.1416)	a_n	a sub n
( )	Parentheses	[ ]	Brackets
		{ }	Braces

POSITIVE AND NEGATIVE QUALITIES
IN ADDITION AND SUBTRACTION

+2	+2	-2	-2
+3	-3	+3	-3
+5	-1	+1	-5

In multiplication and division, like signs give a positive product, unlike signs give a negative product:

$+3 \times -2 = -6$	$-6 \div +2 = -3$
$-3 \times -2 = +6$	$-6 \div -2 = +3$
$-3 \times +2 = -6$	$+6 \div +2 = +3$
$+3 \times +2 = +6$	$+6 \div -2 = -3$

ORDER OF ARITHMETIC OPERATIONS

When a formula or equation contains signs indicating addition, subtraction, multiplication and division, the order in which they should be performed is

1. Calculations inside parentheses
2. Multiplication and division in the order they appear
3. Addition and subtraction in the order they appear

Example:

$$2 + [3 \times (5 - 2)] \div 3 + 5 \times 6 =$$
$$2 + [3 \times \quad 3 \quad] \div 3 + \quad 30 \quad =$$
$$2 + \quad 9 \quad \div 3 + \quad 30 \quad =$$
$$2 + \quad 3 \quad + \quad 30 \quad = 35$$

QUADRATIC EQUATION

If A, B, and C are real numbers, A≠0, and $AX^2 + BX + C = 0$ then $X = \dfrac{-B \pm \sqrt{(B^2 - 4AC)}}{2A}$

LAWS AND EXAMPLES

Commutative Law of Addition and Multiplication

$A+B = B+A$ $AB = BA$
$A+B+C = C+B+A$ $ABC = CBA$

Associative Law of Addition and Multiplication

$A+(B+C) = (A+B)+C = A+B+C$ $A(BC) = (AB)C = ABC$

Distributive Law

$A(B+C) = AB+AC$

Examples of Multiplication and Division of Exponents

$AB^2 = A \times B^2$ $(A+B)^2 = A^2+2AB+B^2$

$A^2 \times A^5 = A^{2+5} = A^7$ $(A-B)^2 = A^2-2AB+B^2$

$A^5 \div A^2 = A^{5-2} = A^3$ $A^{-x} = 1 \div A^x$

$(A^5)^2 = A^{5x2} = A^{10}$ $A^2 - B^2 = (A+B)(A-B)$

$(AA)^5 = A^5 A^5 = A^{5+5} = A^{10}$

Scientific Notation Examples

$10^1 =$ 10	$10^{-1} = .1$ $= ^1/_{10}$		$3.2 \times 10^{11} = 320,000,000,000$
$10^2 =$ 100	$10^{-2} = .01$ $= ^1/_{100}$		$32 \times 10^{10} = 320,000,000,000$
$10^3 =$ 1000	$10^{-3} = .001$ $= ^1/_{1000}$		

INTERNATIONAL SYSTEM (SI) UNITS

Physical Quantity	Unit Symbol	Name of Unit	Definition
Mass	kg	kilogram	Mass of the international prototype is in the custody of the Bureau International des Poids et Mesures (BIPM) at Sevres, near Paris.
Time	s	second	The duration of 9,192,631,770 periods of the radiation corresponding to the transition between the two hyperfine levels of the ground state of the cesium-133 atom.
Length	m	meter	1,650,763.73 wavelengths in vacuo of the radiation corresponding to the transition between the energy levels 2p10 and 5d5 of the krypton-86 atom.
Electric Current	A	ampere	The constant current which, if maintained in two parallel rectilinear conductors of infinite length, of negligible circular cross section, and placed at a distance of one meter apart in a vacuum, would produce between these conductors a force equal to 2×10^{-7} N/m length.
Thermodynamic Temperature	K	degree (Kelvin)	The fraction $1/273.16$ of the thermodynamic temperature of the triple point of water.
Amount of Substance	mol	mole	The amount of substance of a system which contains as many elementary entities as there are atoms in 0.012 kilograms of carbon-12.
Luminous Intensity	cd	candela	The luminous intensity, in the perpendicular direction, of a surface of 1/600,000 square meter of a black body at the temperature of freezing platinum under a pressure of 101.325 newtons per square meter.

Source: MH

INTERNATIONAL SYSTEM (SI) PHYSICAL QUANTITIES

Physical Quantity	Unit Symbol	SI Unit
Area	m^2	square meter
Volume	m^3	cubic meter
Frequency	Hz	hertz (cycle/second)
Density	kg/m^3	kilogram per cubic meter
Velocity	m/s	meter per second
Acceleration	m/s^2	meter per second squared
Pressure	Pa	pascal (newton/meter^2)
Luminance	cd/m^2	candela per square meter

DERIVED (SI) UNITS

Physical Quantity	Unit Symbol	Name of Unit	Definition
Force	$N = kg\ m/s^2$	newton	That force which, when applied to a body having a mass of one kilogram, gives it an acceleration of one meter per second squared.
Work, Energy, Quantity, of Heat	$J = N\ m$	joule	The work done when the point of application of a force of one newton is displaced through a distance of one meter in the direction of the force.
Power	$W = J \div s$	watt	One joule per second.
Electric Charge	$C = A\ s$	coulomb	The quantity of electricity transported in one second by a current of one ampere.
Electric Potential	$V = W \div A$	volt	The difference of potential between two points of a conducting wire carrying a constant current of one ampere, when the power dissipated between these points is equal to one coulomb.
Electric Capacitance	$F = C \div V$	farad	The capacitance of a capacitor between the plates of which there appears a difference of potential of one volt when it is charged by a quantity of electricity equal to one coulomb.
Electric Resistance	$\Omega = V \div A$	ohm	The resistance between two points of a conductor when a constant difference of potential of one volt, applied between these two points, produces in this conductor a current of one ampere, this conductor not being the source of any electro-motive force.
Magnetic Flux	$Wb = V\ s$	weber	The flux which, linking a circuit of one turn produces in it an electromotive force of one volt as it is reduced to zero at a uniform rate in one second.
Inductance	$H = V\ s \div A$	henry	The inductance of a closed circuit in which an electromotive force of one volt is produced when the electric current in the circuit varies uniformly at the rate of one ampere per second.
Luminous Flux	$lm = cd\ sr$	lumen	The flux emitted within a unit solid angle of one steradian by a point source having a uniform intensity of one candela.
Illumination	$lx = lm \div m^2$	lux	An illumination of one lumen per square meter.

Source: MH

PHYSICAL CONSTANTS

Description	Symbol	Constant
Pi	π =	3.1416 or $^{22}/_7$
Light year	=	5.8825 x 10^{12} miles
Velocity of light	c =	2.9978 x 10^8 m/sec.
Energy (energy = mass times the speed of light squared)	e =	mc^2
Velocity of sound (in air)	=	3.3 x 10^2 m/sec.
	=	10.87 x 10^2 ft/sec.
Velocity of sound (in water)	=	14.7 x 10^2 m/sec.
	=	48.23 x 10^2 ft/sec.
Acceleration due to gravity	G =	9.81 x 10^2 m/sec^2
	=	32.174 ft/sec^2
Standard temperature and pressure	s.t.p. =	1.0 atm or 760 mm Hg
Standard volume of a mole of gas	=	22.4 dm^3 at s.t.p.
Faraday constant	F =	96,500 C/mol
Avogadro constant	L =	6.02 x 10^{23}/mol
1 calorie	=	4.18 joules
Specific heat capacity of water	=	4.18 joules/gram/degree Kelvin

VELOCITY OF A FREE FALLING BODY

Velocity (ft. per sec.)	Time (seconds)	Distance Traveled (feet)
0	0	0
32	1	16
64	2	64
96	3	144
128	4	256
160 (max.)	5	400

THE EARTH

Weight of Earth (Mass)	= 5.976 x 10^{24} kg	= 1.317 x 10^{25} lbs
Equatorial Radius	= 6,378.388 km	= 3,963 miles
Average Distance from Sun	= 149,592,000 km	= 92,955,000 miles
Maximum Distance from Sun	= 151,516,000 km	= 94,510,000 miles
Minimum Distance from Sun	= 147,090,000 km	= 91,400,000 miles

Rotation Period	= 23 hours, 56 mins
Revolution Time Around Sun	= 365.26 days
Orbital Velocity	= 18.51 miles/second

FACTS AND FORMULAS

Accelerated Motion Formulas:

$v = a t$ or $v = g t$

$s = \frac{1}{2} a t^2$ or $s = \frac{1}{2} g t^2$

$v = \sqrt{2as}$ or $v = \sqrt{2gs}$

where:
v is final velocity
a is acceleration
g is acceleration due to gravity
t is time
s is total distance

Centrifugal Force:

$$c.f. = m \ \frac{v^2}{r}$$

where:
c.f. is centrifugal force
m is mass
v is velocity
r is radius of path

Work:

$w = f s$
where:
w is work
f is force
s is distance

Kinetic Energy:

$k.e. = \frac{1}{2} m v^2$
where:
k.e. is kinetic energy
m is mass
v is velocity

Velocity = **distance ÷ time**

Velocity of Air from Nozzle

$v = cfm ÷ 60a$
where:
cfm is air volume in cubic feet per minute
v is velocity of air at nozzle
a is cross section of nozzle in square feet.

Newton's Second Law of Motion:

$f = m·a$
where:
f is force
m is mass
a is acceleration

Impulse and Momentum:

$f t$ (impulse) $= m v$ (momentum)
where:
f is force
t is time
m is mass
v is velocity

Potential Energy:

$p.e. = m g h$
where:
p.e. is potential energy
m is mass
g is acceleration due to gravity
h is vertical distance

Liquid Pressure = **force ÷ area**

Momentum = **mass x velocity**

Force = **mass x velocity ÷ time**

Acceleration $= v_2 - v_1 ÷ t$
         = **change in velocity ÷ time**

See page 46 for Energy Converting Machine formulas.

Measures of Length

1 mile	= 1760 yards	= 5280 feet
1 yard	= 3 feet	= 36 inches
1 mil	= 0.001 inch	
1 fathom	= 2 yards	= 6 feet
1 rod	= 5.5 yards	= 16.5 feet
1 hand	= 4 inches	
1 span	= 9 inches	

Surveyor's Measure

1 mile	= 8 furlongs	= 80 chains
1 furlong	= 10 chains	= 220 yards
1 chain	= 4 rods	= 22 yards
	= 66 feet	= 100 links
1 link	= 7.92 inches	

Nautical Measure

1 league	= 3 nautical miles
1 nautical mile	= 1.1508 statute miles
	= 6076.11549 feet
1 knot	= 1 nautical mile per hour
1 degree	= 60 nautical miles (at equator)
360 degrees	= 24856.8 statute miles
	= circumference of the earth

1 nautical mile is approx. equal to one minute of longitude

Square Measure

1 square mile	= 640 acres
	= 6400 square chains
1 acre	= 10 square chains
	= 4840 square yards
	= 43560 square feet
1 square yard	= 9 square feet
1 square foot	= 144 square inches

Dry Measure

1 bushel	= 1.2445 cubic foot
	= 4 pecks = 32 quarts
	= 64 pints
1 peck	= 8 quarts = 16 pints
1 quart	= 2 pints
1 heaped bushel	= $1^1/4$ bushels
1 cubic foot	= 0.8036 bushel

Commercial Weight (Avoirdupois)

1 pound	= 16 ounces	= 7000 grains
1 ounce	= 16 drachms	= 437.5 grains
1 quarter	= 28 pounds	
1 stone	= 14 pounds	
1 quintal	= 100 pounds	
1 long ton	= 20 hundred-weights	
1 gross (long ton)	= 2240 pounds	
1 net (short ton)	= 2000 pounds	
1 hundred-weight	= 4 quarters	
	= 112 pounds	

Liquid Measure

1 US gallon	= 0.1337 cu. ft.	= 231 cu. in.
	= 4 quarts	= 8 pints
1 quart	= 2 pints	= 8 gills
1 pint	= 4 gills	
1 cubic foot	= 7.48 US gallons	
1 British Imperial Gallon	= 1.2009 US gals.	

Old Liquid Measure

1 tun	= 2 pipes	= 3 puncheons
1 pipe or butt	= 2 hogsheads	= 4 barrels
	= 126 gallons	
1 puncheon	= 2 tierces	= 84 gallons
1 hogshead	= 2 barrels	= 63 gallons
1 barrel	= $31^1/2$ gallons	

Apothecaries' Fluid Measure

1 US fluid ounce	= 8 drachms
	= 1.805 cu. in.
1 fluid drachm	= 60 minims

Troy Weight (for gold and silver)

1 pound	= 12 ounces
	= 5760 grains
1 ounce	= 20 pennyweights
	= 480 grains
1 pennyweight	= 24 grains
1 carat	= 3.086 grains
	(used for weighing gems)
1 grain Troy	= 1 grain avoirdupois
	= 1 grain apothecaries' weight

Apothecaries' Weight

1 pound	= 12 ounces	= 5760 grains
1 ounce	= 8 drachms	= 480 grains
1 drachm	= 3 scruples	= 60 grains
1 scruple	= 20 grains	

Other Measures

1 dozen	= 12 units	
1 bakers dozen	= 13 units	= 1 laniappe
1 gross	= 12 dozen	= 144 units
1 great gross	= 12 gross	= 144 dozen
1 score	= 20 units	
1 cord of wood	= 4 ft. x 4 ft. x 8 ft.	
	= 128 cubic feet	
1 face cord	= 4 ft. x 16 in. x 8 ft.	
1 lb./sq. in.	= 144 lb./sq.ft.	
	= 0.068 atmospheres	
1 quire	= 24 sheets	
1 ream	= 20 quires	= 480 sheets
1 ream printing paper		= 500 sheets

TYPES OF ANGLES

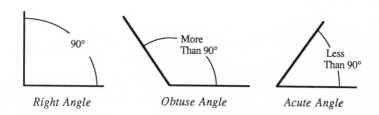

Right Angle   *Obtuse Angle*   *Acute Angle*

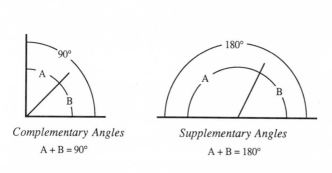

Complementary Angles   *Supplementary Angles*
A + B = 90°   A + B = 180°

TYPES OF LINES

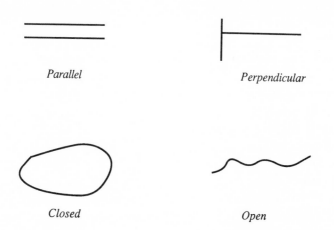

Parallel   *Perpendicular*

Closed   *Open*

CIRCLE PARTS AND FORMULAS

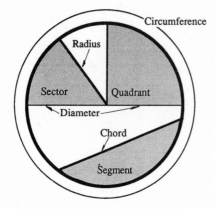

Pi (π) ≈ 3.141593

$\approx \dfrac{22}{7}$

Diameter $= 2\,R$

Area $= \pi R^2$

$= D^2 \times \dfrac{\pi}{4}$

Circumference $= \pi\,D$

$= 2\,\pi\,R$

DRAWING GEOMETRIC SHAPES USING CHORDS

Any regular geometric shape with sides of equal length can be drawn by dividing the circumference of a circle into a given number of equal parts using chords (a line segment which touches the circumference in two places). The table below can be used to determine the length of each chord if you know the radius of the circle and the number of sides of the regular geometric shape. Multiply the number in column A by the radius of the circle. The product will be the length of the chord to lay off on the circumference to achieve the desired shape.

No. of Sides	A		No. of Sides	A	No. of Sides	A
3	1.732	(Triangle)	15	.4158	40	.1569
4	1.414	(Square)	16	.3902	45	.1395
5	1.175	(Pentagon)	17	.3675	50	.1256
6	1.000	(Hexagon)	18	.3473	54	.1163
7	.8677	(Heptagon)	19	.3292	60	.1047
8	.7653	(Octagon)	20	.3129	72	.0872
9	.6840	(Nonagon)	22	.2846	80	.0785
10	.6180	(Decagon)	24	.2610	90	.0698
11	.5634	(Undecagon)	25	.2506	100	.0628
12	.5176	(Duodecagon)	27	.2322	108	.0582
13	.4782	(Tridecagon)	30	.2090	120	.0523
14	.4451	(Tetradecagon)	36	.1743	150	.0419

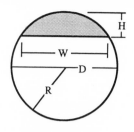

Segment

Height $= R - \sqrt{R^2 - (\frac{1}{2} W)^2}$

$\qquad = \dfrac{D - \sqrt{(D^2 - W^2)}}{2}$

Width $= \sqrt{D^2 - (D - 2H)^2}$

Area $\quad = \dfrac{H(\frac{4}{3}W^2 + H^2)}{2W}$

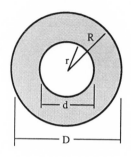

Ring

Area $= \pi (R^2 - r^2)$

$\qquad = \pi (R + r)(R - r)$

$\qquad = \dfrac{\pi}{4} (D + d)(D - d)$

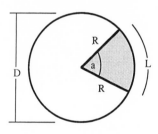

Sector

Length of arc $= \dfrac{\pi R a}{180}$

$\qquad\qquad\quad = \dfrac{\pi D a}{360}$

Area $\qquad\quad = \dfrac{a}{360} \pi R^2$

$\qquad\qquad\quad = \frac{1}{2} RL$

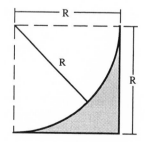

Fillet

Area $\qquad = R^2 - \dfrac{\pi R^2}{4}$

$\qquad\qquad = 0.215 R^2$

Perimeter $= 2 R + \dfrac{\pi R^2}{2}$

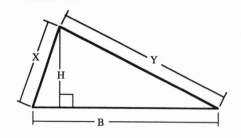

Scalene Triangle

No equal sides, no equal angles

Perimeter $= X + Y + B$

Area $= \frac{1}{2} B H$

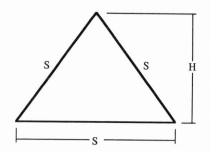

Equilateral Triangle

Three equal sides and angles

Perimeter $= 3S$

Area $= \frac{1}{2} S H$

$= \frac{S^2}{4} \sqrt{3}$

Height $= \frac{S}{2} \sqrt{3}$

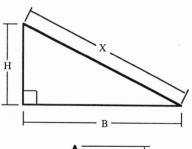

Right Triangle

One angle equal to 90°

Perimeter $= B + H + X$

Area $= \frac{1}{2} B H$

$X = \sqrt{B^2 + H^2}$

$B = \sqrt{X^2 - H^2}$

$H = \sqrt{X^2 - B^2}$

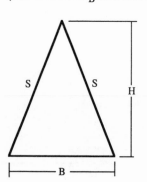

Isosceles Triangle

Two equal sides, two equal angles.

Perimeter $= S + S + B$

Area $= \frac{1}{2} BH$

Not illustrated:

Acute Triangle
All angles less than 90°.

Obtuse Triangle
One angle greater than 90°.

Note: The sum of the three inside angles of a triangle always equals 180°.

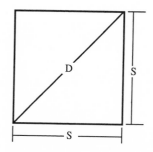

Square

Perimeter $= 4\,S$
Area $= S^2$
Diagonal $= S\sqrt{2}$
Side $= \frac{1}{2}\,D\sqrt{2}$

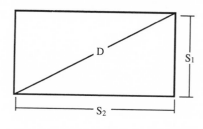

Rectangle

Perimeter $= 2\,(S_1 + S_2)$
Area $= S_1\,S_2$
Diagonal $= \sqrt{S_1{}^2 + S_2{}^2}$

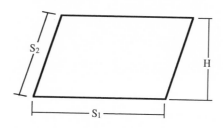

Rhomboid (Parallelogram)

Perimeter $= 2\,(S_1 + S_2)$
Area $= S_1\,H$

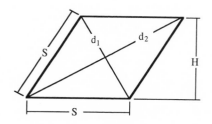

Rhombus (Equilateral Parallelogram)

Perimeter $= 4\,S$
Area $= S\,H$
$= \frac{1}{2}\,d_1 d_2$

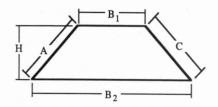

Trapezoid

Perimeter $= A + C + B_1 + B_2$

Area $= \frac{1}{2} H (B_1 + B_2)$

Regular Hexagon

Perimeter $= 6S$

Radius $(R) = S$

Radius $(r) = \frac{S}{2} \sqrt{3}$

Area $= \frac{3S^2}{2} \sqrt{3}$

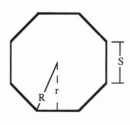

Regular n-gon
(n = number of sides)

Perimeter $= nS$

Area $= \frac{1}{2} Pr = \frac{1}{2} nSr$

$= \frac{1}{2}(nS) \sqrt{R^2 - \frac{S^2}{4}}$

Radius $(r) = \sqrt{R^2 - \frac{S^2}{4}}$

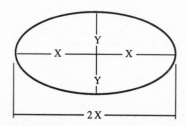

Ellipse

Perimeter $\approx \pi \sqrt{2(X^2 + Y^2)}$

Area $= \pi X Y$

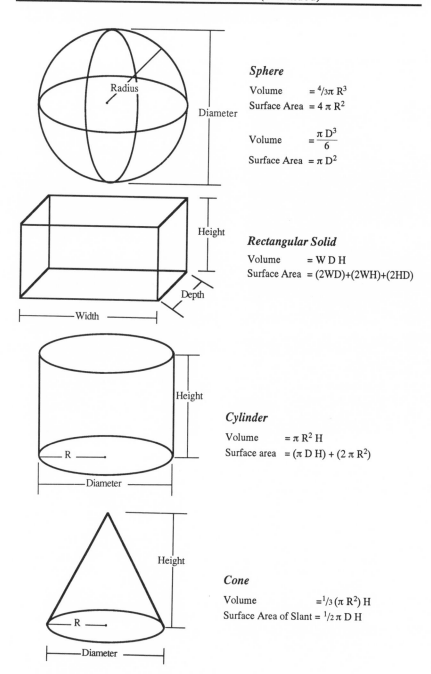

Sphere

Volume $= \frac{4}{3}\pi R^3$

Surface Area $= 4\pi R^2$

Volume $= \frac{\pi D^3}{6}$

Surface Area $= \pi D^2$

Rectangular Solid

Volume $= W D H$

Surface Area $= (2WD)+(2WH)+(2HD)$

Cylinder

Volume $= \pi R^2 H$

Surface area $= (\pi D H) + (2\pi R^2)$

Cone

Volume $= \frac{1}{3}(\pi R^2) H$

Surface Area of Slant $= \frac{1}{2}\pi D H$

LENGTH OF CIRCULAR ARCS FOR UNIT RADIUS

The length of any arc may be determined if the length of the radius and the angle of the segment are known. Using the table below, multiply the figure in column A opposite the given degree of angle of the segment by the length of the radius.

Example: To determine the length of arc of a 45° segment with a radius of 12 ft. 6 in. multiply 0.7853982 (the figure in column A opposite 45°) by 12.5 ft. The result, 9.8174775 ft., is the length of arc of this segment.

Degree	A	Degree	A	Degree	A	Degree	A
1	.017 4533	46	.802 8515	91	1.588 2496	136	2.373 6478
2	.034 9066	47	.820 3047	92	1.605 7029	137	2.391 1011
3	.052 3599	48	.837 7580	93	1.623 1562	138	2.408 5544
4	.069 8132	49	.855 2113	94	1.640 6095	139	2.426 0077
5	.087 2665	50	.872 6646	95	1.658 0628	140	2.443 4610
6	.104 7198	51	.890 1179	96	1.675 5161	141	2.460 9142
7	.122 1730	52	.907 5712	97	1.692 9694	142	2.478 3675
8	.139 6263	53	.925 0245	98	1.710 4227	143	2.495 8208
9	.157 0796	54	.942 4778	99	1.727 8760	144	2.513 2741
10	.174 5329	55	.959 9311	100	1.745 3293	145	2.530 7274
11	.191 9862	56	.977 3844	101	1.762 7825	146	2.548 1807
12	.209 4395	57	.994 8377	102	1.780 2358	147	2.565 6340
13	.226 8928	58	1.012 2910	103	1.797 6891	148	2.583 0873
14	.244 3461	59	1.029 7443	104	1.815 1424	149	2.600 5406
15	.261 7994	60	1.047 1976	105	1.832 5957	150	2.617 9939
16	.279 2527	61	1.064 6508	106	1.850 0490	151	2.635 4472
17	.296 7060	62	1.082 1041	107	1.867 5023	152	2.652 9005
18	.314 1593	63	1.099 5574	108	1.884 9556	153	2.670 3538
19	.331 6126	64	1.117 0107	109	1.902 4089	154	2.687 8070
20	.349 0659	65	1.134 4640	110	1.919 8622	155	2.705 2603
21	.366 5191	66	1.151 9173	111	1.937 3155	156	2.722 7136
22	.383 9724	67	1.169 3706	112	1.954 7688	157	2.740 1669
23	.401 4257	68	1.186 8239	113	1.972 2221	158	2.757 6202
24	.418 8790	69	1.204 2772	114	1.989 6753	159	2.775 0735
25	.436 3323	70	1.221 7304	115	2.007 1286	160	2.792 5268
26	.453 7856	71	1.239 1838	116	2.024 5819	161	2.809 9801
27	.471 2389	72	1.256 6371	117	2.042 0352	162	2.827 4334
28	.488 6922	73	1.274 0904	118	2.059 4885	163	2.844 8867
29	.506 1455	74	1.291 5436	119	2.076 9418	164	2.862 3400
30	.523 5988	75	1.308 9969	120	2.094 3951	165	2.879 7933
31	.541 0521	76	1.326 4502	121	2.111 8484	166	2.897 2466
32	.558 5054	77	1.343 9035	122	2.129 3017	167	2.914 6999
33	.575 9587	78	1.361 3568	123	2.146 7550	168	2.932 1531
34	.593 4119	79	1.378 8101	124	2.164 2083	169	2.949 6064
35	.610 8652	80	1.396 2634	125	2.181 6616	170	2.967 0597
36	.628 3185	81	1.413 7167	126	2.199 1149	171	2.984 5130
37	.645 7718	82	1.431 1700	127	2.216 5682	172	3.001 9663
38	.663 2251	83	1.448 6233	128	2.234 0214	173	3.019 4196
39	.680 6784	84	1.466 0766	129	2.251 4747	174	3.036 8729
40	.698 1317	85	1.483 5299	130	2.268 9280	175	3.054 3262
41	.715 5850	86	1.500 9832	131	2.286 3813	176	3.071 7795
42	.733 0383	87	1.518 4364	132	2.303 8346	177	3.089 2328
43	.750 4916	88	1.535 8897	133	2.321 2879	178	3.106 6861
44	.767 9449	89	1.553 3430	134	2.338 7412	179	3.124 1394
45	.785 3982	90	1.570 7963	135	2.356 1945	180	3.141 5927

"3-4-5" TRIANGLES

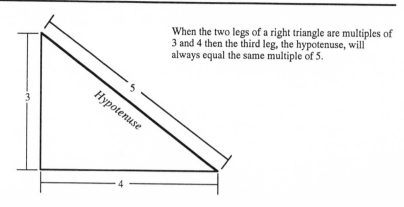

When the two legs of a right triangle are multiples of 3 and 4 then the third leg, the hypotenuse, will always equal the same multiple of 5.

TRIGONOMETRY OF RIGHT TRIANGLES

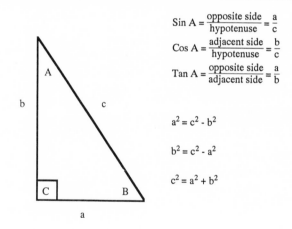

$$\text{Sin } A = \frac{\text{opposite side}}{\text{hypotenuse}} = \frac{a}{c}$$

$$\text{Cos } A = \frac{\text{adjacent side}}{\text{hypotenuse}} = \frac{b}{c}$$

$$\text{Tan } A = \frac{\text{opposite side}}{\text{adjacent side}} = \frac{a}{b}$$

$$a^2 = c^2 - b^2$$

$$b^2 = c^2 - a^2$$

$$c^2 = a^2 + b^2$$

If two parts of a right triangle are known (sides or angles) the following formulas can be used to find the required information.

Known	A	B	a	b	c	Area
				Required		
a, b	$\tan A = \frac{a}{b}$	$\tan B = \frac{b}{a}$			$\sqrt{a^2 + b^2}$	$\frac{ab}{2}$
a, c	$\sin A = \frac{a}{c}$	$\cos B = \frac{a}{c}$		$\sqrt{c^2 - a^2}$		$\frac{a \sqrt{c^2 - a^2}}{2}$
A, a		$90° - A$		$a \cot A$	$\frac{a}{\sin A}$	$\frac{a^2 \cot A}{2}$
A, b		$90° - A$	$b \tan A$		$\frac{b}{\cos A}$	$\frac{b^2 \tan A}{2}$
A, c		$90° - A$	$c \sin A$	$c \cos A$		$\frac{c^2 \sin 2A}{4}$

NATURAL TRIGONOMETRIC FUNCTIONS
FOR DECIMAL FRACTIONS OF A DEGREE

Degrees	sin	cos	tan	Degrees	sin	cos	tan
0.5	0.0087	1.0000	0.0087	30.5	0.5075	0.8616	0.5890
1.0	0.0175	0.9998	0.0175	31.0	0.5150	0.8572	0.6009
1.5	0.0262	0.9997	0.0262	31.5	0.5225	0.8526	0.6128
2.0	0.0349	0.9994	0.0349	32.0	0.5299	0.8480	0.6249
2.5	0.0436	0.9990	0.0437	32.5	0.5373	0.8434	0.6371
3.0	0.0523	0.9986	0.0524	33.0	0.5446	0.8387	0.6494
3.5	0.0610	0.9981	0.0612	33.5	0.5519	0.8339	0.6619
4.0	0.0698	0.9976	0.0699	34.0	0.5592	0.8290	0.6745
4.5	0.0785	0.9969	0.0787	34.5	0.5664	0.8241	0.6873
5.0	0.0872	0.9962	0.0875	35.0	0.5736	0.8192	0.7002
5.5	0.0958	0.9954	0.0963	35.5	0.5807	0.8141	0.7133
6.0	0.1045	0.9945	0.1051	36.0	0.5878	0.8090	0.7265
6.5	0.1132	0.9936	0.1139	36.5	0.5948	0.8039	0.7400
7.0	0.1219	0.9925	0.1228	37.0	0.6018	0.7986	0.7536
7.5	0.1305	0.9914	0.1317	37.5	0.6088	0.7934	0.7673
8.0	0.1392	0.9903	0.1405	38.0	0.6157	0.7880	0.7813
8.5	0.1478	0.9890	0.1495	38.5	0.6225	0.7826	0.7954
9.0	0.1564	0.9877	0.1584	39.0	0.6293	0.7771	0.8098
9.5	0.1650	0.9863	0.1673	39.5	0.6361	0.7716	0.8243
10.0	0.1736	0.9848	0.1763	40.0	0.6428	0.7660	0.8391
10.5	0.1822	0.9833	0.1853	40.5	0.6494	0.7604	0.8541
11.0	0.1908	0.9816	0.1944	41.0	0.6561	0.7547	0.8693
11.5	0.1994	0.9799	0.2035	41.5	0.6626	0.7490	0.8847
12.0	0.2079	0.9781	0.2126	42.0	0.6691	0.7431	0.9004
12.5	0.2164	0.9763	0.2217	42.5	0.6756	0.7373	0.9163
13.0	0.2250	0.9744	0.2309	43.0	0.6820	0.7314	0.9325
13.5	0.2334	0.9724	0.2401	43.5	0.6884	0.7254	0.9490
14.0	0.2419	0.9703	0.2493	44.0	0.6947	0.7193	0.9657
14.5	0.2504	0.9681	0.2586	44.5	0.7009	0.7133	0.9827
15.0	0.2588	0.9659	0.2679	45.0	0.7071	0.7071	1.0000
15.5	0.2672	0.9636	0.2773	45.5	0.7133	0.7009	1.0176
16.0	0.2756	0.9613	0.2867	46.0	0.7193	0.6947	1.0355
16.5	0.2840	0.9588	0.2962	46.5	0.7254	0.6884	1.0538
17.0	0.2924	0.9563	0.3057	47.0	0.7314	0.6820	1.0724
17.5	0.3007	0.9537	0.3153	47.5	0.7373	0.6756	1.0913
18.0	0.3090	0.9511	0.3249	48.0	0.7431	0.6691	1.1106
18.5	0.3173	0.9483	0.3346	48.5	0.7490	0.6626	1.1303
19.0	0.3256	0.9455	0.3443	49.0	0.7547	0.6561	1.1504
19.5	0.3338	0.9426	0.3541	49.5	0.7604	0.6494	1.1708
20.0	0.3420	0.9397	0.3640	50.0	0.7660	0.6428	1.1918
20.5	0.3502	0.9367	0.3739	50.5	0.7716	0.6361	1.2131
21.0	0.3584	0.9336	0.3839	51.0	0.7771	0.6293	1.2349
21.5	0.3665	0.9304	0.3939	51.5	0.7826	0.6225	1.2572
22.0	0.3746	0.9272	0.4040	52.0	0.7880	0.6157	1.2799
22.5	0.3827	0.9239	0.4142	52.5	0.7934	0.6088	1.3032
23.0	0.3907	0.9205	0.4245	53.0	0.7986	0.6018	1.3270
23.5	0.3987	0.9171	0.4348	53.5	0.8039	0.5948	1.3514
24.0	0.4067	0.9135	0.4452	54.0	0.8090	0.5878	1.3764
24.5	0.4147	0.9100	0.4557	54.5	0.8141	0.5807	1.4019
25.0	0.4226	0.9063	0.4663	55.0	0.8192	0.5736	1.4281
25.5	0.4305	0.9026	0.4770	55.5	0.8241	0.5664	1.4550
26.0	0.4384	0.8988	0.4877	56.0	0.8290	0.5592	1.4826
26.5	0.4462	0.8949	0.4986	56.5	0.8339	0.5519	1.5108
27.0	0.4540	0.8910	0.5095	57.0	0.8387	0.5446	1.5399
27.5	0.4617	0.8870	0.5206	57.5	0.8434	0.5373	1.5697
28.0	0.4695	0.8829	0.5317	58.0	0.8480	0.5299	1.6003
28.5	0.4772	0.8788	0.5430	58.5	0.8526	0.5225	1.6319
29.0	0.4848	0.8746	0.5543	59.0	0.8572	0.5150	1.6643
29.5	0.4924	0.8704	0.5658	59.5	0.8616	0.5075	1.6977
30.0	0.5000	0.8660	0.5774	60.0	0.8660	0.5000	1.7321

DETERMINING TENSIONS IN BRIDLING LINES

Bridling with rope, chain, or cable is often used to stabilize a load when only one lifting line is available or desirable. When supporting a load with two or more bridling lines the tension in each line is *greater* than the load divided by the number of lines. This is because each bridling line pulls against the other(s) in addition to supporting its share of the load. As the angle between the bridling lines and horizontal decreases, the tension in the lines increases.

The following table provides multiplying factors used to determine the tension in each of the bridling lines. To use the table: 1) divide the load by the number of bridling lines, 2) multiply that figure by the factor listed for the angle between the bridling line and the horizontal.

For example: If there are three bridling lines, at 45° angles, supporting a 500 lb. load, each line supports $^1/_3$ of the load (166 lbs.) *plus* the "pull" from the other lines. 1) 500 lbs. + 3 = 166 lbs. 2) 166 lbs. x 1.41 (the multiplying factor of 45°) = 235 lbs.

Angle	Multiplying Factor
10°	5.76
15°	3.86
20°	2.92
25°	2.37
30°	2.00
35°	1.74
40°	1.56
45°	1.41
50°	1.31
55°	1.22
60°	1.15
65°	1.10
70°	1.064
75°	1.035
80°	1.015
85°	1.004
90°	1.000

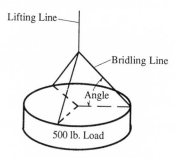

Lifting Line

Bridling Line

Angle

500 lb. Load

TO DRAW AN ELLIPSE

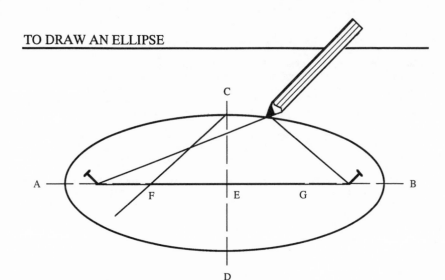

1. Draw major axis (AB) and minor axis (CD).
2. Draw arc from C using a radius that is AE long.
3. Put pins at points F & G where arc intersects axis AB.
4. Using a string FCG long, draw an ellipse by holding pencil against string.

TO DIVIDE A LINE INTO EQUAL PARTS

To divide a given line, AB, into equal sections without having to measure and calculate each section:

1. Draw line, AC, at any convenient length and angle from AB.

2. Set off equal divisions (in this case 3, marked D, E, F) along AC.

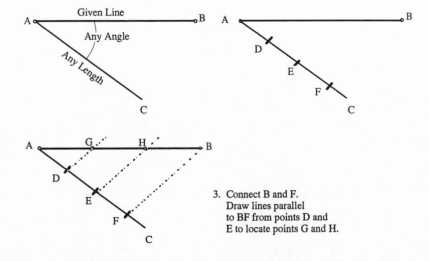

3. Connect B and F.
   Draw lines parallel
   to BF from points D and
   E to locate points G and H.

TO BISECT A LINE OR ANGLE

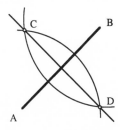
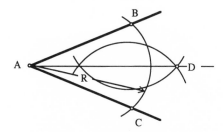

Line, AB

1. Draw two equal arcs from end points A and B, using a radius of more than half AB.
2. Draw the perpendicular bisector, CD, through the intersection points of the two arcs.

Angle, BAC

1. Locate points B and C by drawing arc from angle A using any convenient radius.
2. Locate point D by drawing two equal arcs from end points B and C, using a radius of more than half BC.
3. Draw the angle bisector through points A and D.

TO COPY AN ANGLE

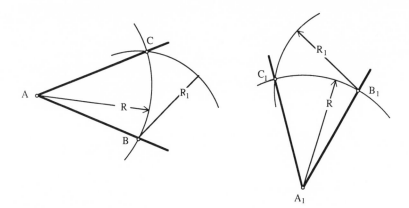

1. On given angle draw arc from A with any convenient radius R to establish points B and C.
2. Copy line AB to new location A_1B_1.
3. Draw arc with radius R from A_1 to establish B_1.
4. Draw arc with radius R_1 from B through C.
5. Draw arc with radius R_1 from B_1 which will locate point C_1.

TO DRAW A CIRCLE THROUGH THREE GIVEN POINTS

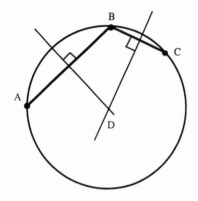

1. Connect A and B, and B and C.
2. Draw perpendicular bisectors of AB and BC using the method described in table above.
3. Draw circle with center D, through A, B, and C.

TO FIND THE CENTER OF A CIRCLE

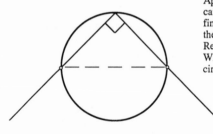

Apply a right angle to the circle as shown. A carpenter's square or a sheet of paper will do fine. Mark the points where the square crosses the circumference and connect the points. Repeat the process to get another diameter. Where the diameters cross is the center of the circle.

TO DRAW A CIRCLE IN A SQUARE

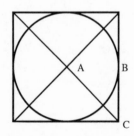

1. Find the center of the square using diagonals.
2. Draw a circle inside the square using radius AB.

Note: to draw a circle outside the square, use radius AC.

TO DRAW A PENTAGON IN A CIRCLE

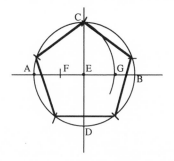

1. Draw two perpendicular lines (AB and CD) through the center of the circle (point E).
2. Bisect the line AE to find point F.
3. Using a compass, swing an arc with radius FC to establish point G.
4. Reset compass to radius CG, then beginning at C, tic off points along the perimeter of the circle.
5. Connect these points to form the pentagon.

TO DRAW A PENTAGON AROUND A CIRCLE

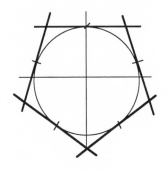

1. Repeat steps 1, 2, 3 and 4 above.
2. Draw lines tangent to the circle at the tic marks.

TO DRAW AN OCTAGON IN A CIRCLE

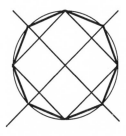

1. Draw two perpendicular lines through the center of the circle.
2. Draw a square along the centerline of these two lines.
3. Connect the four corners of the square with the four points where the perpendicular lines cross the circle.

ARCHITECTURE

•

PARTS OF A STAIRCASE

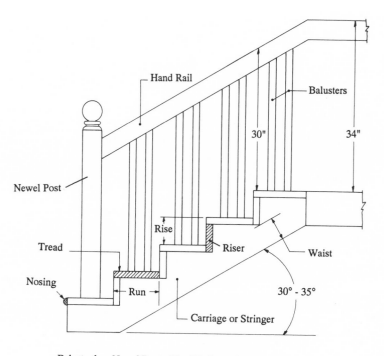

Balustrade = Newel Post + Hand Rail + Balusters

To determine the rise and run of a non-stock stair unit, first determine the height of the stair unit - this is usually equal to the distance between the upper and lower levels, although sometimes stair units are one "step" shorter than the total rise because the last step is onto the upper level. Next, divide this total rise by the ideal rise of each step - 7" is best, 6" or 8" may be used. Last, ignore any fraction and divide the total rise by this number to get the actual unit rise. (*Example*: Total rise is 7'-6": 90" divided by 7" = 12.86": 90" divided by 12" = 7.5". Thus there will be 12 risers (steps), each 7.5" high.) To find the standard tread width, subtract the unit rise (height of each step) from 17^1/$_2$. This is the unit run (width of each tread). To find the total run, multiply the unit run by the number of treads.

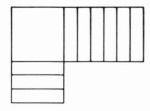
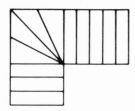

Straight   *Quarter Turn w/ Landing*   *Quarter Turn w/ Windings*

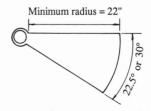

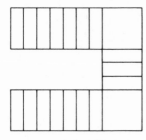

Dog Leg or 'U' Return

Tread Degree	Number of Treads in 360°	Minimum Riser Height	Headroom
22.5°	16	7^1/$_2$	7' 6"
30°	12	8^1/$_2$	6' 4"

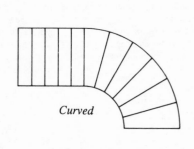

Half Turn w/ Landings

Spiral

Curved

LADDER, RAMP AND STAIR ANGLES

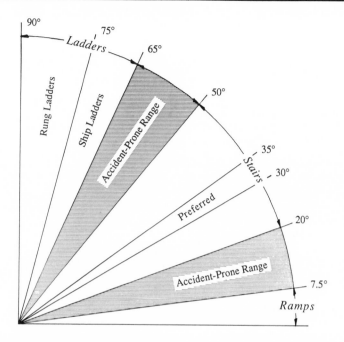

RISER AND TREAD DIMENSIONS

Rise	Tread	Pitch (angle from horizontal)
5"	12$^{1}/_{2}$"	22.00°
5$^{1}/_{4}$"	12$^{1}/_{4}$"	23.23°
5$^{1}/_{2}$"	12"	24.63°
5$^{3}/_{4}$"	11$^{3}/_{4}$"	26.00°
6"	11$^{1}/_{2}$"	27.55°
6$^{1}/_{4}$"	11$^{1}/_{4}$"	29.05°
6$^{1}/_{2}$"	11"	30.58°
6$^{3}/_{4}$"	10$^{3}/_{4}$"	32.13°
7"	10$^{1}/_{2}$"	33.68°
7$^{1}/_{4}$"	10$^{1}/_{4}$"	35.27°
7$^{1}/_{2}$"	10"	36.87°
7$^{3}/_{4}$"	9$^{3}/_{4}$"	38.48°
8"	9$^{1}/_{2}$"	40.13°
8$^{1}/_{4}$"	9$^{1}/_{4}$"	41.73°
8$^{1}/_{2}$"	9"	43.37°
8$^{3}/_{4}$"	8$^{3}/_{4}$"	45.00°
9"	8$^{1}/_{2}$"	46.63°
9$^{1}/_{4}$"	8$^{1}/_{4}$"	48.27°
9$^{1}/_{2}$"	8"	49.90°

Rule of thumb for stair dimensions:
Rise + Run = 17" to 17$^{1}/_{2}$"

Note: This table assumes Rise + Run = 17$^{1}/_{2}$"

STOCK STAIR SPECIFICATIONS

	No. of Risers	Total Rise	Total Run
6" Rise x 11^1/$_4$" Run	1	0'-6"	0'-11^1/$_4$"
	2	1'-0"	1'-10^1/$_2$"
	3	1'-6"	2'-9^3/$_4$"
	4	2'-0"	3'-9"
	5	2'-6"	4'-8^1/$_4$"
	6	3'-0"	5'-7^1/$_2$"
	7	3'-6"	6'-6^3/$_4$"
	8	4'-0"	7'-6"
	9	4'-6"	8'-5^1/$_4$"
	10	5'-0"	9'-4^1/$_2$"
	11	5'-6"	10'-3^3/$_4$"
	12	6'-0"	11'-3"
7" Rise x 10^1/$_2$" Run	1	0'-7"	0'-10^1/$_2$"
	2	1'-2"	1'-9"
	3	1'-9"	2'-7^1/$_2$"
	4	2'-4"	3'-6"
	5	2'-11"	4'-4^1/$_2$"
	6	3'-6"	5'-3"
	7	4'-1"	6'-1^1/$_2$"
	8	4'-8"	7'-0"
	9	5'-3"	7'-10^1/$_2$"
	10	5'-10"	8'-9^1/$_2$"
	11	6'-5"	9'-7^1/$_2$"
	12	7'-0"	10'-6"
8" Rise x 9^1/$_2$" Run	1	8"	0'-9^1/$_2$"
	2	1'-4"	1'-7"
	3	2'-0"	2'-4^1/$_2$"
	4	2'-8"	3'-2"
	5	3'-4"	3'-11^1/$_2$"
	6	4'-0"	4'-9"
	7	4'-8"	5'-6^1/$_2$"
	8	5'-4"	6'-4"
	9	6'-0"	7'-1^1/$_2$"
	10	6'-8"	7'-11"
	11	7'-4"	8'-8^1/$_2$"
	12	8'-0"	9'-6"

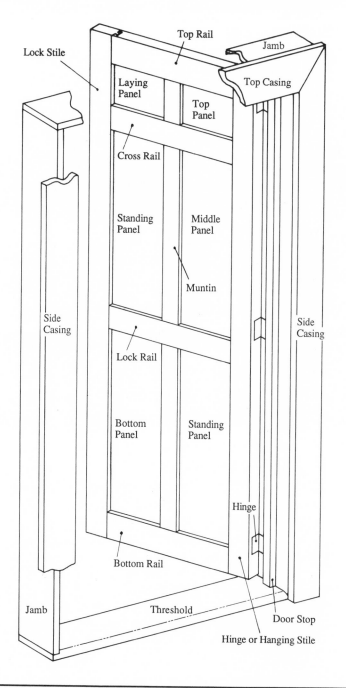

PARTS OF A WINDOW

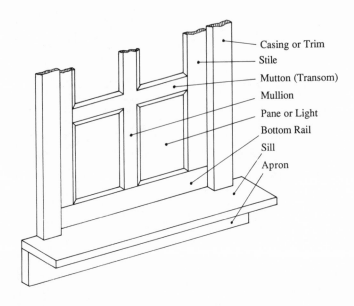

- Casing or Trim
- Stile
- Mutton (Transom)
- Mullion
- Pane or Light
- Bottom Rail
- Sill
- Apron

WINDOW TYPES

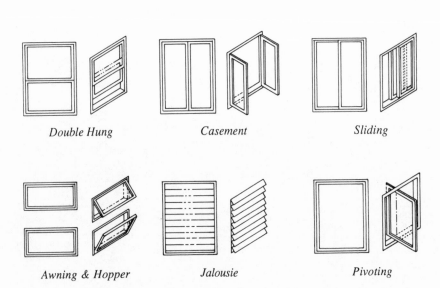

Double Hung   *Casement*   *Sliding*

Awning & Hopper   *Jalousie*   *Pivoting*

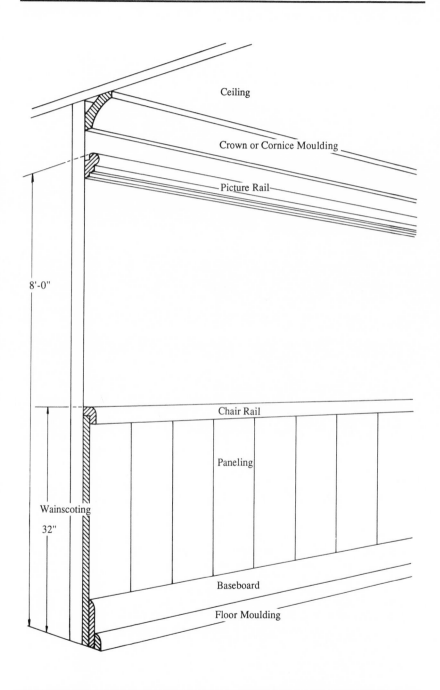

Ceiling

Crown or Cornice Moulding

Picture Rail

8'-0"

Chair Rail

Paneling

Wainscoting

32"

Baseboard

Floor Moulding

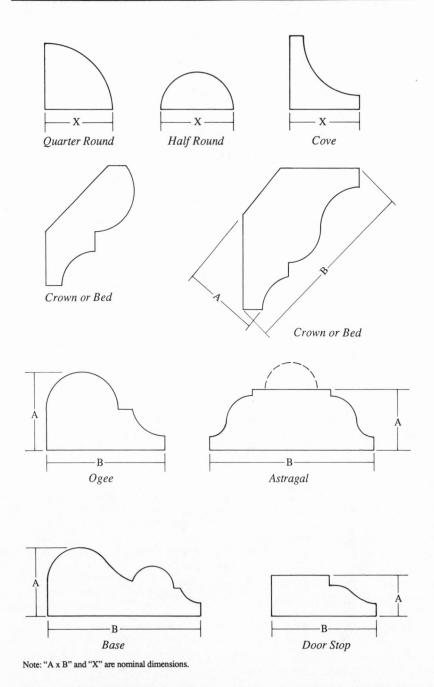

Quarter Round

Half Round

Cove

Crown or Bed

Crown or Bed

Ogee

Astragal

Base

Door Stop

Note: "A x B" and "X" are nominal dimensions.

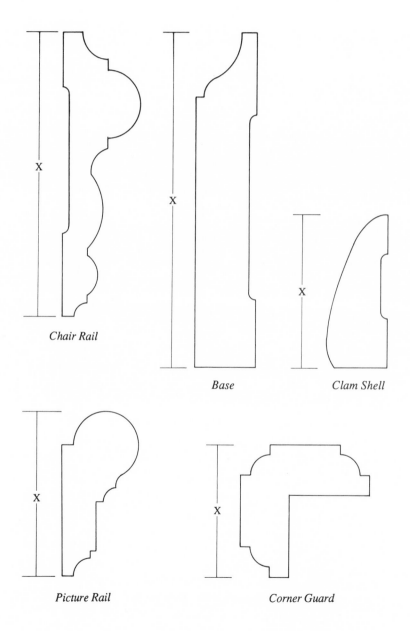

Chair Rail

Base

Clam Shell

Picture Rail

Corner Guard

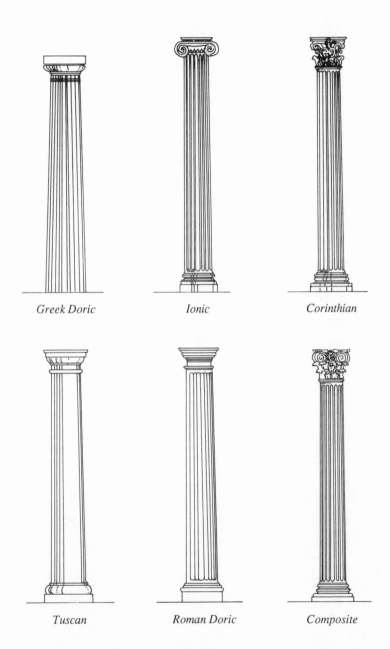

Greek Doric   Ionic   Corinthian

Tuscan   Roman Doric   Composite

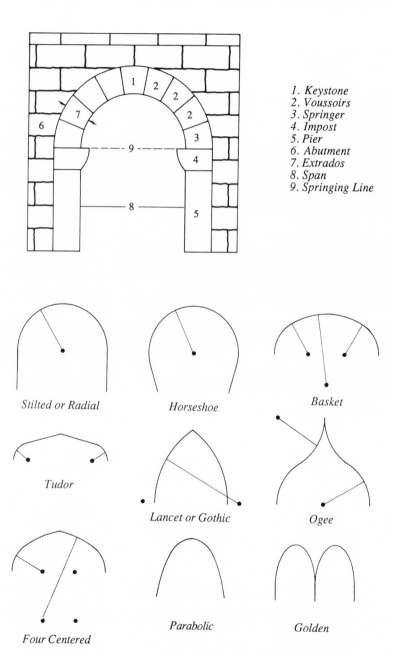

1. Keystone
2. Voussoirs
3. Springer
4. Impost
5. Pier
6. Abutment
7. Extrados
8. Span
9. Springing Line

Stilted or Radial

Horseshoe

Basket

Tudor

Lancet or Gothic

Ogee

Four Centered

Parabolic

Golden

BRICK DIMENSIONS

	Actual Size			Joint Thickness	Nominal* Size			Modular Coursing
W	H	L			W	H	L	
$3^5/_8$"	$2^1/_4$"	$7^5/_8$"		$^3/_8$"				
					4"	$2^2/_3$"	8"	3 courses = 8"
$3^1/_2$"	$2^3/_{16}$"	$7^1/_2$"		$^1/_2$"				

* The nominal size of modular brick *includes* the thickness of the mortar joint, either $^3/_8$" or $^1/_2$".

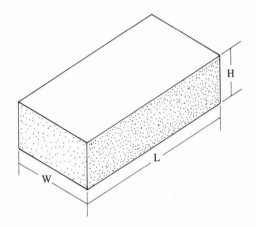

BRICK WALL PATTERNS

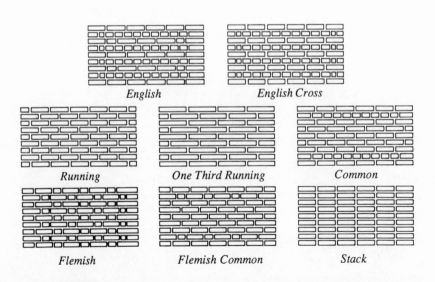

English

English Cross

Running

One Third Running

Common

Flemish

Flemish Common

Stack

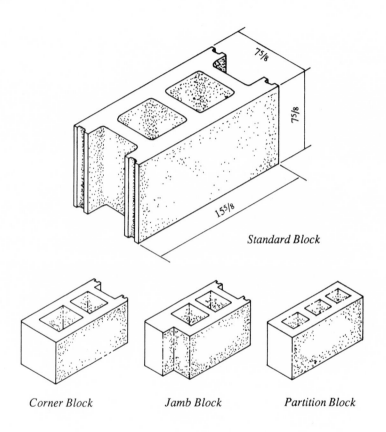

75/8

75/8

15 5/8

Standard Block

Corner Block   *Jamb Block*   *Partition Block*

PITCHED ROOF TYPES

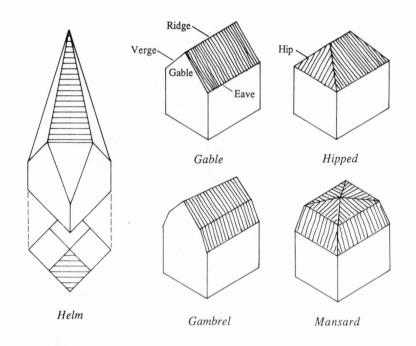

Helm

Gable

Hipped

Gambrel

Mansard

SHINGLE PATTERNS

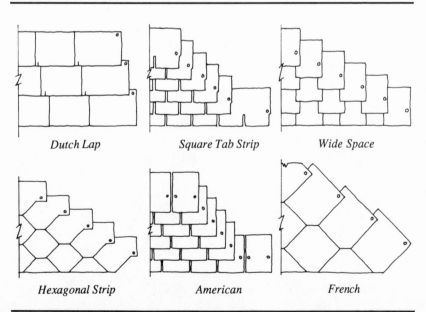

Dutch Lap

Square Tab Strip

Wide Space

Hexagonal Strip

American

French

DRAFTING PROJECTIONS OF SQUARE CUBES

Oblique Projection
Face is in true size and shape. Angle *x* is usually 30 degrees or 45 degrees; in this case it is 30 degrees.

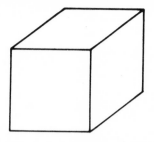

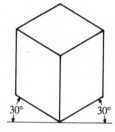

Isometric Projection
"Equal Measure" - three principal faces of the object are equally inclined to the plane of projection; typically 30 degrees.

Axiometric Projection
"30/60 Degrees" - one face of drawing inclined 30 degrees and one 60 degrees.

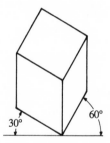

PENCIL GRADES

Hard	9H	8H	7H	6H	5H	4H
Medium	3H	2H	H	F	HB	B
Soft	2B	3B	4B	5B	6B	7B

DRAFTING PAPER STANDARD SIZES

Size	Dimensions inches	Size	Dimensions millimeters (mm)	inches
A	8^1/$_2$ x 11	A0	841 x 1189	33^7/$_{64}$ x 46^{13}/$_{16}$
B	11 x 17	A1	594 x 841	23^{25}/$_{64}$ x 33^7/$_{64}$
C	17 x 22	A2	420 x 594	16^{17}/$_{32}$ x 23^{25}/$_{64}$
D	22 x 34	A3	297 x 420	11^{11}/$_{16}$ x 16^{17}/$_{32}$
E	34 x 44	A4	210 x 297	8^{17}/$_{64}$ x 11^{11}/$_{16}$
		A5	148 x 210	5^{53}/$_{64}$ x 8^{17}/$_{64}$
		A6	105 x 148	4^9/$_{64}$ x 5^{53}/$_{64}$

RISE PER INCH/DEGREE ANGLE CONVERSIONS

Rise (per foot)	Angle	Formula
$^1/_8$"	0.6°	Rise (in inches) divided by 12 = *tan* of angle
$^1/_4$"	1.2°	
$^1/_2$"	2.4°	
$^3/_4$"	3.6°	
1"	4.8°	

Angle	Rise (per foot)		Formula
1°	.21"	($^7/_{32}$")	*Tan* of angle multiplied by 12 = rise (in inches/ft.)
5°	1.05"	($1^3/_{64}$")	
10°	2.1156"	($2^7/_{32}$")	
15°	3.2148"	($3^7/_{32}$")	
30°	6.9288"	($6^{59}/_{64}$")	
45°	12.0"	(1' 0")	

METRIC / IMPERIAL ARCHITECT'S SCALE CONVERSIONS

To Convert	To	Multiply By		To Convert	To	Multiply By
$^1/_4$" scale	1:50 scale	.96		1:50 scale	$^1/_4$" scale	1.042
$^1/_8$" scale	1:100 scale	.96		1:100 scale	$^1/_8$" scale	1.042

Example: If a drawing is in 1:50 scale, measure the dimensions with a $^1/_4$" scale rule and multiply the results by 1.042.

PHOTOCOPYING

------------ *Enlargements* ------------			------------ *Reductions* ------------		
Desired % **of Original**	Copy At	No. Times	**Desired %** **of Original**	Copy At	No. Times
150%	122.5%	2	10%	75%	8
175%	132.3%	2	25%	70.71%	4
200%	141.4%	2	33%	69.35%	3
225%	150.0%	2	50%	70.71%	2
250%	158.1%	2	75%	75%	1
250%	135.7%	3	100%	100%	1
275%	165.8%	2			
275%	140.1%	3			
300%	173.2%	2			
300%	144.3%	3			
300%	131.7%	4			

STANDARD DIMENSIONS

	Height	*Width*	*Depth/Length*
Kitchen			
Base cabinets			
(from floor, incl. countertops)	36"	---	25"
Kickspace	4"	---	4"-6"
Over countertop to upper cabs.	18"	---	---
Upper cabinets	18"-42"	---	15"
Dishwasher	36"	---	
Oven	36"	---	28"-30"
Refrigerator	61"	28"	28"-30"
Sink - single or double	36"	---	28"-30"
Bathroom			
Bathtub	---	30"-33"	60"-66"
Curtain rod	78"	---	---
Medicine cabinet (from floor)	48"-54"	---	---
Shower head	74"	---	---
Sinks	31"-36"	---	---
Tiling ($4^1/4$"x $4^1/4$")			
-room walls, plus trim	10 tiles		
-tub area, plus trim	16 tiles		
Doors			
Door bell	45"	---	---
Door hinges: top	9" below top of door		
center	centered between hinges		
bottom	10" above bottom of door		
Doorknob	38"		
Doors (standard sizes)	6'-8"	2'-6"	$1^3/4$"
	7'-0"	2'-8"	$1^3/4$"
	7'-0"	2'-10"	$1^3/4$"
	7'-0"	3'-0"	$1^3/4$"
Beds (mattresses)			
-Single (twin)	20"-21"	39"	75"
-Double (full)	20"-21"	54"	75"
-Queen	20"-21"	60"	80"
-King	20"-21"	72"-76"	80"-84"
Pianos			
-Grand, apartment	3'-6"	3'-8"	4'-0"
-Grand, baby	3'-6"	4'-10"	5'-4"
-Grand, parlour	3'-6"	5'-0"	5'-10"
-Grand, concert	3'-6"	5'-4"	9'-0"
-Upright, apartment	3'-6"	5'-4"	2'-0" - 2'-4"
-Upright, regular	4'-3" - 4'-7"	5'-1"	2'-0" - 2'-4"
-Bench	1'-7"	2'-6"	1'-2"
Misc. Architecture & Furniture			
Bar stool	24"-25"		
Chair: seat	18"	14"-16"	---
back	30"-34"	14"-16"	---
Closet rod	5'-3"	---	---
Desk	30"-32"		
Light switch	48"	---	---
Table	30"	---	---
Wainscoting	30"-32"	---	---
Work bench	32"-34"	---	---

STANDARD DOOR HARDWARE LOCATIONS

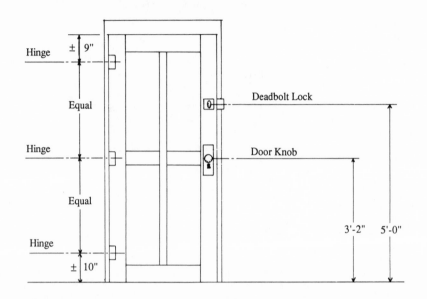

FURNITURE LEGS

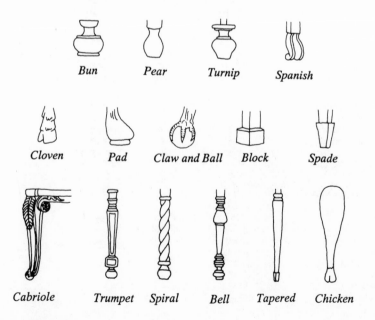

Bun   Pear   Turnip   Spanish

Cloven   Pad   Claw and Ball   Block   Spade

Cabriole   Trumpet   Spiral   Bell   Tapered   Chicken

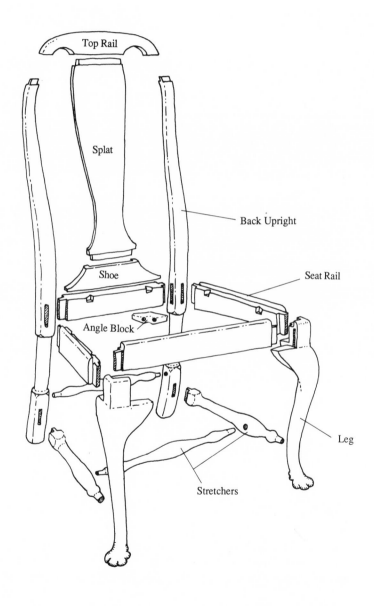

Top Rail

Splat

Back Upright

Shoe

Seat Rail

Angle Block

Leg

Stretchers

THEATRE

(Rear Of Stage)

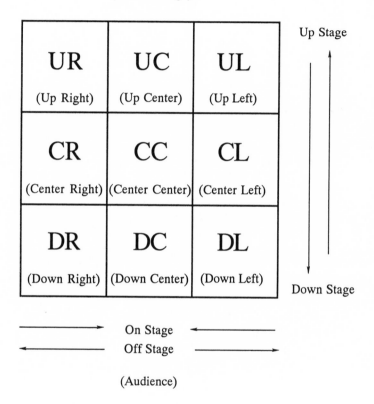

Up Stage

UR (Up Right)	UC (Up Center)	UL (Up Left)
CR (Center Right)	CC (Center Center)	CL (Center Left)
DR (Down Right)	DC (Down Center)	DL (Down Left)

Down Stage

On Stage

Off Stage

(Audience)

Stage-right (SR) and stage-left (SL) are from the performer's view point when facing the audience.

In film and television, directions are commonly given as "camera right" and "camera left" which, being from the camera point of view, are exactly opposite stage directions.

Up-stage (US) is toward the rear of the theatre. Down-stage is toward the audience. Stages built before the 1900's where often "raked" or tilted higher at the rear; thus "up"-stage.

Proscenium Stage

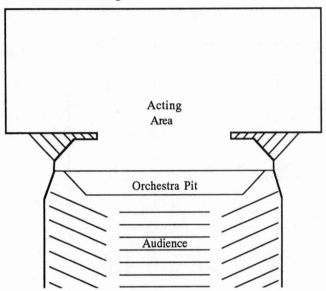

Thrust Stage

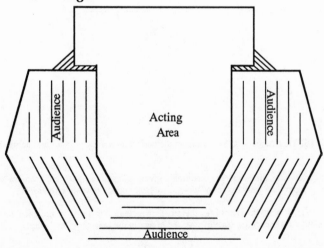

Flexible Stage Or Black Box

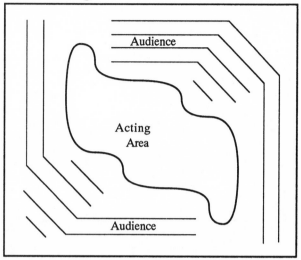

Note: Black Box theatres are empty spaces in which the audience configuration and acting area can be rearranged to suit the needs of the production.

Arena Stage Or Theatre-In-The-Round

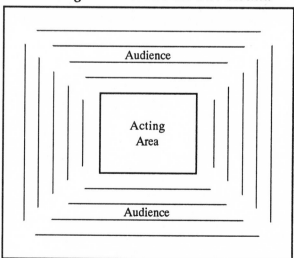

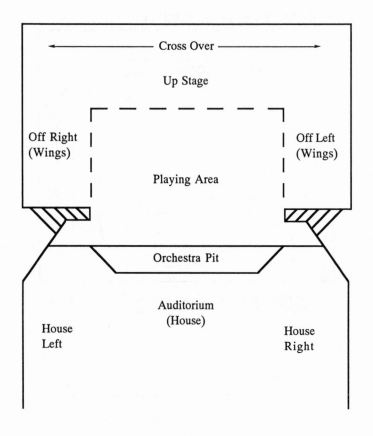

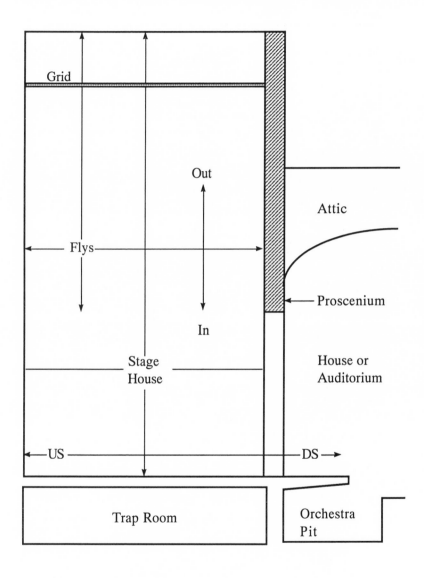

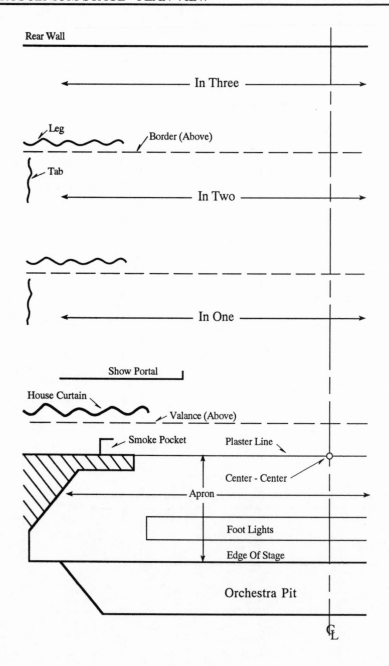

PROSCENIUM STAGE - SECTION VIEW

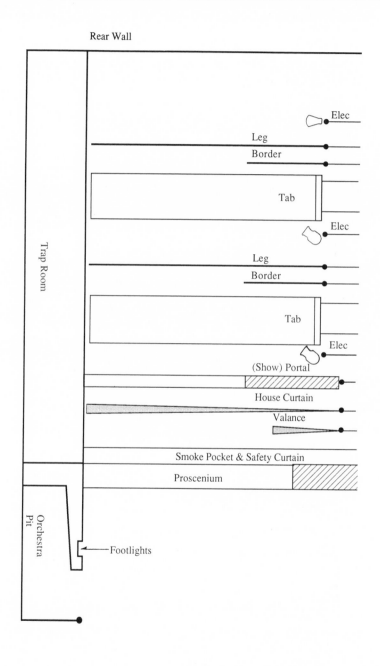

COUNTERWEIGHT SYSTEM - FRONT ELEVATION

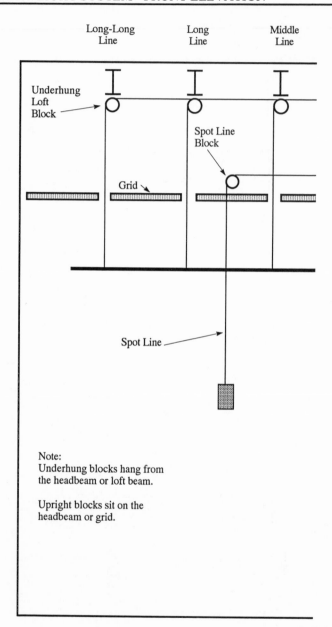

Long-Long
Line

Long
Line

Middle
Line

Underhung
Loft
Block

Spot Line
Block

Grid

Spot Line

Note:
Underhung blocks hang from
the headbeam or loft beam.

Upright blocks sit on the
headbeam or grid.

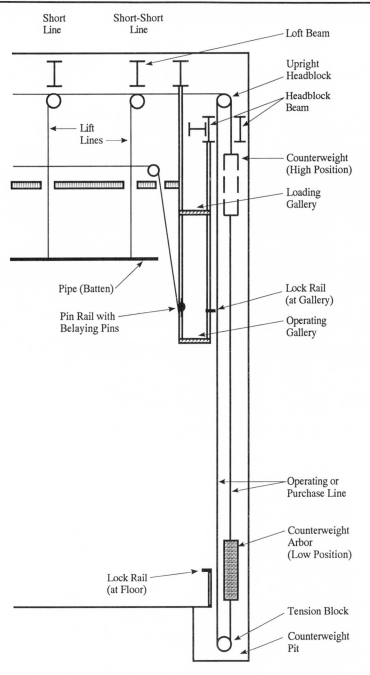

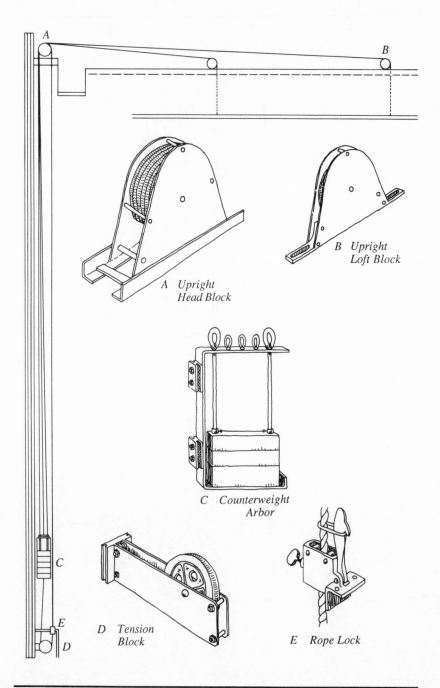

A Upright
Head Block

B Upright
Loft Block

C Counterweight
Arbor

D Tension
Block

E Rope Lock

TYPES OF COUNTERWEIGHT LINE SETS

Standard

1/4" Wire Rope
Lift Lines
Pipe
Combination Lift and Operating Lines
3/4" Hemp Operating Line

- Counterweight equals scenery weight.
- Operating line travel equals pipe travel.
- Distance from head block to tension block (minus the length of the arbor and fittings) is approximately equal to pipe travel.

Double Purchase

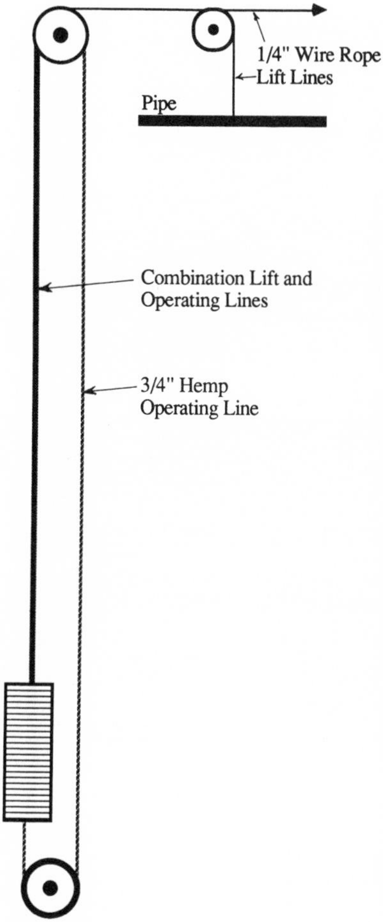

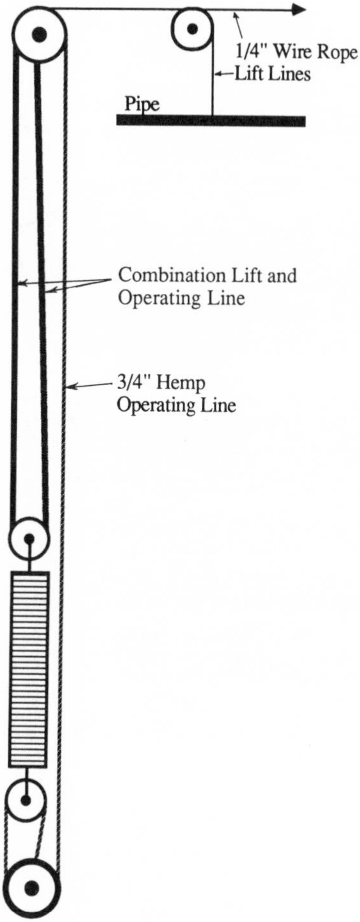

1/4" Wire Rope
Lift Lines
Pipe
Combination Lift and Operating Line
3/4" Hemp Operating Line

- Counterweight equals two times scenery weight.
- Operating line travel equals pipe travel equals two times arbor travel.
- Distance from head block to tension block (minus the length of the arbor and fittings) is approximately equal to one-half pipe travel.

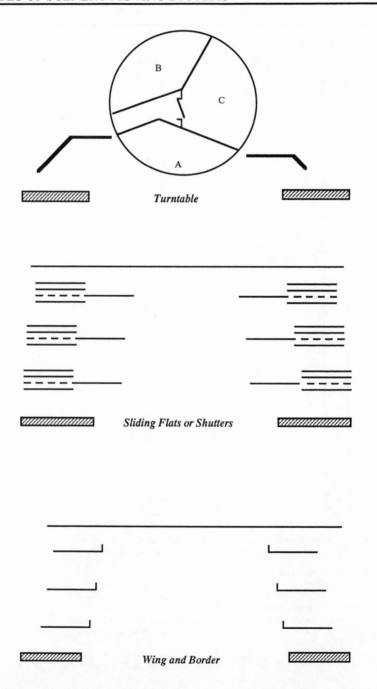

Turntable

Sliding Flats or Shutters

Wing and Border

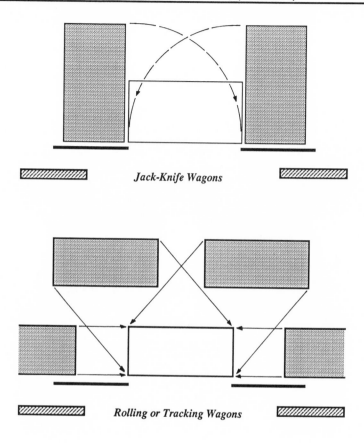

Jack-Knife Wagons

Rolling or Tracking Wagons

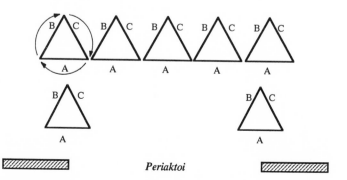

Periaktoi

Line Types

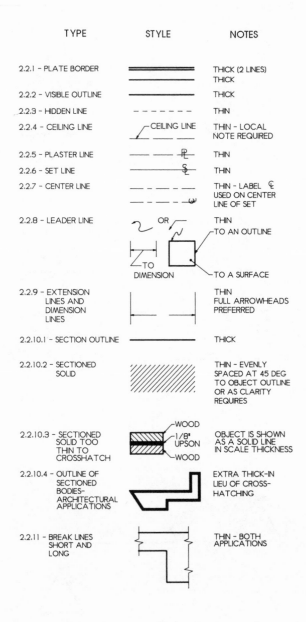

TYPE	STYLE	NOTES
2.2.1 – PLATE BORDER		THICK (2 LINES) / THICK
2.2.2 – VISIBLE OUTLINE		THICK
2.2.3 – HIDDEN LINE		THIN
2.2.4 – CEILING LINE	CEILING LINE	THIN – LOCAL NOTE REQUIRED
2.2.5 – PLASTER LINE	P̶L̶	THIN
2.2.6 – SET LINE	S̶	THIN
2.2.7 – CENTER LINE		THIN – LABEL ℄ USED ON CENTER LINE OF SET
2.2.8 – LEADER LINE	OR / TO DIMENSION	THIN / TO AN OUTLINE / TO A SURFACE
2.2.9 – EXTENSION LINES AND DIMENSION LINES		THIN FULL ARROWHEADS PREFERRED
2.2.10.1 – SECTION OUTLINE		THICK
2.2.10.2 – SECTIONED SOLID		THIN – EVENLY SPACED AT 45 DEG TO OBJECT OUTLINE OR AS CLARITY REQUIRES
2.2.10.3 – SECTIONED SOLID TOO THIN TO CROSSHATCH	WOOD / 1/8" UPSON / WOOD	OBJECT IS SHOWN AS A SOLID LINE IN SCALE THICKNESS
2.2.10.4 – OUTLINE OF SECTIONED BODIES– ARCHITECTURAL APPLICATIONS		EXTRA THICK–IN LIEU OF CROSS-HATCHING
2.2.11 – BREAK LINES SHORT AND LONG		THIN – BOTH APPLICATIONS

Line Types (continued)

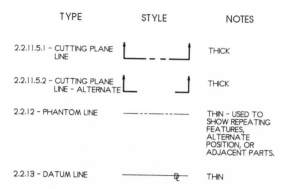

TYPE	STYLE	NOTES
2.2.11.5.1 – CUTTING PLANE LINE		THICK
2.2.11.5.2 – CUTTING PLANE LINE – ALTERNATE		THICK
2.2.12 – PHANTOM LINE		THIN – USED TO SHOW REPEATING FEATURES, ALTERNATE POSITION, OR ADJACENT PARTS.
2.2.13 – DATUM LINE		THIN

Hardware Symbols In Elevation

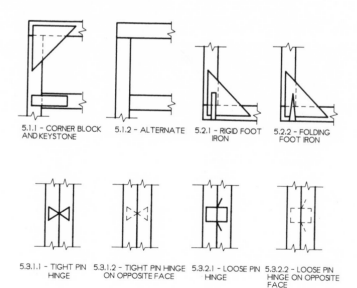

5.1.1 – CORNER BLOCK AND KEYSTONE   5.1.2 – ALTERNATE   5.2.1 – RIGID FOOT IRON   5.2.2 – FOLDING FOOT IRON

5.3.1.1 – TIGHT PIN HINGE   5.3.1.2 – TIGHT PIN HINGE ON OPPOSITE FACE   5.3.2.1 – LOOSE PIN HINGE   5.3.2.2 – LOOSE PIN HINGE ON OPPOSITE FACE

Hardware Symbols In Elevation (continued)

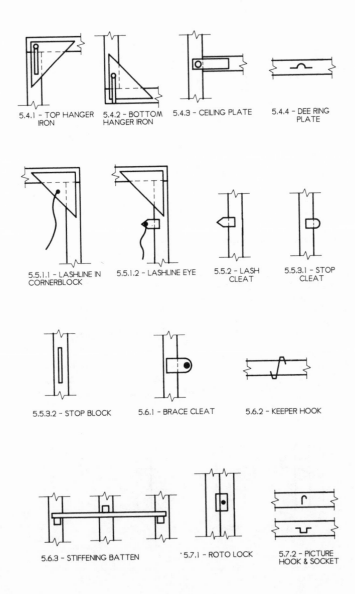

5.4.1 – TOP HANGER IRON

5.4.2 – BOTTOM HANGER IRON

5.4.3 – CEILING PLATE

5.4.4 – DEE RING PLATE

5.5.1.1 – LASHLINE IN CORNERBLOCK

5.5.1.2 – LASHLINE EYE

5.5.2 – LASH CLEAT

5.5.3.1 – STOP CLEAT

5.5.3.2 – STOP BLOCK

5.6.1 – BRACE CLEAT

5.6.2 – KEEPER HOOK

5.6.3 – STIFFENING BATTEN

· 5.7.1 – ROTO LOCK

5.7.2 – PICTURE HOOK & SOCKET

Dimensioning

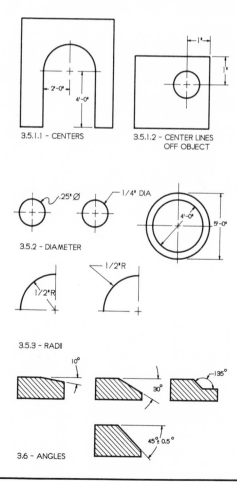

3.4 - ALL OF THE ABOVE FOR CROWDED DIMENSIONS ONLY

3.5.1.1 - CENTERS

3.5.1.2 - CENTER LINES
OFF OBJECT

3.5.2 - DIAMETER

3.5.3 - RADII

3.6 - ANGLES

Scenery Symbols In Plan

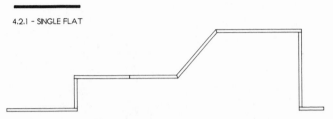

4.2.1 - SINGLE FLAT

THE DRAWING ABOVE ILLUSTRATES THE DERIVATION OF THE RESPECTIVE PARTIAL
GROUNDPLAN BELOW.

4.2.1.1 - FLAT JOINTS/DIVISIONS
NOTE: SOME DETAILS ENLARGED FOR CLARITY.

4.2.2.1 - ARCHWAY

4.2.2.2 - DOORWAY
(SHUTTER DRAWN AS
IT WILL BE HUNG)

4.2.2.3 - WINDOW
(SHOW MUNTINS AND
MULLIONS OF
WINDOW AS
DESIGNED)

4.2.2.4 - FLAT WITH
SLIDING DOOR

4.2.2.5 - FLAT WITH
DOUBLE ACTING
DOOR

4.2.2.6 - FLAT WITH
CASEMENT WINDOW
(SHOW MUNTINS AND
MULLIONS OF WINDOW
AS DESIGNED)

Note: Line thicknesses are exaggerated for comparison purposes.

Scenery Symbols In Plan (continued)

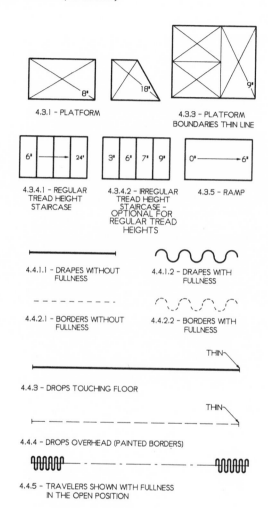

4.3.1 - PLATFORM

4.3.3 - PLATFORM BOUNDARIES THIN LINE

4.3.4.1 - REGULAR TREAD HEIGHT STAIRCASE

4.3.4.2 - IRREGULAR TREAD HEIGHT STAIRCASE - OPTIONAL FOR REGULAR TREAD HEIGHTS

4.3.5 - RAMP

4.4.1.1 - DRAPES WITHOUT FULLNESS

4.4.1.2 - DRAPES WITH FULLNESS

4.4.2.1 - BORDERS WITHOUT FULLNESS

4.4.2.2 - BORDERS WITH FULLNESS

4.4.3 - DROPS TOUCHING FLOOR

4.4.4 - DROPS OVERHEAD (PAINTED BORDERS)

4.4.5 - TRAVELERS SHOWN WITH FULLNESS IN THE OPEN POSITION

Lettering

ABCDEFGHIJKLMNO
PQRSTUVWXYZ
0123456789

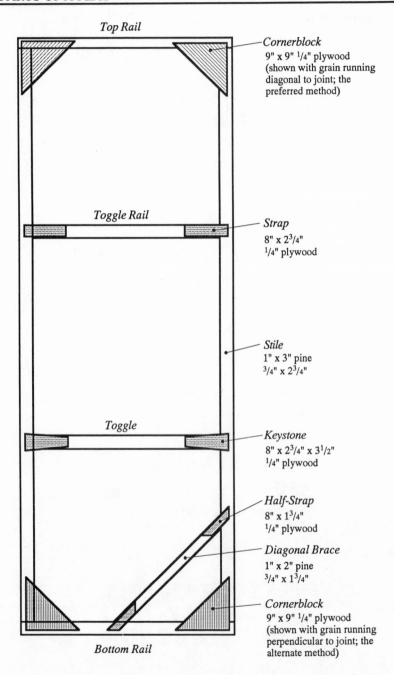

Top Rail

Cornerblock
9" x 9" 1/4" plywood
(shown with grain running
diagonal to joint; the
preferred method)

Toggle Rail

Strap
8" x 2 3/4"
1/4" plywood

Stile
1" x 3" pine
3/4" x 2 3/4"

Toggle

Keystone
8" x 2 3/4" x 3 1/2"
1/4" plywood

Half-Strap
8" x 1 3/4"
1/4" plywood

Diagonal Brace
1" x 2" pine
3/4" x 1 3/4"

Cornerblock
9" x 9" 1/4" plywood
(shown with grain running
perpendicular to joint; the
alternate method)

Bottom Rail

CORNERBLOCK, KEYSTONE, STRAP, AND HALF-STRAP DIMENSIONS AND CUTTING YIELDS

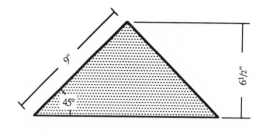

Cornerblock

Yield: 90 per 4' x 8' sheet of plywood.
Rip 6$\frac{1}{2}$" strips along 8' side, then cross-cut at 45° angles.

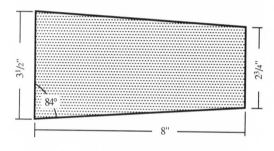

Keystone

Yield: 143 per 4' x 8' sheet of plywood.
Rip 8" strips along 8' side, then cross-cut at 84° angles.

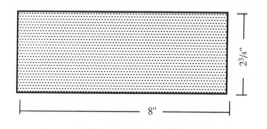

Strap

Yield: 192 per 4' x 8' sheet of plywood.
Rip 2$\frac{3}{4}$" strips along 8' side, then cross-cut 8" pieces.

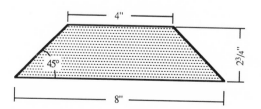

Half-Strap

Yield: 350 per 4' x 8' sheet of plywood.
Rip 1$\frac{3}{4}$" strips along 8' side, then cross-cut at 45° angles.

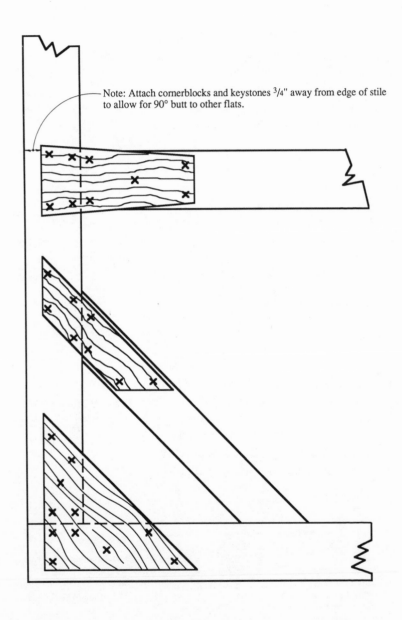

Note: Attach cornerblocks and keystones $3/4$" away from edge of stile to allow for 90° butt to other flats.

HARD COVERED FLATS - STAGE

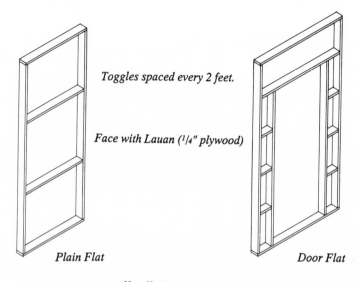

Toggles spaced every 2 feet.

Face with Lauan ($^1/_4$" plywood)

Plain Flat

Door Flat

Note: Hard covered flats are sometimes called "Hollywoods."

HARD COVERED FLATS - FILM

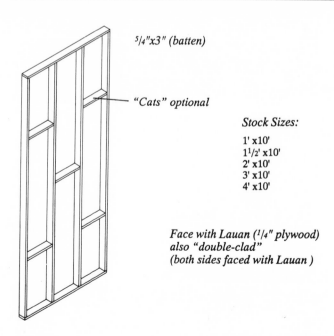

$^5/_4$"x3" (batten)

"Cats" optional

Stock Sizes:

1' x10'
1$^1/_2$' x10'
2' x10'
3' x10'
4' x10'

*Face with Lauan ($^1/_4$" plywood)
also "double-clad"
(both sides faced with Lauan)*

TYPES OF HOUSE CURTAINS

The four most common types of house or front curtains are described below.

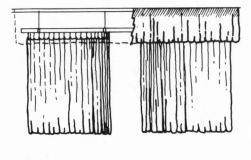

The Traveler or Draw curtain is the most common. It opens and closes horizontally. If hung on a batten, it can be flown out as well. When flown, it is sometimes called a bounce or guillotine curtain.

The Tableau or Tab consists of two overlapping panels. It is opened by pulling the lower inside corners diagonally upward and outward.

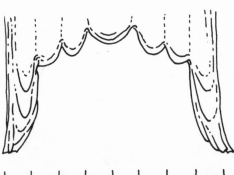

The Venetian, Profile or Contour curtain consists of a single pleated panel which can be opened to various heights and configurations because the vertical pull ropes are individually adjustable.

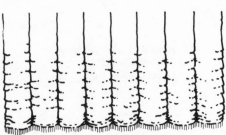

The Austrian curtain is also raised by multiple vertical riggings. Permanent swagging pleats are sewn between the riggings and the bottom edge is often trimmed in fancy fringe or tassels.

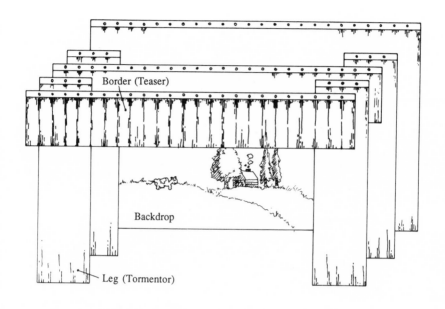

Border (Teaser)

Backdrop

Leg (Tormentor)

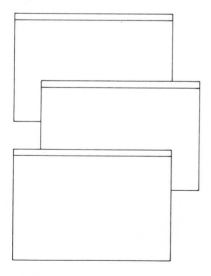

Bounce - Used to "bounce" the light onto the back of a scrim or translucent. A bounce is usually made of canvas or muslin.

Plastic - Used behind a scrim or translucent drop to soften and even the lighting from strip-lights.

Scrim - Used to provide a painted scenic, or neutral background that can be lit so as to appear either opaque or translucent. Also used to give a sense of depth.

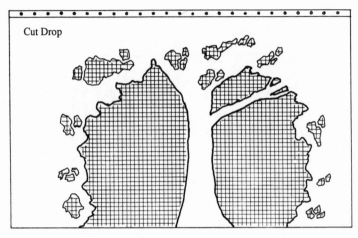

Cut Drop

Cut Border

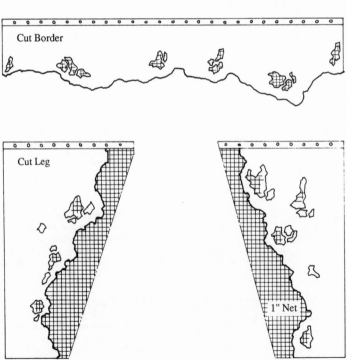

Cut Leg

1" Net

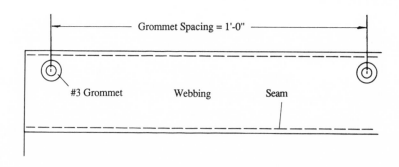

Standard Drop Specifications:

3" jute webbing at top.

#3 grommets on 1'-0" centers (from center).
Black tie lines 3'-0" in length.
White tie line at centerline of drop.

#140 weight, flame-proofed, muslin, sewn horizontally.

¹/₂" pipe pocket and skirt at bottom.
Skirt extends 1' below pocket.

Drop is 6" wider at bottom (to help counteract hourglass effect).

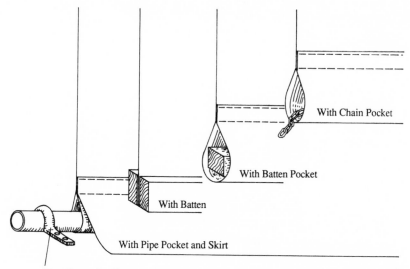

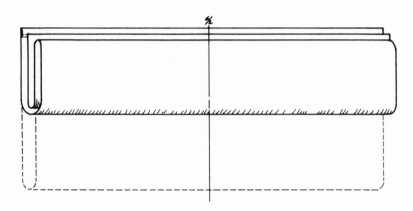

1. With drop on its back, fold bottom up to the top (webbing). Repeat until drop is folded to a $2^1/2'$ to 4' strip.

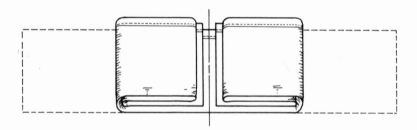

2. Fold side ends in to 4" from the center. Repeat until folds are $2^1/2'$ to 4' wide.

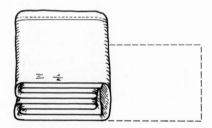

3. Fold one side over onto the other half. Note that the name and dimensions of the drop (written on the webbing) will be visible when the drop is folded in this manner.

ORDER OF TACKING DROPS FOR PAINTING

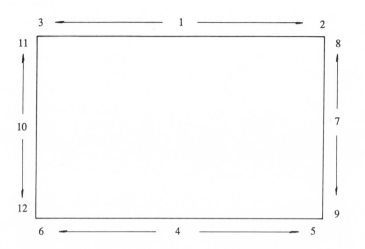

ROLL OR "OLIO" DROP

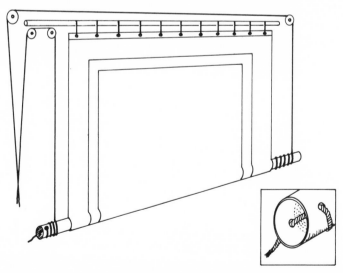

As the drop rolls down (unwinds), the ropes are wound around the bottom pipe. Pulling on the end of the ropes unwinds them thereby rolling up the drop. Half the weight of the drop is supported by the rope and the other half by the drop itself. The tube is usually 6" to 8" diameter plastic pipe.

CONVERSIONS

Multiply	By	To get	Converse: Mulitply by
Acres	0.4047	Hectares	2.471
Acres	43,560	Square feet	0.00002295
Acres	4047	Square metres	0.0002471
Acres	0.001563	Square miles	640
Acres	4840	Square yards	0.0002066
Atmospheres	76.0	Centimeters of mercury	0.01316
Atmospheres	29.92	Inches of mercury	0.03342
Atmospheres	33.90	Feet of water	0.02949
Atmospheres	10,332	Kilograms/sq. metre	0.00009678
Atmospheres	14.70	Pounds/sq. inch	0.06803
Barrels (oil)	42	Gallons (oil)	0.02381
Board feet	144	Cubic inches	0.006944
BTUs	778.26	Foot - pounds	0.001285
BTUs	107.5	Kilogram - metres	0.009302
BTUs	0.0002928	Kilowatt - hours	3414.4
BTU/min.	12.96	Foot-pounds/sec	0.07716
BTU/min.	0.02356	Horsepower	42.44
BTU/min.	0.01757	Kilowatts	56.907
BTU/min.	17.57	Watts	0.05692
Centigrade	*	Farenheit	*
Centigrams	0.01	Grams	100
Centilitres	0.01	Litres	100
Centimeters	0.01	Meters	100
Centimeters	0.3937	Inches	2.54

* Look under "Temp." in this table. See also page 161.

Multiply	By	To get	Converse: Mulitply by
Centimeters/sec.	1.969	Feet/min.	0.5079
Centimeters/sec.	0.03281	Feet/sec.	30.48
Centimeters/sec.	0.03600	Kilometers/hr.	27.7778
Centimeters/sec.	0.6	Meters/hr.	1.6667
Centimeters/sec.	0.02237	Miles/hr.	44.70
Centimeters/sec.	0.0003728	Miles/min.	2682
Centimeters/sec./sec.	0.03281	Feet/sec./sec.	30.48
Cubic centimeters	0.00003510	Cubic feet	28,490.0285
Cubic centimeters	0.06102	Cubic inches	16.39
Cubic centimeters	0.000001	Cubic meters	1,000,000
Cubic centimeters	0.0002642	Gallons	37.85
Cubic centimeters	0.0009999	Liters	1,000
Cubic centimeters	0.001057	Quarts (liq.)	946.0738
Cubic feet	1728	Cubic inches	0.0005787
Cubic feet	0.02832	Cubic meters	35.31
Cubic feet	0.03704	Cubic yards	27
Cubic feet	7.48052	Gallons	0.1337
Cubic Feet	28.32	Liters	0.03531
Cubic feet	59.84	Pints (liq.)	0.01671
Cubic feet	29.92	Quarts (liq.)	0.03342
Cubic feet/min.	472.0	Cubic cms./sec.	0.002119
Cubic feet/min.	0.1247	Gallons/sec.	8.0192
Cubic feet/min.	0.4719	Liters/sec.	2.1191
Cubic feet/min	62.43	Pounds of water/min	0.01602
Cubic feet/sec.	0.6463	Millions gals./day	1.5472
Cubic feet/sec.	448.831	Gallons/min.	0.002228
Cubic inches	0.00001639	Cubic meters	61,023
Cubic inches	0.00002143	Cubic yards	46,656
Cubic inches	0.004329	Gallons	231
Cubic inches	0.01639	Liters	61.02
Cubic inches	0.03463	Pints (liq.)	28.8767
Cubic inches	0.01732	Quarts (liq.)	57.7367
Cubic meters	1.308	Cubic yards	0.7646
Cubic meters	264.2	Gallons	0.003785
Cubic meters	999.97	Liters	0.001000
Cubic meters	1,057	Quarts (liq.)	0.0009461
Cubic yards	202.0	Gallons	0.004951
Cubic yards	764.5	Liters	0.001308
Cubic yards	1616	Pints (liq.)	0.0006188
Cubic yards	807.9	Quarts (liq.)	0.001238
Decigrams	0.1	Grams	10
Deciliters	0.1	Liters	10
Decimeters	0.1	Meters	10

Multiply	By	To get	Converse: Mulitply by
Degrees (angle)	60	Minutes	0.0167
Degrees (angle)	0.01745	Radians	57.30
Degrees (angle)	3600	Seconds	0.0002778
Degrees/sec.	0.01745	Radians/sec.	57.30
Degrees/sec.	0.1667	Revolutions/min.	6
Degrees/sec.	0.002778	Revoluton/sec.	360
Dekagrams	10	Grams	0.1
Dekaliters	10	Liers	0.1
Dekameters	10	Meters	0.1
Farenheit	*	Centigrade	*
Fathoms	6	Feet	0.1667
Feet	12	Inches	0.0833
Feet	0.3048	Meters	3.281
Feet	0.3333	Yards	3
Feet of water	0.8826	Inches of mercury	1.133
Feet of water	304.8	Kilograms/sq. meter	0.003281
Feet of water	62.43	Pounds/sq. ft.	0.01601
Feet of water	0.4335	Pounds/sq. inch	2.307
Feet/min.	0.01667	Feet/sec.	60
Feet/min.	0.01829	Kilometers/hr.	54.68
Feet/min.	0.3048	Meters/min.	3.281
Feet/min.	0.01136	Miles/hr.	88
Feet/sec.	1.097	Kilometers/hr.	0.9133
Feet/sec.	0.5924	Knots	1.6880
Feet/sec.	18.29	Meters/min.	0.05468
Feet/sec.	0.6818	Miles/hr.	1.467
Feet/sec.	0.01136	Miles/min.	88
Feet/sec./sec.	0.3048	Meters/sec./sec.	3.2808
Footcandles	10.76391	Lux	0.0929
Foot-pounds	0.0003240	Kilogram-calories	3,086
Foot-pounds	0.1383	Kilogram-meters	7.231
Foot-pounds/min.	0.01667	Foot-pounds/sec.	59.9880
Foot-pounds/min.	0.00003030	Horsepower	33,000
Foot-pounds/min.	0.00002260	Kilowatts	44,250
Foot-pounds/sec.	0.001818	Horsepower	550
Foot-pounds/sec.	0.001356	Kilowatts	737.6
Gallons	3.785	Liters	0.2642
Gallons	8	Pints (liq.)	0.1250
Gallons	4	Quarts (liq.)	0.2500

* Look under "Temp." in this table. See also page 161.

Multiply	By	To get	Converse: Mulitply by
Gallons, Imperial	1.20095	U.S. gallons	0.08327
Gallons of water	8.345	Pounds of water	0.1198
Gallons/min.	0.06308	Liters/sec.	15.8529
Grams	0.001	Kilograms	1,000
Grams	1,000	Milligrams	0.001
Grams	0.03527	Ounces	28.3495
Grams	0.002205	Pounds	453.5924
Grams/cm.	0.005599	Pounds/inch	178.58
Grams/cu. cm.	62.43	Pounds/cubic foot	0.01602
Grams/cu. cm.	0.03613	Pounds/cubic inch	27.68
Grams/liter	0.06242	Pounds/cubic foot	16.0205
Grams/liter	1,000	Parts/million	0.001
Hectograms	100	Grams	0.01
Hectoliters	100	Liters	0.01
Hectometers	100	Meters	0.01
Hectowatts	100	Watts	0.01
Horsepower	42.44	B.T.U./min.	0.02356
Horsepower	1.014	Horsepower (metric)	0.9862
Horsepower	10.547	Kilogram.- cal./min.	0.09481
Horsepower	0.7457	Kilowatts	1.3410
Horsepower	745.7	Watts	0.001341
Horsepower-hours	0.7457	Kilowatt-hours	1.3410
Inches	2.540	Centimeters	0.3937
Inches	25.40	Milimeters	0.03937
Inches of mercury	345.3	Kilograms/sq. meter	0.002896
Inches of mercury	70.73	Pounds/sq. ft.	0.01414
Inches of mercury (32°F)	0.4912	Pounds/sq. inch	2.036
Inches of mercury	13.5962	Inches of water	0.07355
Inches of water	25.40	Kilograms/sq. meter	0.03937
Inches of water	0.5780	Ounces/sq. inch	1.7301
Inches of water	5.202	Pounds/sq. foot	0.1922
Inches of water	0.03613	Pounds/sq. inch	27.6778
Kilograms	1,000	Grams	0.001
Kiloliters	1,000	Liters	0.001
Kilometers	1,000	Meters	0.001
Kilograms	2.205	Pounds	0.4536
Kilograms/meter	0.6720	Pounds/foot	1.488
Kilograms/sq. meter	0.2048	Pounds/sq. foot	4.881
Kilograms/sq. meter	0.001422	Pounds/sq. inch	703.1

Multiply	By	To get	Converse: Mulitply by
Kilometers	3281	Feet	0.0003048
Kilometers	0.6214	Miles	1.6093
Kilometers	1094	Yards	0.0009141
Kilometers/hr.	0.5399	Knots	1.8522
Kilometers/hr.	16.67	Meters/min.	0.05999
Kilometers/hr.	0.6214	Miles/hr.	1.609
Kilometers/hr./sec.	0.2778	Meters/sec./sec.	3.5997
Kilowatts	1,000	Watts	0.001
Liters	2.113	Pints (liq.)	0.4733
Liters	1.057	Quarts (liq.)	0.9461
Lux	0.0929	Footcandles	10.76391
Meters	1.094	Yards	0.9144
Meters/min.	0.03728	Miles/hr.	26.82
Meters/sec.	2.237	Miles/hr.	0.4470
Meters/sec.	0.03728	Miles/min.	26.8240
Microns	1,000,000	Meters	0.0000001
Miles	1760	Yards	0.0005682
Miles/min.	60	Miles/hr.	0.01667
Milligrams	0.001	Grams	1,000
Milliliters	0.001	Liters	1,000
Millimeters	0.1	Meters	1,000
Minutes (angle)	0.0002909	Radians	3438
Ounces	0.06250	Pounds	16
Ounces (fluid)	1.805	Cubic inches	0.5540
Pounds	0.0005000	Tons (short)	2000
Pounds	0.0004464	Tons.(long)	2240
Pounds	453.5924	Grams	0.002205
Pounds	0.4535924	Kilograms	2.2046
Pounds/sq. foot	0.006944	Pounds/sq. inch	144
Quadrants (angle)	90	Degrees	0.01111
Quadrants (angle)	5400	Minutes	0.0001852
Quadrants (angle)	1.571	Radians	0.6365
Quires	25	Sheets	0.04000
Radians/sec.	57.30	Degrees/sec.	0.01745
Radians/sec.	0.1592	Revolutions/sec.	6.283
Radians/sec.	9.549	Revolutions/min.	0.1047

Multiply	By	To get	Converse: Mulitply by
Radians/sec./sec.	573.0	Revolutions/min./min.	0.001745
Radians/sec./sec.	0.1592	Revolutions/sec./sec.	6.283
Reams	500	Sheets	0.002000
Revolutions/min.	0.01667	Revolutions/sec.	60
Revolutons/min./min.	0.0002778	Revolutions/sec./sec.	3600
Square centimeters	0.001076	Square feet	929
Square centimeters	0.1550	Square inches	6.452
Square centimeters	10,000	Square meters	0.0001
Square feet	144	Square inches	0.006944
Square feet	0.09294	Square meters	10.76
Square feet	0.1111	Square yards	9
Sq. kilometers	1,000,000	Square meters	0.000001
Sq. kilometers	0.3861	Square miles	2.590
Sq. kilometers	0.000001196	Square yards	836,120
Square meters	1.196	Square yards	0.8361
Temp.(°C.) + 17.78	1.8	Temp. (°F.) -32	0.5556
Tons (short)	2000	Pounds	0.0005000
Tons (long)	2240	Pounds	0.0004464
Tons (metric)	2205	Pounds	0.0004535
Tons (short)	0.90718	Tons (metric)	1.1023
Tons (long)	1.12000	Tons (short)	0.8929

BIBLIOGRAPHY

The letters in parentheses below are the abbreviations used throughout the book to identify and credit data from sources where it will facilitate further research and corroboration.

(AB) Acco Babcock Inc. *Catalog SH85.* York, PA: ACCO, 1985.

Ball, John E. *Carpenters and Builders Library No. 2.* Indianapolis, IN: Howard W. Sams & Co., Inc., 1976

Box, Harry C. *Set Lighting Technician's Handbook: Film Lighting Equipment, Practice, and Electrical Distribution.* Boston, MA: Focal Press, 1993.

(CC) Campbell Chain Division, McGraw-Edison Co. *Campbell Chain Catalog F-3170.* York, PA: Campbell Chain Division, 1982.

(COH1) Center for Occupational Hazards. *Air Purifying Respirators.* New York, NY: COH, 1982

(COH2) Center for Occupational Hazards. *Solvents in Conservation Labs.* New York, NY: COH, 1985

(BCI) Ching, Francis D.K. *Building Construction Illustrated.* New York, NY: Van Nostrand Reinhold Co.Inc., 1975

(CG) Cordage Group,The, Division of Columbian Rope Co. *Fiber Data Sheet.* Auburn, NY: The Cordage Group, 1981.

(C) Crosby Group Inc., The *General Catalog, January 1987.* Tulsa, OK: The Crosby Group Inc., 1987.

(RM) Dickie, D.E. *Rigging Manual, 1st ed.* Toronto, Ontario: Construction Safety Association of Ontario, 1975.

Dykes Lumber Company. *Catalog of Mouldings & Building Products, No. 85.* New York, NY: Dykes Lumber Company, 1985.

Glerum, Jay O. *Stage Rigging Handbook*. Carbondale, IL: Southern Illinois Press, 1987.

Graf, Don. *Basic Building Data*. New York, NY: Van Nostrand Reinhold Co.Inc., 1949.

Grafstein & Schwarz. *Pictoral Handbook of Technical Devices*. New York, NY: Chemical Publishing Co., Inc., 1971.

(LH) GTE Sylvania. *Lighting Handbook, 5th ed*. Danvers, MA: GTE Sylvania, 1974.

Hayward, Charles H. *Woodwork Joints*. New York, NY: Drake Publishers Inc., 1970.

(H)   Hubbell Incorporated. *Catalog No. 35-R-2*. Bridgeport, CT: Hubbell, 1987.

Janovic/Plaza, Inc. *Incomplete Catalogue for Decorative and Scenic Painters*. New York, NY: Janovic/Plaza, Inc., 1990.

Leavell & Bungay. *Standard Aircraft Handbook*. Fallbrook, CA: AERO Publishing Inc., 1977.

Macwhyte Company, Division of AMSTED Industries, Inc. *Wire Rope Manual*. Kenosha, WI: Macwhyte Company, 1981.

Matthews Studio Equipment Equipment, Inc. *1993 Dealer Catalog*. Burbank, CA: Matthews Studio Equipment Equipment, Inc., 1993.

Mayer, Ralph. *The Artists Handbook, 4th Edition*. New York, NY: Viking Press, 1980.

Mole-Richardson Co. *Catalog*. Hollywood, CA: Mole-Richardson Co., 1992.

(M)   Mutual Hardware Corp. *Catalog No.88*. Long Island City, NY: Mutual Hardware Corp., 1988.

(NEC) National Fire Protection Association. *National Electrical Code 1987*. Quincy, MA: National Fire Protection Association, 1987.

Nelson, Carl A. *Mechanical Trades Pocket Manual*. Indianapolis, IN: Howard W. Sams & Co., Inc., 1974.

_____. *Millwrights and Mechanics Guide*. Indianapolis, IN: Howard W. Sams & Co., Inc., 1972.

Newberry, W. G. *Handbook for Riggers*. Calgary, Alberta, Canada: Newberry Investments Co. Ltd., 1967.

(MH) Oberg, Jones and Horton. *Machinery's Handbook, 21st Edition*. New York, NY: Industrial Press Inc., 1982.

Padgett, Allen and Smith, Burce. *On Rope: North American Vertical Rope Techniques For Caving, Search & Rescue, and Mountaineering*. Huntsville, AL: Vertical Section, North American Speleological Society, 1987.

Raoul, Bill. *Stock Scenery Construction Handbook*. Louisville, KY: Broadway Press, 1990.

Richter, H.P. *Practical Electrical Wiring*. New York, NY: McGraw Hill Book Co., 1987.

Rossol, Monona. *Stage Fright*. New York, NY: Center for Occupational Hazards, Inc., 1986.

Sands, Leo G. *Electronics Handbook for the Electrician*. Philadelphia, PA: Chilton Book Company, 1968.

Sterling Publishing Co., Inc. *The Encyclopedia of Wood*. New York, NY: Sterling Publishing Co., Inc., 1980.

(TD)   Swezey, Kenneth M. *Formulas, Methods, Tips and Data for Home and Workshop*. New York, NY: Popular Science Publishing Co., Division of Harper & Row Inc., 1979.

(WREH)   U.S. Steel Supply, Division of United States Steel. *Wire Rope Engineering Handbook*. Newark, NJ: U.S. Steel Supply, 1976.

(UC)   Union Connector Co., Inc. *2P&G Receptacle Polarity, Drawing No. 8692201*. Roosevelt, NY: Union Connector Co., Inc., 1986.

(UWP)   Universal Wire Products, Inc. *Catalog UWP 801*. New Haven, CT: Universal Wire Products, Inc, 1984.

(WC)   Wire Rope Corporation of America, Inc. *Wireco Wire Rope Technical Data*. St. Joseph, MO: Wire Rope Corp. of America, Inc., 1985.

INDEX

luminous intensity 171, 212
lux 213

machine screws 58
madras 146
Mafer clamp 15
magic finger 15
magnetic flux 213
mallet 2
manila rope 84, 85, 86, 87
mansard 248
Manufacturers' Standard Gauge 117
marking or mortise gauge 1
marquisette 146
Masonite 125, 155
mass 212
Mastic 11
mat knife 6
material - see fabrics
MATERIAL HANDLING EQUIPMENT 24
MATH SIGNS AND SYMBOLS 209
Matth becky adjustable hanger 17
Matth pole 17
Matthews magic finger 15
Matthews parallel 23
Matthews pop-up stud 15
maxi brute 185
McCloskeys 135
MEASURING AND MARKING TOOLS 1
meat axe 16
MECHANICAL FASTENER POINTS 62
medium lamp base 197
mending iron 68
metal properties 160
metallic fabrics 146
meter 206, 212
methanol 136
methocel 139
METHODS OF SAWING LUMBER 121
methyl acetate 137
methyl ethyl ketone 137
methyl isobutyl ketone 137
**METRIC / IMPERIAL ARCHITECT'S SCALE
    CONVERSIONS 250**
METRIC UNITS 206
mickey 184
middle panel 239
midget 186
**MIDGET LOCKING TYPE (TWISTLOCK)
    RECEPTACLES 195**
midget tubing cutter 41
mig welder 38
mighty 184
mil 216
mile 216
millinery velvet 148
mineral spirits 136
mini phone plug 202
MISCELLANEOUS KNOTS 90
MISCELLANEOUS PAINTING TOOLS 28
MISCELLANEOUS STEEL PRODUCTS 119
miter 127
miter box 6, 36
mogul lamp base 197
mohair 146
moire 146
mole 212
Mole pin 187
Molly fastener 57

momentum 215
monkey's fist 94
monks cloth 146
mooring hitch 92
mortise & tenon joint 128
mortise gauge 1
mosaic tile 151
mottler 26
MOULDING 241-243
mule block 71
mullion 240
muntin 239
muslin 141, 146
mutton 240

N-hexane 136
nail claw 3
nail gauges 50, 51
nail gun 2
nail heads & points 51, 52
nail puller 3
nail set 2
NAIL SIZES 50
nail sizes, common 49
NAIL SPECIFICATIONS 51
NAIL TYPES 50
nail weights 50
NAILING PATTERNS 278
nanometer 172
**NATURAL TRIGONOMETRIC FUNCTIONS
    FOR DECIMAL FRACTIONS OF A DEGREE
    226**
nautical measure 216
nautical mile 216
needle nose pliers 5
net (short ton) 216
net (fabric) 146
NET / SCRIM CHARACTERISTICS 21
neutral density filters 174
newel post 235
newton 213
Newton's Second Law of Motion 215
NICOPRESS SLEEVES AND TOOLS 104
nippers 7
nipple 113
NM cable 169
NMC cable 169
noils 147
NON-GROUNDING RECEPTACLES 190
nook light 184
nosing 235
Nu-Rail pipe fittings 83
nut driver 4
NUTS 62
nylon 131
nylon fabric 147
nylon rope 84, 85, 86

O-ring 82
oblique projection 249
**OBSOLETE LOCKING TYPE (TWISTLOCK)
    RECEPTACLES 195**
obtuse angle 217
obtuse triangle 220
octagon, how to draw 231
octave 200
off stage 257

This handy reference book brings together under one cover an incredible variety of information useful to designers, technicians and students who work behind the scenes in theatre, film and television.

Backstage Handbook is truly an almanac of technical information. It covers *Tools, Hardware, Materials, Electrics, Shop Math, Architecture,* and *Theatre.* There are hundreds of illustrations, tables and charts which cover everything from the stock sizes and specs of wood screws, to safe working loads for several kinds of rope, to illustrations of twenty-two types of standard lamp bases (with names and standard abbreviations, of course.)

Paul Carter (1956-1990) was a theatre planning consultant with Artec Consultants Inc. of New York City. He worked on such projects as the Raymond F. Kravis Center for the Performing Arts, Palm Beach, Florida, the International Convention Centre, Birmingham, England and the Harbourfront Arts Centre, Toronto, Canada. Before joining Artec, Mr. Carter served as Production Manager for the Cleveland Ballet, and as Assistant Technical Director for the New York City Opera and the Denver Center Theatre Company. In addition, he spent several years working backstage at the Metropolitan Opera House and the State Theatre at Lincoln Center.

Mr. Carter held an M.F.A. from the Yale School of Drama and had one of the largest stage screw collections in the world.

George Chiang began his career as an illustrator in his native San Francisco, where he received his degree in the fine arts. He now lives in New York City with his wife, Sheri, and their daughter, Ariel Zhi-Han.

Broadway Press
3001 Springcrest Dr.
Louisville, KY 40241

800-869-6372
www.broadwaypress.com

ISBN: 0-911747-39-7

ISBN 0-911747-39-7

51650

9 780911 747393

$16.50